Life is constantly handing [...]
marriage, a new child, i[...]
community. In her hig[...]
Harper Neeld helped thousands deal with mourning and loss.
Now, in this inspirational new book, she teaches us how to over-
come all kinds of challenges.

Discover:

- What issues you're likely to face with different kinds of change

- How your body, mind, and emotions are affected by transition

- New thinking and new behaviors that can transform your life

- The difference between surviving and thriving—and the se-
crets that will make you a thriver.

This book comforts and inspires—
and illuminates the path ahead.

TOUGH TRANSITIONS

PRAISE FOR ELIZABETH HARPER NEELD'S
SEVEN CHOICES

"A deeply healing book about loss and grief from a writer . . . with
a very rare and precious vision."
    —Hugh and Gayle Prather, authors of *Notes to Each Other*

"A highly original and meaningful approach to the grieving process."
    —*Psychology Today*

"A useful, wide-ranging work . . . trenchant . . . pertinent."
    —*Kirkus Reviews*

"Readers will welcome Elizabeth Neeld's guide . . . It offers sound
advice to change and to form new life patterns and human bonds."
    —*Publishers Weekly*

Elizabeth Harper Neeld has twenty publications to her credit, including:

Seven Choices: Finding Daylight After Loss Shatters Your World, a critically acclaimed book on loss and grief that was the subject of two public television hourlong programs, including *Seven Choices for Healing Your Grief*, and was given to families of 9/11 by the American Red Cross.

The Challenge of Grief, a one-hour video documentary based on *Seven Choices* shown on public television.

Managing Change, video, text, posters, and art multimedia offerings for Fortune 500 and Fortune 100 companies throughout the United States as well as numerous foreign organizations and companies.

A Sacred Primer: The Essential Guide to Quiet Time and Prayer, about which critics wrote, "original and eloquent . . . reflect[ing] years of research . . . absolute gems of wisdom."

Writing, a college textbook that has been used in hundreds of American colleges and universities, including Harvard, Pasadena City College, Boston University, Goucher College, the University of Illinois, the University of Houston, the University of Maine, the University of North Carolina, the University of Nebraska, Purdue University, the University of Richmond, the State University of New York, the University of Minnesota, and West Virginia University.

Yes! You Can Write, a six-audiocassette program written for adults who want to write.

Either Way Will Hurt & Other Essays on English, published by the Modern Language Association in New York for college and university English department leaders.

Sister Bernadette: Cowboy Nun of Texas, a rollicking story of a contemplative nun who breeds miniature horses, published by Centerpoint Press. (coauthor)

From the Plow to the Pulpit: The Spiritual Autobiography of Tommie Harper, an oral history of a farmer and community hellion who becomes a preacher, set in the rural South, 1908 to 1986. Published by Centerpoint Press. (editor)

TOUGH
TRANSITIONS

Navigating Your Way
Through Difficult Times

ELIZABETH HARPER NEELD, PH.D.

WARNER BOOKS

NEW YORK   BOSTON

Grateful acknowledgment is made to the following for permission to reprint previously published material:

Thomas Merton, from *Raids on the Unspeakable*, copyright © 1966 by The Abbey of Gethsemani, Inc. Reprinted by permission of New Directions Publishing Corp.

Elie Wiesel, "A Prayer for the Days of Awe," from the *New York Times*, October 2, 1997, p. A15. Reprinted by permission of The New York Times Co.

"The Five Steps of Freeze-Frame," p. 67 from *The HeartMath Solution* by Doc Childre and Howard Martin. Copyright © 1999 by the Institute of HeartMath. Reprinted by permission of Harper-Collins Publishers.

Warner Books
Hachette Book Group USA
1271 Avenue of the Americas, New York, NY 10020
Visit our Web site at www.HachetteBookGroupUSA.com.

Printed in the United States of America

Originally published in hardcover by Warner Books.

First Trade Edition: September 2006
10 9 8 7 6 5 4 3 2 1

Warner Books and the "W" logo are trademarks of Time Warner, Inc. or an affiliated company. Used under license by Hachette Book Group USA, which is not affiliated with Time Warner Inc.

The Library of Congress has cataloged the hardcover edition as follows:

Neeld, Elizabeth Harper.
    Tough transitions : navigating your way through difficult times / Elizabeth Harper Neeld.—1st ed.
      p. cm.
    Includes bibliographical references.
    ISBN 0-446-53149-9
  1. Life change events.   I. Title.
    BF637.L53N44 2005
    158.1—dc22
                                         2004029440

Book design by Giorgetta Bell McRee
Map concept by Erik Kuntz

ISBN-10: 0-446-69455-X (pbk.)
ISBN-13: 978-0-446-69455-1 (pbk.)

For
Christine Tomasino

ACKNOWLEDGMENTS

May I thank first the generous people who met on a regular basis with me for over a year as I wrote this book? We discussed and clarified and examined the central distinctions. We explored and created and discovered new ideas and connections. Because of these people, I have confidence that this book reflects both broad and deep implications that tough transitions have for all of our lives. Gratitude upon gratitude, then, to: Zosia Hunt, Alison Adams, Elizabeth Newell, Patricia Thomas, Gail Daniels, Marlene Clark, Kerry Cowlishaw, Lucy Ross, Beth Webster, Judy Rohde, Carla Raper, Janey Marks, Brigid Kleber, Jeanie Forsyth, Kelly Porterfield, Mary Elizabeth Owen, and Beverly Scott.

The dozens of individuals who contributed their true stories to this book remain unnamed but are deeply honored and appreciated. To each of you, thank you for making a contribution from your own tough transition by telling your story. The readers of this book will be enriched by the gift of your experience.

Chris Tomasino, my agent, and Caryn Karmatz Rudy, my editor, read every word I write and offer suggestions that allow me to true up my opinions and enlarge my thinking. Their belief in my work provides a plank of support that I stand on every day that I'm at my desk.

What would an author do without the professionals who make her work always look better? Erik Kuntz designed and maintains my Web site, www.elizabethharperneeld.com. Hal Kooistra keeps my computers and all my electronic equipment in top-notch shape and handles every technical issue immediately, even on the weekends. Ann Rachlin advises me on music. Mimi Bark designed the cover of the book. Erik Kuntz drew the map that structures *Tough Transitions*. Giorgetta Bell McRee designed the text and embellished the map. Roland Ottewell copyedited the text. Linda Duggins made sure people knew the book existed. I thank each of these talented professionals.

When I needed to decide on a final title for the book in a very short period of time, it was Howard Butt, Barbara Dan Butt, Judy Parker, Deborah Butt Rogers, Eva Archer-Smith, Yvonne Donaldson, Hope Fonte, and Carole Murdock who came to my rescue. It does take a village to write a book! Thank you, members of my village.

Friends. I am so blessed by these treasures. Yvonne Donaldson broadcasts far and wide her support and creates new cadres of readers for my work wherever she goes. She also provides a home away from home when I travel to her neighborhood. Lee Herrick will change any date at a moment's notice if I need to work rather than play; and she, like Yvonne, throws a great book party. Eva Archer-Smith has been there from the beginning, when my first trade book was about to be published in 1989; and I am in debt to her forever for the support and lift she gave me then and continues to give me today. Kathi Appelt, Joan Bohls, Alison Adams, Christine Reel, Darlene Walker, Judi Mayne, Kelley Jemison, Carla Raper, Betty Unterberger, Brigid Kleber, Gail Daniels, Sher Patterson, Mary Breslin, and Beth and Joe Mercer help balance my life—shared breakfasts and lunches; jokes and cartoons; prayers, movies, art, and music.

My family always have me on their radar screen. Sheri Harper, my sister-in-law, sends e-mails the entire time I'm writing a book, checking to see how things are going. My brother, Frank Harper, contacts me every day or so while I'm meeting a timeline to see if all is well. My sister, Barbara Walker, sends congratulations cards and surprise gifts when I mail in a manuscript, get a manuscript back, finish a revision, send in the final product. My Aunt Frances sends very frequent messages of support and, on occasion, has been known to suggest—a welcome voice of conscience—that it seems to her as if I am doing a lot of other things rather than finishing my book. My husband, Jerele, gives me everything I need to have a wonderful writing life and cares deeply that I am productive and happy in my work. He is my love.

CONTENTS

Author's Note

There's an old Inuit legend that says, "The Great Spirit must love stories, because the Great Spirit made a lot of people." And for this book the Great Spirit inspired a lot of people with a lot of stories to be truly generous. Each of the four sections of Part II in *Tough Transitions: Navigating Your Way Through Difficult Times* concludes with true stories women and men shared with me. (The only exception is the story in "Responding" told by a mother of an injured soldier. That true account was sent to me as an e-mail from a friend who had received it from the soldier's mother.) While I changed details to provide anonymity, melded stories on the same topic to avoid repetition, selected, divided, and interpreted for applicability and relevance, every story remains at its core the story someone told me. On three occasions a story told to me for an earlier book, *Seven Choices: Finding Daylight After Loss Shatters Your World*, is repeated here because I felt it was the perfect story for the spot. And in rare instances the story told is one of my own. While all emphases in the published accounts are mine and not to be attributed to the storytellers, the authenticity, the lived experience, and the specificity of detail belong solely to the women and men who told the stories. For their generosity I am deeply grateful.

TOUGH
TRANSITIONS

PART ONE

PRELIMINARIES

1

Introducing the Challenge

Not in their goals but in their transitions are people great.

adapted from RALPH WALDO EMERSON

Why read a book about tough transitions? Aren't these rough patches as count-on-able as rain and as normal as crabgrass? What more needs to be offered than perhaps a gentle admonition to buck up and move on or, on a really difficult day, a steady hand of support? No one wants to give time to words that only belabor the obvious, even if those words do aim to be inspirational or encouraging.

This book is about something more than inspiration or encouragement (though I hope it's that, too). Its purpose is to distill the most current information available related to tough transitions—from science, philosophy, the arts, ancient spiritual thought, medical studies—and to show how individuals have used this information to navigate their way through some of life's most difficult times.

Tough transitions are inevitable. But the fact that they are inevitable does not mean that they have only to be suffered through with clenched teeth and fisted fingers. Information exists—if we can find it—and ways of thinking and behaving—if we can do them—that can give us a facility to navigate through tough times with more insight, understanding, and sense of direction. I've written this book to offer just such a possibility.

Your Transition Is Not My Transition

If we look back over our lives, each of us can make a long list of transitions we've experienced. Some of us can create a list just by calling out what we're in the middle of right now. Try putting a mark by the side of every situation listed here that you've dealt with or are experiencing now, and you'll see what I mean:

_____ moving

_____ losing a job

_____ dealing with illness (yours or someone close to you)

_____ taking a new job

_____ losing someone by death

_____ facing one's own aging

_____ experiencing failure

_____ dealing with financial loss

_____ looking for work

_____ living in a country you weren't born in

_____ going to or coming from war

_____ choosing a public alternative lifestyle

_____ becoming a stay-at-home mom

_____ changing careers by choice

_____ getting married

_____ experiencing an empty nest

_____ caring for elders

_____ retiring

_____ being divorced, separated, or left

_____ downsizing

_____ having a baby

_____ having someone go to war or come home from war

_____ losing sense of security

_____ having a new grandchild

_____ losing a baby

_____ finding adoptive birth parents/child

_____ blending two families

As you look at your own list of transitions, you note that each is a different kind of challenge: this one hurt for years . . . that one is a challenge but a bit exhilarating . . . this one shook everything in my life . . . that one brought at least as much joy as hard work . . . this one makes me angry as a buzzing bee . . . that one knocked the breath out of me. A short list of three or four transitions matched with the challenge or emotion or experience will illustrate this variety in intensity, pain, duration, and effect on well-being.

Here are a few of my own transitions matched to my experience:

- Moving to a strange city for a two-year job assignment in my husband's work: disoriented, feeling of emptiness, excited, challenged by daily essentials, feeling I had stepped out of my real life into a vacuum, lonely, sense of enormous opportunity. Looking back, now that I've been home a couple of years, I'd say that that transition, though difficult, particularly at first, was much more positive than negative.

- Caring for elderly parents with health problems: discouraged, tired, confronted, sad, watching for any breakthroughs made in medicine or science that might help, anxious about their daily well-being, angry when they wouldn't accept help that was available in the community, wanting to be with them as much as possible because I loved them so much. That transition was many years long—ended only by their deaths eight days apart and the start of a new transition—and was mostly hard, though there are many memories from that time that warm my heart today. And now I am a font of information for my friends who are just starting into a similar transition with their elders.

- Changing careers: scared, excited, surprised, jolted by ideas and ideals slamming into reality, experiencing loss, supported by others, required to learn over and over, gratified. This transition had a long blank spot in the middle; it was several years after I left my position as a tenured, full professor before I felt grounded in my new career as a writer. Because I initiated the change entirely, I had expected a much quicker and smoother transition. But I didn't know what I didn't know. I really didn't have a clue what personal fears I would face, what I would have to learn to become a woman good at the business aspects of another career, what long, up-front investment I would have to make of my time and hard work before I could hope for any return.

> When each thing is unique in itself, there can be no comparison made.
>
> D. H. Lawrence

Your list of transitions will show a similar variety of pluses and minuses, loss and gain, pain and satisfaction, long and longer duration.

When we talk about transitions, then, we are not talking about cookie-cutter situations. Every transition concerns a particular individual living a specific set of experiences. That set of experiences varies just as personally and uniquely as individuals themselves differ from every other human being on the planet.

A Paradox: Different, Yet the Same

Even while each of us lives out a tough transition in our own unique way, we are all standing on the same threshold. A threshold that marks the passage from how things *were* to how things are *going to be*. Anthropologists write a lot about thresholds, those times that mark an individual's leaving one way of life and beginning another. Any of us would smile if we look at the origin of the word *threshold* in Old English, where it refers to a thorn, then going all the way back to the Danish, where it means *to thresh or beat with a stick*. That's how a lot of transitions feel when we're experiencing a tough time.

What is living on a threshold like? What is normal when we find ourselves propelled into a tough transition?

People who study such things say this: Standing on a threshold and living a transition is a time of "betwixt and between," a time when we feel as if we are traveling through a realm or dimension that has few or none of the qualities our lives will have in the fu-

> The word *threshold* in Old English refers to a thorn. In ancient Danish it means to thresh or beat with a stick.

ture, a time that can be compared to feeling invisible, being in the wilderness, falling into the dark, living in floating worlds. There can be terrible ambiguity and confusion.

At the same time, finding ourselves on the threshold in a tough transition can be viewed as an enormous opportunity. It is a time when we can be inwardly transformed and outwardly changed. A time associated with major reformulation, open-endedness, and possibility. Instead of a time of *what is*, it is a time of *what can be*. At any moment the way we ordered our thoughts and actions in the past can be revised. There is a strong chance that we will come up with ways of thinking, ways of making connections and relationships, that we have never experienced before. We may break free from old ways of thinking and come up with new ways we want to live.

It is all this that we share in common, no matter the specificity of our individual transitions. We share the experience of living a threshold event, of navigating ourselves in that "floating world" between how they used to be and how things will be.

> Leaving the old, both worlds at once they view
> That stand upon the threshold of the new.
>
> Edmund Waller

The Promise of This Book

Once I joined a small group of women in exploring a part of the Mojave Desert. We left behind the world we knew so well—asphalt highways, running water, road maps with markings printed in different colors, bathrooms, and Starbucks coffee—to enter a wilderness. There were no set markings and no clear path. Even our guides got lost on several occasions and we had to retrace our route to attempt to find some kind of landmark.

Gradually, however, all of us—guides and neophytes alike—got better at reading the terrain and recognizing the signs that nature provided. We learned to make a distinction between a dry creek bed that would be safe to camp by and a wide crevice that was likely to become a rushing torrent when the rain fell. What had begun as only twenty shades of brown—ground, bushes, cacti, jackrabbits, roots—became, as we grew more and more familiar with the wilderness we were exploring, purple and gray and red and soft sage green. We were learning the territory. Over the days we came to know more and more what to expect and could appreciate the diversity that lay before us rather than fear it.

> Life offstage has sometimes been a wilderness of unpredictables in an unchoreographed world.
>
> Margot Fonteyn, dancer

This book exists as a guide through the unfamiliar terrain of tough transitions—a way to help us recognize the potential that change brings; for whether you are literally or figuratively in the desert, the mere knowledge that a trail exists can help immeasurably. Many experts have studied these wildernesses of change that we traverse as we retire, blend families, lose money, change jobs, move house, age, tend elders, grieve the absence of family and friends, deal with chronic illnesses, and watch the kids grow up and leave home (or come back home, as is often the case now).

In addition to reading experts' findings, I have personally experienced my share of tough transitions: divorce, sudden death of a young husband, job loss, career change, suicide of a grandfather, remarriage including blending families, several moves, illness of parents and then death of parents eight days apart, to name a few. And I have talked to dozens of friends and acquaintances about their tough transitions.

From the research of the experts, from my own experience, and from the wisdom of friends and acquaintances, I describe in this book the territory of a tough transition—the terrain that is similar for all of us, even though our individual transitions are personal and specific. No matter the exact nature of our transitions, we share many things in common.

We all start the transition in a place of uncertainty, newness, unfamiliarity, and potential strain. We all must, at some point, take stock of what our options are, what we can and can't do in a particular situation, what will help us move forward and what will suck us down into the quicksand of apathy. We all take steps into new places as part of navigating a tough transition, practice, fall back, practice again new ways of thinking and new models of living. We all have the opportunity to create a life that includes in an honest way the implications of the tough transition without our being defined by or identified by that tough transition. And we all have the possibility of achieving what Dr. Heinz Kohut calls "victorious outcomes" from our tough transitions. We can all be not just survivors but, in spite of the hard times, thrivers.

> . . . through ditches, over hedges, through chiffons, through waiters, over saxophones, to the victorious finish . . .
> Edna St. Vincent Millay

If you let it, this book will serve as your guide to describing the passage through tough transitions. You can learn what people have done who have stood on the threshold and then stepped out into the unknown and the unfamiliar. You can be taught—and inspired—by people who walked out into the wilderness and lived to tell the tale.

2

Surveying the Terrain

A plague upon it! I have forgot the map.

HOTSPUR, in HENRY IV PART I

A wife speaks of her husband's job loss:

What a Valentine's present. Fortunately, we had exchanged our gifts and cards that morning before he went to work. He told me after supper, "I've got some bad news. I lost my job today."

"What in the world happened? I can't believe this."

"I couldn't either," my husband replied. "Sam walked in my office out of the blue and said, 'The merger's gone through and duplicate jobs are being eliminated. I'm afraid yours was one we lost.' I just sat there stunned."

He went on with more details about the merger—how many people were losing their jobs on both sides, other friends of his who were also affected, the kind of outplacement services that were being provided. But everything he said sounded to my ears like blah, blah, blah. All I could think about was that this was it for six years of hard work with this company. Moving the kids a thousand miles away from their grandparents so he could take this job. Working on the weekends. Being gone on business trips sometimes three weeks at a time.

Now, it's find another job. Move again, just when the kids are ready for junior and senior high school. Uproot, give up, start over . . . I felt like throwing the dishes on the table against the wall.

A husband talks about his divorce:

I was standing in front of the bathroom mirror, combing my hair. She was in the doorway, her head tilted, leaning up against the doorjamb.

"I think I'm destroying our lives," she said, her voice so low I could hardly hear it.

"You're not destroying our lives," I retorted. "You're just moving to another city for a temporary job assignment. A job assignment, I might add, that lets you use the talents and skills you've worked hard to develop over the past several years."

Maybe I was trying to be the modern, sophisticated partner; but I also in that moment meant exactly what I said. A year was not a long time in the span of an entire career. We would meet on most weekends, either here or there. And I had always loved the architecture in the city where this job assignment was taking her. Now I would have many opportunities to visit.

But perhaps that afternoon she knew something deep inside her that I didn't. Something about the dangers of tilting a couple's equilibrium. Something about where she wanted to go in life and thought that I didn't. Or she might have just been giving voice to the kind of fears that come anytime human beings face the risk of making a change.

Whatever the source, my wife's remark about our life being destroyed proved prescient. For that's exactly what happened. There was never anything really dramatic. She didn't fall in love with someone else. I didn't decide I preferred the role of a bachelor. She just moved on.

Moved on in her interests ("I've cut back on my eating-out budget," she told me one night on the phone, "just so I could buy a season ticket to the opera. I've discovered I love opera!"). Moved on in her relationships (I didn't have a clue after two or three months who the Betsy was she went to yoga with every Tuesday or what Mark and Meredith looked like who came over to her apartment on Sunday nights for supper). Moved on in her goals ("They want me to stay on here for a few more months . . . I think I'm being considered for a big promotion").

So was the beginning of the end of a marriage. It took nearly three years before I could accept that this was the way things were going to go. I think she was ambivalent, too, at the beginning. It's nobody's fault, really. But that didn't make filing for a divorce one whit easier. And how it all came about doesn't matter when I'm sitting in my apartment at night thinking about how I've got to get a whole new future.

An adult daughter talks of her aging parents:

Between the squeaking of the pedals and the lapping of the Frio River against the sides of the paddleboat, my husband and I did not at first hear the voice from the side of the bank. Finally the sound was loud enough for us to catch the words: "Yoo-hoo! Yoo-hoo!" someone was calling.

It took a few minutes to turn the boat in the current. In fact, we had to go almost as far as the Blue Hole at the bend of the river before we had enough berth to make a circle and head back toward the lodge and the stranger calling to us from the bank.

It was a trip that took way too long not to imagine a hundred different scenarios of what could be important enough that someone had needed to come to summon us.

I was anything if not alert when we got back to the dock. In fact, it was as if everything were in crisp Technicolor. The peeling gray paint on the side of the paddleboat, the knurls of the brown-almost-black roots growing out of the side of the riverbank, the blue skirt of the woman who was waving.

"An emergency telephone call just came in for you," the messenger said, reaching for my hand. "Your father has had a stroke."

So began the saga of the last epoch of my parents' lives. From that day on the Frio River forward for more than a decade, my husband and I, my parents, my siblings . . . all of us were required to reorganize most everything around us to respond to the winding down of two beautiful people's lives.

And so begin our tough transitions.

Powerful situations, one commentator calls them.

Cornered horror, another asserts.

A crucible, is a poet's description.

It's like entering another country, says a researcher. *A country that is a speechless, undefined, empty place.*

Somehow, transitions are bigger than problems. Transitions are also more than just a change. Yes, we are required to solve problems, lots of them, when we are in tough transitions. And, yes, transitions require many, many changes. But tough transitions are different. They are just what the term *transition* suggests: a time when *we ourselves* are *in transit*.

No Guide in This Territory

My dictionary tells me that to *transit* is to *pass over, across, or through*. I read into this definition that there is some kind of barrier present, maybe a high granite mountain to climb over, a rushing river to ford. Or at least a distance to travel where you are neither at the place you left nor the place you are going to.

And when my friend says to me while we're having a cup of coffee on her back porch, "During a *time of transit* it's natural for everything to seem foreign and weird," she means these words as comfort. What she is suggesting is that a tough transition is a *process* . . . just as my dictionary also confirms: *transit (noun): the process of passing from one form, state, or stage to another. A passage.*

And it only stands to reason that when something—or someone—is in process, going from one form, state, or stage to another, things will be pretty much a mess. Formless, changing by the moment. Like that amoeba we used to watch under the microscope in high school biology—a blob of squirming protoplasm that kept shape-shifting, extending what my science teacher used to call a "finger" of protoplasm here, a "false foot" there.

To make matters more difficult, we are expected to be brilliant at work, have fun at our cousin's wedding party, and keep the household running smoothly through all this upheaval. "Regular life" marches right on. We may be ricocheting like a silver shot in a kid's pinball game, but we still have to catch the bus at 9:04 and decide whether or not to sign the kids up for summer camp by the fifteenth. No matter that we are dealing with a situation that has knocked us winding—the "world out there" will cut us no slack.

And I'm afraid—in spite of the fact that we *are* transiting in *another country, a country that is an undefined, empty place*—there are no signs that say, "Go this way." There is nothing that looks familiar. What we need is some kind of map of the terrain. But who has been into this territory and lived to tell a coherent tale?

Well, it does happen in the movies. As a metaphor at least. Remember the heroine Nicole Kidman plays in *Cold Mountain* who goes through all kinds of travails as she waits for her beloved to return from fighting in the War between the States? Though there are pains and dangers, upheavals and despairs, we see her in the last frames of the movie, out under the trees playing with her little daughter, enjoying a meal with family and friends. If you like the classics, you'll probably remember *Jeremiah Johnson*. The Robert Redford character, who came to be called the Mountain Man, goes into the Rockies shortly after the Civil War and lives to come out a dozen years later knowing how to navigate the roaring rivers and to make a fire in a blowing snow. "You've come a far piece, pilgrim," the old trapper tells him near the end of the movie. "Feels like far," answers Jeremiah Johnson.

And Lewis and Clark—with a lot of help from Sacagawea—did finally make it to Astoria, where they could stand on the cliff and see the Pacific Ocean. They went south sometimes when they should have gone north; carried their boats on their heads across the rocks to a river that then turned out to be missing; ran into black bears and lost their compasses. But they did finally traverse the unknown continent. And we have their maps and journals to prove it.

So Many Tough Transitions

Life gives all of us a curriculum. What we glean from our experiences with this curriculum may be called common sense, accumulated wisdom, or just barn raising and quilt making in the village. But regardless of what we call the learning, when individual experiences amass from enough of us, they become a wellspring of knowledge. And sharing this knowledge is what makes us a community.

I learned this personally a number of years ago when my young husband, in perfect health, dropped dead one late July afternoon. I found my way out of that undefined, empty country only because of the generosity of people around me who told me their stories and gave me their clues. From these others' experiences, I made my own map for moving through and out of the territory; and I've spent my time ever since trying to add my contribution to the wellspring of knowledge. Isn't that the best way any of us can say "thank you"?

Like everyone else, I didn't get just one chance to learn about tough transitions. They do seem to come in all shapes and sizes. And we seem never to get to the end of them. There's changing careers, moving to another city (or another country), losing a job, taking care of (and then losing) parents, being left by someone we had committed to or ourselves doing the leaving. There's the kids moving out (or back in), our own aging, the retirement account crashing, rebel cells that act up and wreak havoc in the body. There's changing careers, having a baby, blending two families, and retiring. There's the loss of memory, of flexibility, of patience. There's the shock from betrayal, the anger from unprovoked attack, the confusion that comes when what we had always been able to count on in a moment disappears. There's death, disaster, and despair. Yes, I'm afraid we all know what it is like to live in what seems like at times nothing but a series of—or worse, a set of simultaneous—tough transitions.

Drawing a Map of the Terrain of Tough Transitions

Over the years I've tried to understand as much as possible about these tough transitions. I've wanted to survive, of course; but I've wanted to do more than that. I've wanted to survive with well-being. Since on any given day I—like you—am likely to find myself in the beginning of yet another tough transition, is there anything that, if I could know it, would guide me through the undefined country? Anything that would say, not "Here is what you are supposed to do," not "Here are the 1–2–3 clear and simple steps," but "Here is some accumulated wisdom from people who have traversed this terrain and reflected upon it. Here are offerings of experiences from people who have paid attention."? I wanted those experiences culled into one usable implement . . . but none existed.

So, after reflecting on the challenges of tough transitions for more than twenty years, I sat down with a talented friend of mine and said, "Help me draw a map of the terrain of tough transitions." I had in mind something like what Aristotle used when he wrote his how-to manual for students preparing to give public speeches. He covered subjects such as how to make emotional yet ethical appeals to the listeners and how to deliver a speech most effectively. In addition to giving sensible and useful advice on organization and presentation of these public orations, Aristotle also offered guidance on how to find something to say, or finding the "best" thing to say.

Aristotle's advice went something like this:

Picture your mind as a land with several kinds of places or regions or haunts in it. These places (called *topoi* in Greek; "topics" for a loose translation) stand for different kinds of ways to view or think about a subject. Just as each part of the country—desert or mountain—would have a climate of its own, Aristotle said, so each area of the mind has its characteristic way of thinking.

It was this figurative, picturesque way of describing different

What we want from a map is help in getting someplace, not description and analysis of the soil. That can come later after we find out where we are.

James Peterson

mental processes that I wanted to use as a model in "mapping" the terrain of tough transitions: What were the different "places or regions or haunts" that one moved through while going through the process of transition? What would the "climate" of each of these particular places be? What could one expect to find in the different locales that make up such a map?

See pages 24 and 25 for the map we came up with.

Identifying a Map of Orientation

There are maps that we use to determine a route to some destination. There are also maps that we use to orient ourselves. Think about arriving at a shopping mall or a state park. You enter and find your way to a display. On this display will be a map. This will be an orientation map. If you are at a mall, the map will show you where all the stores are, where the restrooms are located, where the escalators go up and down. And there will be the words "You are here," with a bold X marking the spot. You now see where you are standing in reference to the various options on the map and can decide what you want to do next. If you are at a state park, the map will show you the names of various buildings—here's the canteen where you can get a cup of coffee, here's the visitors' center where you can see an educational video. You'll also be able to see the names, locations, and probably length of the hiking trails. The waterfalls, the lakes, the scenic drive will all be indicated on the map. Again, you'll see the words, "You are here," and X will mark the spot. Based on your own plans and interests, once you see clearly where you are, you set out to enjoy yourself in the park.

The map of the Terrain of Tough Transitions is a map of orientation. It is not a map that shows you how to get somewhere. This map identifies the kinds of experiences that are normal when we are moving through a time of change. This map offers clues as to what we can expect at different points as we process through the transition. It tells us what clusters of experiences predominate at different points on the map. We can place our own X on this orienting map and say, "At this moment I am here." We can determine, based on our own needs and interests and wishes, how and when we move around on the map.

Turning a Map Into an Illusion

If someone attempts to turn an orienting map into a route-describing map, such an action creates an illusion. A map of orientation does not begin to suggest where the visitor will go or what the visitor needs to do. It merely details what is present at the site. Everything else is left up to the individual. The map is a static depiction of the location. But let's say that we take this orienting map—we're at the state park—and mark on it our movements through the day. We might first have gone for a hike on the

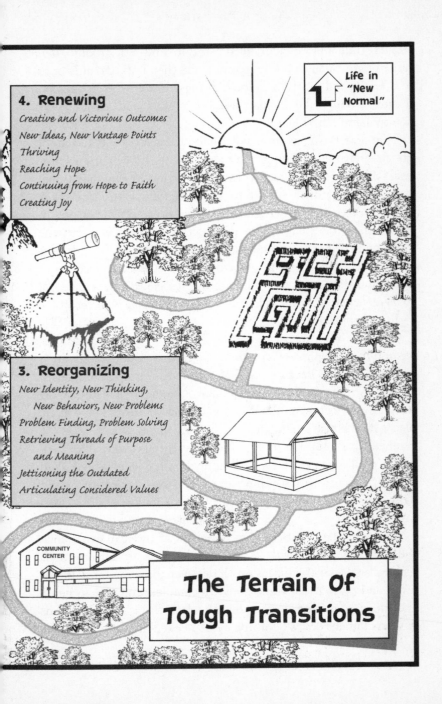

Life in "New Normal"

4. Renewing

Creative and Victorious Outcomes
New Ideas, New Vantage Points
Thriving
Reaching Hope
Continuing from Hope to Faith
Creating Joy

3. Reorganizing

New Identity, New Thinking,
New Behaviors, New Problems
Problem Finding, Problem Solving
Retrieving Threads of Purpose
and Meaning
Jettisoning the Outdated
Articulating Considered Values

COMMUNITY CENTER

The Terrain Of Tough Transitions

Azalea Trail and then doubled back to find a restroom, then turned right to buy a bottle of water, and then walked a mile or so to the lake and rented a canoe. All these movements marked on the map would make the map look very messy—and certainly very personal and individual.

The same is true as we move around the map of the Terrain of Tough Transitions. Though our movement through the experiences depicted on this map occurs more or less in a unidirectional sequence—we usually start in Responding, for instance, and rarely find ourselves at Renewing before we've been in at least one or two of the other places. This does not mean, however, that the movement through a tough transition is clear, 1–2–3–4, do this today, and then do that tomorrow. And it especially does not mean that the map is route-describing: *you should be here, you will go there, here is the order to follow as you go shopping in the mall*.

To the contrary.

Using an orienting map like the Terrain of Tough Transitions, we find that the process is often messy, recursive, unpredictable; it overlaps, doubles back on itself. We don't "do" Responding, mark those experiences off our list, and make a note to "do" Reviewing next Tuesday before dinner. We don't know where and how many places on the map we might be on any given day. We think we've reached a certain point in our progress only to find ourselves back where we were a month ago. All normal. All to be expected. And we can find ourselves in a transition where the practicalities of our daily experiences would put us smack in the middle of Reorganizing while our experiences of making meaning of the situation would put us in our inner life in Renewing. So we can experience the same transition—with its different demands, its different ramifications—in several places on the map at the same time, in our inner and outer lives. Transitions are complex; the human being and the human spirit are complex. We deal with tough transitions at many dimensions, so nothing can be boxed and tidy.

Making a Map of Orientation Useful

An orienting map can't predict where we will go. It can't direct what we should do. What such a map offers is a way to check in, locate oneself, and identify what people and research says is normal at various stops on the way. The map offers distinctions. It provides a cluster of experiences that are common: this is what you may expect; this is what people have done that worked when they found themselves in this place. In a sponsored study of change, loss, and transition, the National Academy of Sciences asserts that there is a process through which people can move: "Although observers divide the process into various numbers of phases and use different terminology to label them, there is general agreement about the nature of reactions over time."

"Oh, these are the experiences, thoughts, questions, emotions I have at this moment," one of us might say. "Let me remember what facts are known about this; let me remember what stories real people have told about this; let me remember what is normal so I won't think I am off-the-wall." Or we might think this way about the usefulness of the map: "At the emotional level I feel this, but at the take-action level I have to make some important decisions tomorrow. Let me remember the map and think about the tensions between how I feel and what decisions I am being required to make now. How have others lived out tensions like this?" The Map of the Terrain of Tough Transitions with all the commentary about it, then, serves as a reference tool that we can return to as we experience yet another aspect of the transition.

Now let's explore the map. What are the characteristics of the distinct areas on it? Where will we locate ourselves? It would be a good thing for each of us to choose a tough transition we have already experienced in our own lives and track that transition on the map as we go from location to location. Test out the research findings for ourselves. Determine what parts of people's stories correspond to our own and what value we can find in that correspondence. Perhaps draw our own maps if we find deviations or differences.

As murky as a tough transition can be on any given day, there is also a lot of clarity available in research and in people's lived experience about the ways of thinking and acting that help us move through these transitions. Thank goodness, we don't have to reinvent the wheel. And there is good news about the end of the process. More than one researcher asserts that it is possible to find yourself at some point feeling that the tough transition is now integrated into a "new normal." That you experience equilibrium again. That you can make some kind of meaning out of the whole experience. *Creative outcomes, victorious outcomes, what we can reasonably expect* . . . these are the terms scientists use to describe the achievements and accomplishments we find in our lives as a result of the hard work we do in moving through the tough transition. I must say for myself that when I'm slogging through a tough transition even the *possibility* of achieving creative and victorious outcomes at some point in the process is enough to make me feel, if not certain, at least optimistic.

PART TWO

NAVIGATING THE MAP

1

Responding

Blue soul, dark road.

GEORG TREKL

Life as it Was

1. Responding

Emotions Haywire
Emotions Numbed
Assumptive World Disappears
Transitions Out of Our Control

For most of us, the first responses we have to the news of a tough transition do not reflect our best performance. While we'd like to be calm, we're unsettled and upset. While we know we'd do better if we were centered and stable, we instead tilt and spin. Instead of focus and concentration and wise decision-making, we experience the inability to sit still or remember useful things or find what we are looking for. It's difficult to consider the situation from different perspectives while we are being swept along what feels like the rapids on a Class VI river.

Two important shifts occur simultaneously when we are required to respond to some news or event that launches a tough transition. First, our physical bodies go into emergency mode. We can do nothing about this. It happens involuntarily. We can, however, work to understand what is happening and make decisions that intervene in or assuage the dangerous results of this physical assault. At the same time, our *assumptive* world—the way we expected things to be, the way we had worked for things to be, the way life is supposed to be—shatters like a glass globe hitting a stone floor. Depending on the kind of transition presenting itself, we are surprised, euphorically lifted out of ourselves, taken aback, confused, startled, confronted, unsure, mad, resigned, overwhelmed. Our personal world, as we knew it, has changed. We can only notice that what gave us meaning and what provided a sense of direction are no longer present and count-on-able. Until we are able to create a new center that holds, we feel in limbo, or at least in a very strange and new place.

If knowledge is power, it will help us enormously to approach the terrain of the Responding experience with as much information as possible about the body's reaction to tough transitions and the challenges we face when we lose our assumptive world. Let's begin with our emotions.

Emotions Haywire

You'd think that we humans would be wired to begin problem solving immediately when a disrupting change occurs in our lives. But instead we are wired to react with our emotions. The triggering of our emotions can do us a world of good if we need to run to get out of the way of a fast-moving bus, but they can cause a problem when we need to make well-thought-out decisions or step back from a situation and get our bearings. Our emotions exist, of course, to help us stay alive. Scientists tell us that there is always some part of us—our emotional center—that is trying hard to keep us "in a positively regulated life." They tell us that this regulation, in fact, is "a deep and defining part of who we are." Emotions exist to keep danger away or to help us take advantage of opportunities. They help us "maintain the coherence of [life's] structures and function against life-threatening odds."

But to have our physical body go into emergency mode, causing a cascade of biochemical and neuronal responses just when we need to be able to marshal every rational resource we have, only adds to our problems. (Researchers have even pinpointed where in the brain these responses occur: If we're sad, that emotion was probably evoked, for instance, in the ventromedial prefrontal region. Negative emotions like fear and anger usually trigger in the right frontal cortices.)

So when we find out that we have lost a job or a parent has to go into a nursing home or retiring turns out to be a disappointment or a relationship falls apart or the reality of moving to a new city sets in, our emotions fire into action immediately—perhaps as quickly as 120 milliseconds after being triggered. Realizing that there are one thousand milliseconds in a second, it's difficult to grasp

How fast is emotion triggered? 120 milliseconds (millisecond is .001 second) Hummingbird wingbeat: .02 seconds Blink of an eye: .025 seconds

how quickly the emotions spark. But if a hummingbird wingbeat rate is .02 seconds and the blink of my eye is .025 seconds, clearly 120 milliseconds (where a millisecond is .001 second) is too fleeting a time for a human being consciously to obtain control of these emotions.

When the emotions respond to the disequilibrium of a tough transition—and these tough transitions can be good events like getting a promotion or making a windfall on an investment as well as bad events like being betrayed or losing a family member—the body immediately secretes various hormones. For instance, in the brain trauma center where arousal, responses, and memories are integrated, there is an increased production of CRH, corticotropin-releasing hormone, which produces anxiety-like symptoms. Chemicals such as catecholamines are released, "emergency-mobilizing" chemicals that synthesize in the neuronal cells of the brain and the sympathetic nervous system. As we become more and more stressed by the tough transition—again, whether we consider the transition good or bad—the chemical levels increase and our central nervous system becomes highly stimulated. Perhaps we feel giddily euphoric and may act devil-may-care. Perhaps we're anxious and can't sit still or concentrate.

So much is happening in our body that it is little wonder we overreact when someone speaks normally to us or we feel so despondent that we don't think we'll ever have a good day again. How can we be our smartest and best selves when our hearts are beating faster, when our blood vessels are literally constricting and even rerouting the blood flow? No wonder we tense up, for our emotional responses are causing our muscles to contract. We come down with a cold or the flu because the T cells that protect our immune system have changed roles. Our breathing may become defective. The autonomic, physiologic, biochemical, and endocrinologic systems are all affected. The adrenal system is activated. The body's homeostasis has been disturbed. We're in a chronic hyperarousal state. So we don't sleep well; have difficulty concentrating; experience outbursts of anger or irritation; find ourselves jumping at the slightest noise.

What else can we expect as our emotions continue to run amuck? What else is normal?

Upon realizing that we are faced with some circumstance or situation that might affect our life's coherent structure, we get volleys of reactions in the body that actually change the environment in the belly, entrails, intestines, and bowels. "It feels like I've been hit in the gut," we are likely to say. "I've got butterflies in my stomach," another might say. "My stomach's in knots," responds someone else.

These reactions rearrange the muscles, and sometimes even our body's skeleton, in particular patterns for particular lengths of time. We might snarl, frown, grin, grimace, or suddenly see new lines on our face. We might say things spontaneously like, *With this windfall, the world's my oyster; This makes me so mad; Oh no, I can't take this; I'm confused.* We may make all kinds of sounds like moans, giggles, growls, frantic laughter. Our body postures might change as a result of these emotional charges in the brain. We might hug everyone in sight, jump up and down, clap our hands, strike out, clutch our stomach, grab for a chair, bolt, fall down. Our emotions and the responses to them may produce specific patterns of behavior, like calling everyone we can think of on the phone, writing a lot of checks, turning away, running, standing in paralysis, striding back and forth. The brain, too, produces pictures—if it's an unwanted event, the pictures will be the worst scenario possible—and, naturally, these pictures become the focus of our attention.

In this emotionally charged state, we don't have good physical coordination. We can't run our daily lives as smoothly as we did.

Even the simplest thing seems harder to do. Our brain and our eyes don't coordinate the way they did, or our brain and our hands. We don't feel our normal freedom and power to act. Every negative emotion that is triggered by the tough transition puts us outside our regular range of opera-

> Sometimes we feel like a sparrow caught by cat's claw.
>
> Dame Julian of Norwich, fourteenth-century scholar

tions. If the emotion is related to a happy transition—making a great investment or getting engaged, for example—we may find ourselves not taking prudent care, overspending, not paying attention to details, not being responsible in the ways we know to be. If the emotion is related to a less than happy transition—not getting a promotion or hearing a diagnosis of illness, for example—we may find ourselves lashing out in resentment, withdrawing in despair, soldiering on in resignation.

How does all this look in a real-life situation? Let's listen to an adult granddaughter speak of her emotional response to feeling betrayed by her grandparents:

The night after the funeral my cousin handed me the will. I saw that I had been listed with my grandparents' hated ex-daughter-in-law and my stepsiblings who had disowned my grandparents more than twenty years before. Everyone in this list was to receive $100, the bequeath being a legal maneuver to say, "Yes, we know these children and this wife of our late son exist; but we are making sure that they know by this action that they have no part in our lives." I was devastated, not by not getting a lot of money, but by being included in this list of people my grandparents hated. I had not disowned them when the family fell apart after my father's death. In fact, I had given the eulogy at both of my grandparents' funerals. I was family. But, suddenly, with this line in the will, I knew that for more than two decades the relationship with my grandparents had been full of hypocrisy on their part and had ended with this cruel act.

My emotions went wild. I said almost nothing at the time and, I think, showed no emotion outside. But inside my heart was beating so fast and hard I could feel it against my blouse. I felt something like a lava flow of anger move from my stomach up my esophagus to my throat . . . actual heat that I could feel moving up, up, and up. I wanted to scream. And when I got back to my hotel room, I did scream. I took one of the plastic glasses from the sink and crushed it and then threw it across the room, crying all the while. And I yelled, "Was everything for the past twenty years a lie? Have you pretended to love me when all along you considered me one of the group you despised?" For two weeks my emotions continued to shake me violently. And even now, a month later, I have an internal response that feels like nausea when I think straight on about the situation.

Let's extract the emotions this adult granddaughter records experiencing:

My emotions went wild.
My heart was beating so fast and hard I could feel it against my blouse.
Something like a lava flow of anger moved from my stomach up my esophagus to my throat.
I wanted to scream.
I did scream.
I took one of the plastic glasses from the sink and crushed it.
Threw it across the room.
Crying all the while.
I yelled.
Two weeks later emotions shake me violently.
A month later, I have an internal response that feels like nausea.

When we remember that our emotions exist to *help us keep a positively regulated life and to maintain the coherence of life's structures,* it is easy to understand why this educated adult woman reacts in these ways. The coherence of her relationship with two grandparents to whom she had felt so close that she gave both their funeral eulogies has splintered. Her positively regulated life—thinking she was beloved of her grandparents, thinking she was a central part of their lives—now appears to have been an illusion surrounded by hypocrisy. Her emotions have erupted because she has lost the coherence and the positively regulated life she thought she had. Until she finds a way to quiet these ferocious emotions, this granddaughter will be off keel and not able to think and act as productively as she would like. Yet, even though the emotions are causing intense stress and upset, they are a normal response in this life-changing circumstance.

There's another kind of emotion that we often experience during certain types of tough transitions: a low-grade, ongoing, chronic emotion that doesn't slap us around but does always seem to be there, pulling our energy level down and nagging at our sense of well-being. After my father had his first stroke and even though it was a relatively mild one, I had a sadness that stayed with me. I knew that, at his age, this stroke was the beginning of a stage of his life that could only go down and not up. He had to stop driving, which both reduced his independence and created an extra burden on my mother. When he found that he couldn't stand up long enough to work the corn and collard greens he had planted around the yard, he was upset. (Though I might say, not daunted, for he figured out how to keep on gardening, even if he had to raise sweet potatoes in a washtub.) I just knew after that Saturday morning of the stroke that his and Mother's life would never be the same. And I was sad with a kind of sadness that, though it wasn't debilitating, didn't go away.

I've seen mothers of babies who died unexpected crib deaths accommodate the emotion of fear that keeps cropping up when they have other children. I've seen adult children of alcoholics have to keep working to transform their anger at childhood traumas into something useful and productive (and be successful at doing so). Such emotional responses, I've come to see, are just part of the cycle of living and can only be honored, not explained away.

Emotions Numbed

We all know people, however, who, when faced with a tough transition, act as if nothing has changed. They are efficient, calm, seemingly unflustered. Are certain people, then, immune to the commotion of their emotions? Doctors and scientists say this: "It may well be that in time of stress some people's brains secrete special neurohormones that allow them to register or recognize what has happened to them in a piece-by-piece way. Some part of a person may respond to unwanted or disrupting news by closing down so that the situation won't feel so overwhelming."

Yet for the neurohormones and the defenses even to go into action, the individual had to know that something disturbing, disruptive, or unusual had happened. So while those whose brain temporarily fends off the reality of the situation may be protected for a time from realizing the full external implications of the tough transition, nothing protected them from the immediate internal knowledge that something had changed and that their previous equilibrium was threatened. In order to receive temporary protection from reality they must have registered the tough transition on some level. It was the undeniable registering of that immediate internal knowledge that triggered the neurohormones that now allow them to appear calm or unfazed by the transition.

Furthermore, nothing protects these people from the damage of repressed emotion if they do not, at some time, stop to acknowledge the impact of the situation. Fortunately, for most people who at first seem unfazed by a situation, this moving toward acknowledging the event evolves naturally. Slowly, in a time right for each individual, the reality of the transition presents itself. Perhaps she acknowledges how much money she's been spending in celebration of the promotion. Perhaps he realizes that, in response to a loss, he has been irresponsible in taking care of his health. Another person will awaken to the damage she is doing to herself by hanging out with the wrong people. Someone else may realize suddenly one morning that he has not even started to grieve and needs to. For some, this acknowledgment brings collapse after weeks or months (or even years) of being strong and efficient. For some, it brings clarity that a change in behavior is needed. For some, it brings a storm of emotions as powerful as if the situation were happening today. For all who are finally in touch fully with the emotional response to the transition—no matter the challenge of responding to those emotions—their lives can now be lived with freedom and authenticity.

In fall 2004 I spoke to a large group of doctors, nurses, health practitioners, and hospice directors in Mobile, Alabama. I talked some about the purpose of emotions, and I spoke about unacknowledged emotions and the toll they take. Following the question-and-answer period, a highly qualified and experienced nurse approached me at the front of the room with an astonishing story. Her words went something like this:

While you were talking, I realized that I have been stuck in my life for the past twenty-one years because I would not acknowledge my emotions. When my husband left me more than two decades ago, I reacted by acting as if nothing bad had happened. I prided myself on keeping myself together, always showing a sunny face to the world. But today I see how much that has cost me. The anger I have always felt but refused to show has given me an ulcer. I have lines on my face that age me beyond my years. I've gained nothing by living this way. It was such good news today to realize that, even though it is twenty-one years later, I can acknowledge all the emotions I have been denying and start to live a freer life.

This woman's comments demonstrate that the emotions are always present. It is up to us whether we acknowledge them, when, and how.

Emotions and Social Connections

As if the physical upheaval of the brain and body were not enough, there is another set of emotions that are triggered as part of our response to tough transitions. Along with the primary emotions of fear, anger, disgust, euphoria, sadness, and happiness come the social emotions: pride, contempt, jealousy, envy, embarrassment, shame, guilt, indignation, contempt, and sometimes sympathy.

I remember instantaneously being swept up in the emotions of embarrassment and shame the day the new president of the university where I was a faculty member told me that my part-time duties as assistant to the president would end the coming September. It wasn't that I wanted to stay in the president's office. In fact, the previous president and I had exchanged notes some months before, in which I told him that I wanted to return full-time to the department where I was a professor so that I would have the summers off to write. Nevertheless, I descended immediately into an emotional tailspin when the new man said, "Your job will be eliminated." I wanted to be the one who resigned; I didn't want to be someone who had not been chosen. I wanted to instigate my own transition, not have it instigated for me.

Amazing . . . I was a grown woman—in fact, a soon-to-be tenured, full professor—sitting in that chair listening to the university president. But the images that flooded my mind in that moment were of an eight-year-old girl standing on the gravelly red dirt of the school playground with the rest of Miss Flegal's third grade students. Steve Slack and Frances Farmer were choosing people to be on their softball teams. One classmate after another was picked—even Faye Hudson who wasn't big as a minute and hated to run—but I was still standing there. *Total embarrassment. Little yellow pique dress. Not good at this, always throwing my bat. The hot sun coming down, trying to keep my balance on the slope of the hill behind Rossville Elementary. Everyone being picked but me, a bit on the chubby side, stringy hair that would not stay curled no matter what. Miss Flegal standing in the background. Having to play softball whether you wanted to or not . . .* So that day in the president's office at the university, when I was told I was not being chosen (for a job I had already said I didn't even want, for jimminy's sake!), I turned into a blob of upset protoplasm. Embarrassment. Shame.

Why, any sensible adult would wonder, do tough transitions trigger social emotions like shame and embarrassment? Why do we feel guilt related to a transition event, even while our friends argue that the guilt has no rational basis? Emotion, after all, is all about "transition and commotion." So while reason might say that it is silly to be embarrassed because we lose a job we didn't even especially want, our social emotions say otherwise. It may well be that these emotions are "terrible advisors." Yet "advise" us they do.

Identifying Our Assumptive World

When we understand that our emotional system is automatic and hot-wired, we can start to make sense of the immediate—and even recurring—outbursts of energy, displays of anger, feelings of guilt, and even the long nights without sleeping. But why the ongoing sense of emptiness? Why the experience that we are now living our lives in a vacuum? Why, when we know there is nothing to do about this situation except to make changes, take care of business, move on and forward, etc., etc., etc., are we unable to shake this stuff off and get on with it? After all, we know how the world works: life isn't fair, things happen, everybody ages, justice is not always done, things never stay the same, you win some/you lose some, life without change would be stale—all those things we read every January on giveaway desk calendars.

> I want to go home,
> to ride to my
> village gate.
> I want to go back,
> but there's no
> road back.
>
> Mei Sheng and Fu I,
> first century BC

The answer lies beneath the surface. Because in dealing with tough transitions, something else is happening in addition to the obvious. We are "handling" things out there, of course—clearing out a parent's apartment, putting a visit-the-other-parent schedule on a child's calendar, calling the chamber of commerce to prepare to move to a strange city, sitting down at the computer every morning to check Monster.com's new job listings. But on an internal level we are floundering. Our assumptive world has dissolved. We are like a ship without a rudder.

With the outside world, we know what we are losing: our parents' independence, our partner's companionship, our chair at the office, the familiar route we can drive with our eyes closed. But, with this assumptive world, what we are losing is subterranean, down beneath the surface of things.

To try to understand this for myself, I think of the deck on the back of our house. Of course, I, like most of us, don't go around thinking every day about the structural framework of some part of the building where I live. The structure is just there. The frame on which the walls and windows and roofs are placed. The form that determines the shape of the building. Unseen and unthought of.

Until one day the termites swarm.

Fortunately, it was our exterminator who found the pesky insects, and before they had time to do a lot of damage. A few planks of decking replaced here, the ground thoroughly treated there, and things were back to normal. But I've never since been as totally oblivious of the structure shaping and holding up our house as I was before. I'm very aware now that there is something that determines the very stability of our home that we never see and don't even think about, which I need to pay attention to and consider.

The two-by-fours, joists, and rafters make up the internal structural framework of a house. The assumptions we naturally hold about life (but usually take little notice of) are the internal structural framing of our lives. What kinds of assumptions do we plan and live our lives by?

When good things happen, I will be happy.

It is easy to make adjustments if I want the change that is occurring.

People who are sincere and honest will have a good life.

Parents die before children.

People are basically honest.

Family members will be helpful.

People who sacrifice for a good cause will be rewarded.

People who are careful (hardworking, loving, believing, etc.), can avoid misfortune.

Add to these assumptions such as:

I will like the outcomes of good fortune that come my way.

This change is manageable; in fact, I'll probably even enjoy it.

If I want something a lot, I will feel complete when I get it.

If I take care of myself, I won't become ill.

If I pray, God will take care of me and those I pray for.

If I work hard, I will achieve my goals.

If I perform well, I will be rewarded.

If I work hard at relationships, I will have people around me who love me.

Then there are our personal, specific expectations that are part of our assumptive world:

I will grow old with this person.

My retirement plan will take care of my needs when I am elderly.

My children will bury me.

My parents will age well, given their genetics.

This company is fair and well managed.

Moving to a new town will be exciting.

Blending our families will be work, but our dreams of togetherness will always be more powerful than the problems we incur.

Now, if we stop and look directly at these assumptions—with a laser light or a stare—we *know* they are not true. We've cooked more than our share of dinners after work and washed up the dishes—and still our partner said we were selfish and left. We took our vitamins all last winter and still got pneumonia the week before spring. All those overtime hours and weekend-prepared reports full of color graphics didn't amount to a hill of beans when the cost-cutting guys said a thousand people have to go. And, for sure, we know our parents are going to get old and so will we.

But somehow—and I guess in many ways it is a blessing—we live a kind of positive illusion. Our own world is a very limited part of the world at large. And in our relatively contained world, there *is* evidence that hard work pays off, people help when you need them, and we can make good things happen by setting goals and working hard to meet them. Our own experience—our own specific assumptive world—says that we ought to be able to count on certain things. *I did brilliantly at my last assignment; therefore, I can count on an equal or better assignment next time. I deeply love this person; therefore, anything can be worked out.* By these personal assumptions, then, we dream our dreams and make our plans.

It is these mental maps, our assumptions, that shape our daily actions and daily thoughts without our realizing it. Imagine an aunt putting away a family quilt to give to her niece when she gets married, automatically assuming that the niece will get married and the aunt will be alive on that day. If you asked the aunt, she would probably say that either of these things might not be true. But the point is that she automatically acts as if they will be true. Which is well and good. Otherwise she would be paralyzed and could take no action.

Assumptive World Disappearing

When we are hit with a tough transition that shatters our assumptive world, it rocks us. Shakes the foundation. Brings into

question everything we counted
on and trusted previously. We
are suddenly on Pogo's "Land
of the Trembling Earth"—
standing deep in the Okefeno-
kee Swamp on one of those

Congressman Frog to Pogo:
I'll tell you, son, the minority
got us outnumbered.

floating islands of peat that cause even trees and bushes to trem-
ble with the approach of man or beast. And all we can do is try to
find a pole long enough to reach solid earth and hope we can get
there.

I remember how my assumptive world dissolved when my husband was sent abroad on a job assignment and I moved with him.
I had a track record of being a strong and capable person. I had
weathered losses. I had set high goals for myself and worked hard
to reach them. So I naturally assumed—especially since this transition was one we chose and one that stood to be new and exciting—that I would adapt quickly and skip blithely through the
countryside on my new adventures.

Did I ever have a surprise in store! My assumptive world didn't
last two days! I couldn't find any part of my steady foundation to
stand on. The traits and attributes I had counted on just weren't
there. "I've stepped out of my life and into nothingness," was the
refrain that kept circling in my head. I couldn't talk myself into
feeling that I had the unbelievable good fortune of living in a big
foreign city with more museums to visit and plays to see and parks
to walk in than I could ever enjoy. I knew things logically in my
head, but the assumptions I had about how I would react and what
I would do had faded like smoke.

I left a notebook on the train and broke down and cried like a
baby in front of a stranger when I was checking to see if anyone
had found it. I overpaid the old gentleman helping with our yard,
hoping he would like me and stay longer talking. I became irra-
tionally angry when I couldn't find fabric softener on the grocery
store shelf. Strange behavior. *Not myself*, I would say. What I had
assumed about the kind of person I was and about my capability to
adjust didn't hold. And if those assumptions weren't true, what

was? I swirled around in a vacuum until I was able to start to sort out what I could count on about myself and what I couldn't.

We don't rebuild an assumptive world overnight. It took years of experience for the internal structure upon which we base our plans and actions to assemble itself. When this structure falls apart, we find ourselves in a void. Our threads of purpose and meaning are cut. Where we were going has ceased to exist. What we thought was going to happen in our future now won't. The expectations and beliefs that shaped our behavior no longer hold. The faith that underpinned our very existence appears now to be a mirage or, perhaps, even a mockery of our current situation. Of course we feel lost. Of course we feel that life is meaningless and empty. Of course we feel without purpose.

This happens in ways that surprise us.

When my mother, ten years younger than my father and in good health, surprised everyone by dying first, I felt she—and my sister, brother, and I—had been betrayed by life. We had expected to have her with us at least a decade after Daddy died. Perhaps we could help make up some for the years of sacrificial care she gave our ailing father. She'd go with us on trips, which she loved to do. Even in her late seventies she still imagined that she might take a course or two at the local community college. I could imagine helping to make that possible when our father died. I was surprised at how angry I became when we got to do none of these things; I was also surprised at how many years and how much work it took for me to handle that anger. Sensible? No. Understandable? Yes. My assumptive world had been logical; it just had not been realistic.

And I have reeled when the assumptions I held about God did not hold. After my father retired as a minister and he and my mother moved to their little frame house on Possum Creek in Soddy-Daisy, Tennessee, I had a crisis of faith. How could God allow my father and mother to be so

> Can we take a direct flight back to reality or do we have to change planes in Denver?
>
> Tim Allen, comedian

poor after they had sacrificed everything for God's work for over sixty years? Where was the reward for the righteous man talked about in Psalms? Where was the result of "Ask and ye shall receive"? Even though I knew the truth—that the rain falls on both the evil and the good—I had an unexamined assumption that my father and mother's devoted work for God's cause would be rewarded at least with enough money to buy groceries and pay their insurance in the same month. When that assumption proved to be false, I was both angry and confused. It took a conversation with my father one spring morning sitting on the screened-in side porch to start me on the way to building a new assumptive world—when he pointed to the one flower blooming in the yard and said, "You see that lily? God takes care of that lily, and God takes care of your mother and me."

Building a new assumptive world takes time. We have to find new purpose and meaning where the old has been destroyed. We have to examine and reflect on what we now believe, what we now know. We have to establish new patterns. Make new habits. Think new thoughts. In this interim between the shattering of an assumptive world and the building of a new one, we often experience deep sorrow, sadness, sometimes even depression. Often we feel we have lost our identity. We may feel consumed with anger or guilt. We may wonder if anything is ever going to be worthwhile again. Or we may just feel devastatingly tired.

Good Transitions That Bring Loss

It's hard to think of a tough transition that does not include some kind of loss. There's an old saying that "many a good person has been undone by a promotion." And it's true: Good transitions—like new jobs, house moves, marriage, births—can be tough and usually involve losing something we value, even while we are gaining something we desire. We love our new job but we miss the camaraderie we used to have with our former colleagues. The baby has brought more love and joy than we could ever have dreamed of; and we're surprised by how so many things have changed in the marriage. Naturally we want the kids to grow up and go to college, but we are deadened by a sense of uselessness when they are gone.

We don't have trouble understanding the sense of loss when a transition is undesired. But we are often surprised when a transition that we know is a gain also feels like a loss at the same time. Loss almost always brings sadness. Sadness can spiral down to despondency, depression, and despair, particularly if we are not aware of how built-in and strong are our connections and bonds to people and situations that are part of our everyday living. Something as simple as losing our routine can take the punch out of a new job. The challenge of solving new problems that arise after we've established a home with a great partner takes the shine off our bliss.

Probably the best way to hold these happy-yet-sad situations is to acknowledge the paradox. To move on, we often have to leave something desirable behind. The new requires problem solving that makes the old look so attractive. Simple becomes complex when we change from a life as an independent single person to someone with a family. A boon propels us out of what was normal and familiar and into a heady stratosphere where we don't know the rules. A situation that beckons leaves us feeling stranded, at least until things become more familiar. The most important thing is to remember that such contradictions are part of the fabric of change. When we know that the paradoxes are normal, we will not be undone by them.

Transitions We Don't Control

When Mrs. Miller, the librarian, first read us second graders the fairy tale *Little Red Riding Hood*, I thought that "the little girl, the prettiest creature anyone has ever seen" was the main character in the story. Later—certainly by the summer my high school boyfriend left me for one of the most beautiful girls I had ever seen, arriving with her even tan and perfect white teeth from the beaches of California—if asked about the main character, I would probably have said, "Well, it's probably not the little girl in the red velvet hood as much as it is the wolf—that conniving, cheating, crafty animal who would chew you up with his teeth." But today, having been a participant in way too many transitions that I didn't instigate, I think it's the grandmother who is the central figure in *Little Red Riding Hood*.

Can you just imagine?

Here Grandma is, at home in her little cottage in the woods. She's resting in bed, recuperating, probably thanking her lucky stars that she, at her age, has recovered from her most recent serious illness. Grandma is now able to eat again; and one has to imagine how much she is going to enjoy the piece of cake and bottle of wine (and in some versions, little pot of butter) that her granddaughter has swinging in that little basket as she skips through the woods.

But what happens next?

It was nothing the grandmother had done that brought the wicked wolf to her cottage to eat her up. She had no knowledge of the chain of events put into place by the trickery of the wolf and the naiveté of her granddaughter in their encounter in the forest. The danger she was going to be in, the problem she would have to solve to save herself and her granddaughter—of all these she was oblivious. She was just lying in bed, living her life, doing what was wise and natural. Then, *knock, knock, knock*. The wolf was at the door. Suddenly, her life was threatened. Because of someone's else's actions, she was in danger.

Quiz: Who is the main character in *Little Red Riding Hood*?
a) little girl
b) wolf
c) grandmother

The reason I associate the grandmother in *Little Red Riding Hood* with our modern tough transitions is that something similar happens to us in many of these powerful situations. It is someone else's health problems that change my weekly schedule. It is some vote in the European Union, determining the size of apples that can be exported from Denmark, that decreases the sales from my orchard in Wenatchee. It is the need of someone else to spread her wings or declare his independence that leaves me dangling. It is my boss's problems with his superior that results in my position's being discontinued.

This isn't to cry, *Woe, woe, I'm a victim*. It's just to say that, like the story of Grandma resting peacefully in her little cottage, forces are at the door, knocking my life off center, before I hardly know it. And it doesn't matter whether I wanted the change or not; I am suddenly the one dealing with the tough transition.

This has to make it harder. At least if we instigate the change, work for it, decide this is the way to go—taking a job that requires moving the family but stands to create a better future; downsizing because it's the sensible thing to do and we are tired of all the cleaning and maintenance—we are clear about the potential positive outcomes. It may be true that, in time, we will come see the upside of the unwanted, instigated-by-someone-or-something-else tough transition (and most of the time we do). But the fact that the need to make a transition comes from circumstances and situations beyond our control has to make engaging in the process even tougher.

Everyone Goes on a Merry Way

Finally, there's the infuriating fact that for most of the people around us, life goes on the same even while we are reeling and rocking from the slam of the tough transition. It's not that people are callous or uncaring. They are just busy. At first, folks say, "I'm sorry," or "Here's the number of a friend of mine who knows a lot of recruiters," or "I'll help you research assisted living locations for your mother." And they mean to do more. But life intervenes, perhaps bringing them one of their own unexpected tough transi-tions, or if not, certainly filling up their days and nights with more to do than they have time or energy to do it.

W. H. Auden once wrote a poem about how people just natu-rally stay focused on their own life and activities, even when a spectacular something happens to someone right next to them. Auden is not being critical; he's just writing about something that is the way life goes.

In the poem Auden is remembering a painting by Brueghel that he saw displayed in the Brussels Fine Arts Museum. In the painting, Icarus, the young boy whose wings melted when he flew too close to the sun, is shown falling into the water. A big ship is passing in a sealane nearby, and on the shore a farmer is plowing his field. The poem ends poignantly with words about people on a ship who see something amaz-ing—a boy falling through the air to-ward the water—and yet go on calmly with their lives.

> The French philosopher Simone Weil once said that the only suitable question to ask another human being was, "What are you going through?"

Like the people on the ship in the poem, friends and family around us often seem to have somewhere to get to and so they sail calmly on.

Is It Any Wonder

Is it any wonder, then, that with . . .
  Basic emotions like euphoria, anger, fear, and surprise erupting
  Social emotions like pride, guilt, indignation, and embar-rassment hovering
  Factors outside our control often instigating the current situation

Sadness clouding life around us, even when there's good in
the tough transition

And . . .

Folks, even those that love us, not able to give much attention after the first offers of help and expressions of
concern . . .

We feel as if we have been hit by a meteorite when we must
begin responding to a tough transition. And at the very time
that we need to be smart, clearheaded, inventive, centered,
and focused.

And about the only thing we can say to that is: You have
to be kidding.

PEOPLE TELL THEIR STORIES OF RESPONDING

Someone once said that we need stories as much as food. When
we're in the upheaval, chaos, and uncertainty of Responding during a tough transition, hearing stories of others' experiences reminds us of our shared humanity. We see ourselves in their
situations and imagine them in ours. Somehow just knowing what
is normal in other people's lives strengthens us to respond to the
challenges tough transitions bring us. Let's listen, then, to these
true stories . . .

RESPONDING TO A JOB LOSS

He was calm and collected when he told me. He had known since 1:30
that afternoon—his boss came by and put a sticky on his computer
screen—"I need to see you." He said when he saw it he thought, "This
isn't good."

"I kept the note," he said. "I'll put it in my autobiography . . . a real

turning point in my life." He was trying to be funny, but his face was full of pain.

After the first, perhaps, hour of calm, stunned (for me especially—he had had since 1:30 to get used to the news) conversation, we started yelling at each other.

I told him I was so angry at him for risking taking a job in another part of the business and leaving one of the strongest positions in the company to do that . . . that if he hadn't taken that risk he would be back in his old job and not in this predicament. I told him that he hadn't included me fully in the knowledge of that risk two years ago. He said he had. I said he had not given me the full picture.

Then we went upstairs to check on our finances. Well, we have this much here, this much there. We have these stock options to cash in . . . I can't keep from saying, "Look at all the ones we are losing because you have lost your job—options that could in years ahead send the kids to school, options you have already been granted for work well done—and now you will lose them all. This situation is a huge dollar loss for us, potentially. Such a sad, sad situation."

Nothing had changed in his job performance, ability, etc., from being the person granted all those wonderful stock options over the past ten years—and yet he is now out. He does not have a job.

Oh, I was so angry.

So then we started going over the budget to see where we could cut. "I'll not get manicures and pedicures," I said. "We'll clean the house ourselves," he said, "and I'll get the car washed only every other month." I said, "Wash it yourself." He said, "Clean the house yourself," after I had insisted that one cleaning a month be put back in the budget. Then we came to the line in the budget for a vacation already partly paid for to his home state of Wyoming. "We can't do that," I said. "That will cost maybe another $1,500 or $2,000." "I want to go to Wyoming," he said. "I need to go to Wyoming. I haven't been to my home state for two years, and in my spirit I really need to go."

Then we come to vitamins. "You have to cut out all the extra vitamins you started taking in December for weight loss," I say. He answers, "I'm down five pounds since I started taking those extra vitamins." "We can't spend three or four hundred dollars a month on vitamins," I yell. "I am going to get these last ten pounds off," he yells back. "For the good of my health. So I am not giving up those vitamins."

We yell and scream at each other some more.

I put the money for the vitamins back in the budget. He leaves for a minute, comes back and says, "Take it out. I'm not taking the vitamins. And if you order them, you'll just have to send them back."

So that was that uproar and that argument.

Then it's time to go to bed. I go in and sit on the side of the bed while he is closing down his computer. I sit by the bed, putting cream on my face, and I start crying. Really the first time I've cried, except for maybe a few seconds earlier in the evening.

And I get into bed and shake the bed with my sobs.

RESPONDING TO AN AGING PARENT'S ILLNESS:

Family,
GOOD NEWS:
The clan had a very nice visit last week. It was not all fun, however. Here is some insight as to why it is "good news." I will later in this note say why it is sad news.

The original plan for last week was for the Knoxes, Walker Sr.s and Jr.s to go to Daytona Beach for family time at the ocean. The week was to culminate in a celebration of Mom and Dad being married sixty years (their anniversary is actually not until November but we wanted to combine the beach and the celebration). The Knoxes were at the beach for the week (Saturday–Saturday). The Walker Jr.s flew in from Europe on Sunday and rented a Navigator so we could haul Mom, Dad, medical stuff (oxygen tanks, wheelchairs), and assorted other things in comfort. The four of us were going to spend a couple of days (Tuesday–Thursday) at the beach, then return to Mom and Dad's house to rest up for the Saturday night celebration.

Well, Monday of last week (the day before we were to head to Daytona), Mom had difficulty getting her breath. (This has been a problem over the past couple of months.) So into the hospital she went. Ginny

drove back that day. The rest of the Knox clan drove back on Tuesday
to check out the situation. Mom had stabilized and was very alert. We
all had a wonderful time on Tuesday visiting (even though the hospital
environment was not exactly like being at the beach!).

The Knoxes headed back to the beach late Tuesday afternoon. John
and Karen drove down to Daytona and spent Wednesday–Friday a.m.
Karen and I spent most of Friday afternoon with Mom. Friday night we
went to dinner with Dad. I bought the dinner. He bought the drinks. (I
got a better deal.) Saturday the whole clan again spent time with Mom
at the hospital. We all had a great visit.

Saturday evening we proceeded with the dinner at a private dining
room. Mom was still at the hospital so it was not the same but we did
have her on the cell phone for all the toasts. Through the cell phone,
Mom made a toast as well, which she claims she did not prepare but it
was too good for us to believe her. We did sing the family song (but after
Mom hung up as she said she would be embarrassed).

Sunday we took turns visiting.

Karen and I flew back to Europe Sunday evening. I am typing this
from London on Monday evening at around 4 p.m. EDT.

So why is this good news? Our family spent a lot of quality time together over the past week.

SAD NEWS:
The doctors are saying that Mom's condition is deteriorating. The plan
is for Mom to be released from the hospital in the next day or so and return home. Ginny is contacting a hospice to assist with her care. Mom
is comfortable and alert. Frankly she is in better spirits than the rest of
us. The doctors still are not 100 percent sure of the diagnosis. Her lungs
are filling up like she has an infection but all the tests for infection are
negative. The doctors think it is probable that she has an unusual lung
cancer that is not treatable.

So . . . I wanted you to know. Nothing to do . . . Mom is still fight-
ing and I hope and pray the doctors are wrong.
I will keep you informed.
Love, John

RESPONDING TO AN EMPTY NEST

Now That the Old-Enough Child Has Gone . . .

Here are the things that bring me to my knees: the mirror ball still hanging in the corner of his room, casting rainbows against the blue wall; the porch light turned dark before the ten o'clock news; one of his friends in the checkout line at the grocery store, the hug he gives me that is not my son's hug; the name of his new city on the radio; the footfalls of the cat no longer here, a shadow cat; his black nylon shorts still hanging beside the dryer, not the only thing he forgot.

I should have been prepared, and I was for the big things, the whole idea of this boy-becoming-a-man leaving home, off to find his way, this golden one, just a baby only days ago, and now away, taking his pierced ears and his loud music and his blue Dodge pickup with him. Taking the cat.

No question about time, it was past time for him to leave. He was twenty-one years old, after all. And there's my husband to rediscover, yes, his arms open, the beer in the fridge that did not disappear between yesterday and today. The other cat, the one who stayed behind, sleeps between us, happy to be an only cat.

I know this melancholy will pass, but for now I wear it like a loose shirt, not so close as to chafe, but still tucked in. It's a strange thing, this letting go and hanging on, this joy and sorrow all at once. I want to paint his room. But I stand in front of the smudges on the wall by his closet, where his hand must have rested a million times, and suddenly every color imaginable fills the air. How can I change something so sacred? How can I not?

RESPONDING ON THE DAY OF RETIREMENT

I cannot quite believe today sees the close of my music teaching activities, which I have been doing for forty years!

Last day today.

Strange feelings inside.

Many feelings of wishing the day was already over. Other feelings that are nostalgic. I'm very aware that it is the last time I do so much of my routine, which is written in stone and has not changed for over forty years! The last time I go round with the Smarties to reward my three-year-olds and put stickers on their coloring books. The last time I sing, "It's a hap-hap-happy day" with them and play my "tap-a-head" piano (the way I choose the first conductor with my eyes shut). The last quiz and the last toddler story.

But it is also the last time I have to scour the shops for the right size bread for sandwiches (they only make thick slices for toast). The last time I fight for a place to park the car at the church. The last time I lug in the heavy props! The last time I deal with the so-called nannies who had no idea how to handle children or teach them manners!

So, this Grizzly Gran is only half nostalgic. And what is there to do but confess that I feel both sad and happy at the same time. It is a momentous day.

RESPONDING TO THE DEATH OF A YOUNG HUSBAND

I have to change my life and I don't want to. I want my husband back. It's been four months since he died, and I know he can't come back but I want him to come back. He was such a wonderful man, and I will always love him and miss him. I can't imagine how my life will be without him. I feel really empty, with no hope.

I'm afraid I have nothing noble to say. Guilt plagues me because I think I should have seen symptoms sooner and got him to a hospital. I keep thinking there must have been something I could have done. His absence now is such a presence. We had bought this lovely Victorian house that we loved so much. Now it could be anybody's house. In the mornings when I see the light hitting the chair where he always sat, the scene evokes the deepest sorrow I've ever felt. Sleep is like Novocaine and the mornings bring pain waiting in the wings. I feed the cat, make coffee; but it is all so hard for me. I think, "This is another day I won't have him."

The last day we spent together was a golden day in October. We were working in the yard and he commented on the beautiful day. "You know," he said, "the ancient Greeks said that if you put someone who was ill out in the sun, he or she would get better." He planted tulip bulbs that day, and when the tulips bloom this spring it will be such a bittersweet experience. I've now watched the gold leaves turn to red, then snow falling . . . every change reminds me he is not on earth. If I searched all over the earth, he would be nowhere.

I have one friend who is also a young widow (longer than I have been) and she encourages me to be in the moment, no matter how awful that moment is. And I can call her and say the same thing over and over, and she does not try to make me feel better. She honors my grief. I also attend a grief group at the hospital. Some of the people there seem to want just to slog through. But I want growth from this. If I can't be a better person out of all this suffering, then I wouldn't want to go on. So I'm committed to growing as I live this grief process. My brother, whose wife died a few years ago, gave me some excellent advice, too. He suggested that I try every day to see something beautiful in the world, if only for two seconds. I have had those moments a few times, when I felt the awe of nature, the beauty of the snow, and I felt that my husband was somehow talking to me in that beauty.

And there has been the inexplicable. When we bought the place, the light on the barn had not worked for years. The owners said the whole thing would have to be rewired, that it had never worked while they lived there. We said we didn't need the light anyway, so there was no problem. Well, after my husband died, that light came on and is still on now. Many people have seen it. I even called the original owners again, not telling them what had happened, but just asking about the light on the barn again: "Oh, it's busted," they said. So I am in complete reverence in front of this inexplicable event.

RESPONDING TO A FINANCIAL WINDFALL

I've never had so much money at one time in my life before. I am the sole recipient of a relative's estate, and I can hardly believe my good fortune. The best part about the whole thing is the freedom I feel. The Olympics are about to start, and I'm planning to take myself and eight *of my friends to the Games. I've bought myself a new motorcycle, and when we get back from the Olympics I'm going to take a cross-country trip, stopping to see family and friends along the way. And I'm making some investments in some friends' companies. My accountant the other day told me that he bet he'd see me back in his office in a year or less, having lost a lot of money. He is urging me to be conservative, put cash away and buy bonds, things like that. I hear what he is saying, but I don't think I'm going to turn out like some of his other clients. The friends I'm investing with are smart. And I do plan to go back to work in the future.*

RESPONDING TO MENOPAUSE

I'm just entering menopause, so things aren't so bad yet. But I can see what is coming. Occasionally I have hot flashes and night sweats. I hate feeling wet and clammy and, most of all, I get upset that I can't cuddle with my husband. And there are times that I drive the family just about nuts. "I'm dying," I'll say, opening all the windows. "It's ten degrees," one of our teenagers will retort, "there's three feet of snow on the ground, and you are hot!" Then minutes later I'm closing all the windows and turning the heat up because now I'm cold. I know I'm driving my family crazy. Fortunately, these times are not frequent, but I'm sure they will be.

I'm trying to keep a sense of humor. The other day a vendor came in to meet with me and even while she was shaking the snow off her boots she suddenly started fanning herself. "I'm having my personal summer here," she said, and I knew exactly what she meant. I keep a fan by my desk at work, so I turned it on for her and we laughed together.

The thing that is most distressing is my weight gain. The doctor told me that with menopause comes a slowing down of a woman's metabolism. I hate not being able to eat the way I used to without gaining pounds. I hate to cut down a lot of what I eat and still not lose a pound. It seems hopeless. I'm not happy with myself and I feel depressed about ever losing the weight. I don't feel pretty. I can't find clothes that fit and look great. It doesn't help that my mother fusses at me all the time about losing. My high school graduation class will have its thirtieth reunion this summer, and if I haven't lost any weight by then I'm just not going. Although I really do want to see my classmates.

But I struggle with many other issues every day—like adjusting to a new job, trying to get involved in all the activities of our two teenagers—and I'm not able to fight for myself then. I just don't have enough energy. I'm mentally exhausted. It's important that I change this because already I'm seeing some health costs. I have to take blood pressure medicine and I can tell a difference in my knees when I go up stairs since there so much more weight to carry around.

I am looking forward to spring. We can now see the streets around here; the snow is starting to melt. Our family bikes during good weather, and I love the activity. We drive to wonderful trails and go on a twenty-mile ride, which, in this beautiful nature, seems like nothing. Not only do I get good exercise on these rides, but I feel very close to God. I find the surroundings so spiritual. I'm hoping this exercise and the uplift to my spirits in the spring will be just what I need to get mentally energized to lose weight and deal with the symptoms of menopause.

RESPONDING TO A HUSBAND ANNOUNCING DIVORCE

It was his birthday. I had a big cake for him on the kitchen table, and the children had put their gifts to him all around the cake. When he came in, I was still in the bedroom getting dressed. He walked in to where I was sitting on the end of the bed putting my shoes on, pulled a chair directly in front of me, and sat down. "I filed for divorce today," he said. Nothing else. Just "I filed for divorce today." I was totally shocked. At the moment the only thing I could think to say was, "The children have a birthday cake and presents for you." Then I asked, "Why, James, why?" I had no inkling anything like this was going to happen. I was flabbergasted. All James did was stare straight at me and say, "The perfume is stale that you have been wearing for the past twenty-five years." And with that, he got up and walked out of the room. I don't have a clue what I am going to do. I did find out that James has just gotten back from a two-week trip with another woman *when I thought he was on an extended business trip. Right now I'm just getting through each day. Focusing on taking care of the children and wondering what in the world is next. I'm frightened, hurt, and angry, oh, so very, very angry.*

RESPONDING TO THE LOSS OF A PET

Twelve years ago today, Joan and I were married at Gethsemane Lutheran; she walked into the sanctuary to the organ playing Johann Pachelbel's Canon in D. Seven years later, Joan came home with a tiny little puppy who became our very own Pachelbel, or Pachie. I hadn't had much history with pets at home, and he moved in and became an important part of our family, our four grown children having left us with an empty nest. He loved us and we loved him.

He taught us to take time to play and enjoy life. He was still training us how best to enjoy him. He touched the lives of many of you, and you would share what a special dog we were blessed to have. Many have commented on the "amazing wonderful cow dog" (from our answering machine) who loved the ranch and the beach. But mostly he loved people, everyone he could entice to play.

Pachie died today under the care of our gentle veterinarian, and we still are not sure why. We have a sad hole right now, and if you haven't shared this experience yet, you can say (as I would have), "It is only a dog." Our nephew Cameron prayed at tonight's supper, and he said, "God, tell Pachie we miss him." We, too, feel, like Martin Luther, that there is a special place in heaven for four-legged friends who teach us to love unconditionally.

Thanks for the love we share in this journey of life.

Kent & Joan

RESPONDING TO THE ILLNESS OF A SISTER

Unbelievable as it is, after her earlier glowing report, a radiologist picked up something on Kay's chest X-ray that requires a CAT scan.

Hopefully hopefully, it is this lung disorder she's had all along simply progressing—that would be the best possible news. "Is it a rope or a snake in your bed?" the Buddhists ask in a funny story about alarm. So I'm trying to just wait, with trust, to find out. The test is set up for Wednesday morning, and she's supposed to fly in tomorrow . . . but with the pending hurricane waffling around, the whole thing may have to be postponed. I do hope not.

*   *   **

Kay got the CAT scan done early early this morning (6 a.m.), and I put her on the plane about 10:30. It will be at least a day—probably more—before results are read, compared, etc., and she gets word about the next step, which we figure will be one of two things: (1) watchful waiting or (2) a lung biopsy. I'm just trying to stay in the moment . . . as is she. There is no good news or bad news: just what is, and what we do with that. But I do hope she doesn't have to go though something "big" right now. She's as worn down as I've seen her.

In this moment, I am just plain pooped! So I'm going to wash my face and get right in bed. It just takes it out of you, all that worry . . .

RESPONDING TO A MOVE

One of the main things I'm having to grapple with in this move we've just made from one part of the country to another is guilt. We are very blessed. We have so much to be thankful for. I have a great husband. He has a great new job. We have plenty of food while so many people in the world are hungry. Things could be so much worse. Yet I'm in the doldrums. Lethargic. I feel very down. When I used to work, I longed for the time when I could stay home and do all the things I now have the opportunity to do here in our new environment. But those things aren't exciting anymore, now that I have the time to do them. So I feel guilty. I feel like I'm complaining and shouldn't be. I criticize myself for even having any kind of adjustment problems, given the blessings of our life.

My emotions go up and down. I'll be out on a walk and I'll see the beautiful trees and hear the wind blowing through the leaves. I'll tell myself, "The wind is saying, 'It's going to be okay.'" And I'll actually feel in that moment that everything is going to be okay. Then I'll get back to the house and I'll feel like crying. Highs and lows. I've never had such up/down/down/up emotional swings before. Even my husband notices it. The only thing I have to compare to it is a past experience when I took fertility hormones for a short period of time to try to get pregnant. I never expected a move to create this kind of emotional roller coaster.

Probably the biggest surprise I've had is how hard I'm finding it to start over somewhere. The last few moves we've done were overseas assignments; but we always came back to America to a house we knew, to friends we were comfortable with, to an environment we knew. This move from one part of the U.S. to another, however, is permanent. I expected that my experience in moving several times in the past five years would stand me in good stead in this move. In fact, I expected this move to be much easier than the overseas moves. But that past experience doesn't seem to be making any difference at all in the adjusting I'm having to do now. This move's not temporary, and it doesn't come with a plan to return to our old home and old friends. This move is requiring us to start over with everything. And I'd just forgotten how difficult completely starting over can be.

I'm also surprised at how tired I am, and how unexcited. We have a bigger house now. And it's on a concrete slab! So there's none of the swaying and moving that were so aggravating in our old pier-and-beam house. I anticipated that I would love every moment in a new home. But things are still on the floors in the various rooms and I just haven't made myself go in and find a closet to put things in. The euphoria I've known in the past when I've done the things to make a house a home just isn't present.

There are bright spots, however. Nature here is so beautiful. I take long walks in the woods with the dogs. The trees are spectacular. And we live beside a wetlands, so there are birds and wildlife. (One wildlife got a little too close to one of our dogs, who came home the other day full of porcupine quills!) I think these walks are saving me.

RESPONDING TO DIFFERENT WAYS MEN GRIEVE LOSS

I'm watching my father and my father-in-law grieve the death of my wife. My father-in-law is stoic, with no outlet for any emotion except anger. The most outgoing I have ever seen him was when he put his hand on his wife's shoulder when she was crying. He was dazed at the funeral home and didn't think he wanted to see his daughter in her coffin. He represses his emotion. Five months later he has almost died. He had diverticulitis, a ruptured abdominal cavity that was full of abscesses, and had to have his spleen taken out. His wife says she knows this illness is related to his not letting himself grieve. He has no idea that he doesn't know about expressing grief.

Then my father takes the approach that too much attention is paid to emotions. When I cry sometimes without stopping, he says, "Actions are more important. Get up and act happy. That way you can get happy." I have been very critical of men like him and my father-in-law who denied their feelings. But I had a realization the other day. My father is big on genealogy, and he told me he had found out that my grandfather's mother was born in 1858. My grandfather was very important in my own life, as well as my father's. His mother taught him and had enormous impact on him, all of which he passed on to me. She lived in the Civil War era, in a time when you had ten kids so they could work on the farm, when cholera was rampant. So from this existence—which isn't true anymore at all—she, who was born in 1858, taught my grandfather who was a direct bridge to me in the twenty-first century. And if I hadn't worked on becoming more feeling, not repressing myself and life, I could be just like my grandfather, father, and father-in-law. This gave me a new perspective on these men in my life—they were taught by people who lived in totally different circumstances.

RESPONDING TO A MISCARRIAGE

I have had two miscarriages previously. Today's was the third. It was a long day full of ups and downs. But mainly it was a day of completion. After days of bleeding and cramping, I expelled the fetus and Mark and I did a sacred ceremony and buried it beside a tree. It seemed to be the only thing we could do. Afterwards I went to the hospital and had a sonogram that revealed my uterus is clean and healthy. That was wonderful news. Now that the contractions have stopped, the soul/emotional healing begins.

Tonight Mark and I decided to escape reality for a few days by going to the ocean this Sunday. This will give us time to be alone and to get warm and to get a massage. I love to bike while down at the shore, and it will give me the opportunity to feel like a free kid again. And perhaps when I return the shock will have worn off and I can begin to think about moving forward and looking ahead.

RESPONDING TO THE NEWS OF THE DEATH OF A TEENAGE SON

It was the Saturday after Thanksgiving. I was sitting on the back porch with my sister, who was visiting for the weekend. It was a balmy afternoon. The telephone rang and a stranger's voice asked, "Have you been told?" "About what?" I answered. "About the accident," the voice said. "What accident?" I answered. Then the caller asked, "Is this Dawson O'Connor's house?" I answered that it was. "Well, Dawson's been in an accident. Get to the hospital." I asked, "How is he?" and the caller said, "I can't tell you that."

That was how I found out.

We rushed to the hospital, but Dawson never regained consciousness. He lived through the night and then the next morning he died. Our eighteen-year-old son, my "son/sun, moon, and stars," I always called him. That six-foot-three "tall drink of water," as we refer to him. Classical guitar player. That young man grinning in his senior picture, wearing the yellow patterned tie he asked me to tie for him, which I had done with him facing the mirror and my arms coming from behind to knot the tie and both of us looking at each other in the mirror and grinning. That son who tested me everywhere I was weak. Who was a pure joy to carry in the womb . . . I just glowed throughout the pregnancy.

That son was now dead. As we walked away from the hospital that Sunday morning, I said to my family, "I now know how God felt when Jesus died."

RESPONDING TO RETIRING

It has been very hard to let go. Even though I retired three months ago, I'm still going into the office. I'm a lawyer, and some of the cases I was working on are still active, so I can find all kinds of reasons to go help out, even though I'm no longer on the payroll. What I'm realizing is this: I don't know how to retire. I was very excited as my retirement date moved closer. I made preparations, such as visiting with the pastor at church to ask what kinds of volunteer opportunities could best use my skills and experience. I collected travel brochures and wrote to friends about coming to visit. But I just can't let go. It seems so wasteful to sit around the house, feeling as if I'm not a productive member of society. And, so far, all these great things waiting out there for me to do when I finally would have time to do them don't interest me. I think I have an identity problem, too. Who am I if I am not a practicing lawyer? I also don't know what to do with free time. I guess I'm afraid of having free time. I asked someone the other day, "Can a person fail at retiring?" I make a lot of jokes about it, but I do think that, up to this point, I'm failing at retiring.

RESPONDING TO A LIFE-THREATENING ILLNESS

Dear Family,

I have a bit of health news to share with you. For some time I have been bedeviled with what I have been calling "my little spells." With modest exertion, like going shopping or walking a bit fast or a bit long, I would fairly suddenly become very short of breath and start feeling really awful and maybe get dizzy. Symptoms go away with rest and haven't raised their hoary head when I'm not exerting myself.

In the meantime, I have been going to the gym three times a week and working with someone who truly puts me through my paces. I also ride my stationary bike three times a week at a 12 mph clip with faster intervals. I can do all this without getting a spell. Seemed really weird to be able to do some things but not others of equal exertion. I also have been accumulating fluid as of late.

I had been attributing this to residual lung damage from my pulmonary embolus of four years ago, though the blood clots almost always just get absorbed and leave no long-term damage. At my last doctor's visit, I mentioned my spells and my conclusion, to which my wonderful woman said, "Maybe not." As the spells have been escalating, I embarked on a cardiac workup these past couple of weeks.

I have had everything done, short of an angiogram. The really great news is that my lungs are functioning just fine. I also do not have an irregular heartbeat (arrhythmia), nor do I appear to have problems with the blood supply to my heart (ischemia). I do have what they are calling diastolic dysfunction, which translates into English as a stiff heart. Apparently I have little reserve capacity because the heart is stiff and doesn't fill as well as if it was more relaxed when it relaxes. Bursts of exertion interspersed with relative rest I can tolerate. It is when the demands made by the exertion continue for an uninterrupted period that I go into acute congestive heart failure heralded by classic symptoms of shortness of breath, etc.

The cardiologist says I am younger than the usual person who gets this. As for the cause, it usually is "idiopathic," which means the cause is unknown. The good news here is that the condition is treatable. I have started on a water pill (Lasix) and potassium. Will take two to three weeks for this to work. It has been less than twenty-four hours since I started treatment so there have been no dramatic changes yet except that I am peeing my brains out, which is the intended effect.

I haven't told my late brother's family yet. Since it is most unlikely that I will drop dead anytime soon, I want to be able to report success with the treatment when I do tell them. I am still processing the idea that there is something intrinsically wrong with my heart. So far, I'm really pissed. I don't have time for this foolishness. Oh, well, at least I don't need a cath or surgery. I can create a lifestyle designed around rest periods, sit-downs, and lie-downs if necessary.

RESPONDING TO A FUTILE JOB SEARCH

My former employee got the job I had been told I was the front-runner for! The recruiter just called me. I really can't figure this out. How could someone with less experience and a much more erratic work history get the job everyone told me I was the front-runner for? I'm going to meet with the recruiter, and brutally honest feedback will be appreciated. If he's honest, perhaps I'll gain an understanding of what I'm not doing right. Fourteen months is a long time to be looking for a job, when you've held some of the top jobs—nationally visible jobs—in your industry. To say I'm discouraged is the understatement of the year.

I'm meeting tomorrow morning at nine o'clock with a retail shop owner to see if there's some way we can strike a deal. I've put together a list of ideas for how she can improve her establishment and want to see what she thinks about how we can do something together. It would be different and out of the box, away from all the negative parts of corporate life, which is appealing. But it's also hard for me to see myself working in a retail establishment this far along in my career. But a person has to work.

I have an interview at one company on Friday—the thought of the level of work there nauseates me; and yet it's a job. And I'd be thankful for that at this point.

I must be honest . . . I'm lower than low. I'm sick and tired of feeling sick and tired. I'm just out of ideas. Tomorrow I'm going to call a temp agency to see if I can do some kind of office work.

RESPONDING AT THE BEDSIDE OF A YOUNG SON WOUNDED IN WAR

Phil underwent another "washout" surgery around 4 p.m. today. The surgeons said everything looks great internally. The plastic surgeon attended during the surgery and took a look at all of his burn areas. They think they may be able to start some of the arm skin grafts next week, but it will be "much longer" for the groin and hip areas. They will harvest skin from his thighs for the arms.

We are still in a bit of a state of shock as we were informed after his surgery that the abdomen will remain "open" for anywhere from eight to twelve months. Yeah. That was our reaction, too. Apparently, it is because of the issues with the fissure in his stomach and inability to re-join it to the intestine and the swelling associated with the lack of ability to absorb nutrition for so long. We need to pray specifically for that pro-tein to kick in and Phil's body to process all the nutrients as efficiently and quickly as possible.

So we will continue to keep an eye on things with Phil one hour at a time, while keeping the other eye on what this will mean for us for up to one year, logistically, financially, and emotionally. We received word today that the Army approved reimbursement of expenses for us for seven days.

These stories provide windows into the lives of women and men like us, standing on their own thresholds of betwixt and between, just as we are. We listen; we learn; we sigh with relief at the wide range of what is normal. We are encouraged to realize that we are neither weird nor weak. Like the generous women and men who tell us their stories, we take comfort in the truth that we are all just human.

Although every story is different, these women and men share several things in common. They all speak the truth. They do not attempt to camouflage their reality as they see it. They acknowl-edge the emotional responses their tough transitions are trigger-ing. Even while they look into the abyss, they stand there. Observing. Describing. Witnessing to the state of affairs they find themselves in. Probably the most admirable thing is that the peo-ple telling these stories are speaking. To their family, to their best pal, to friends and acquaintances, to an interested stranger. They are reaching out to others. Telling their stories. Connecting—or at least trying to.

WHAT HELPS DURING RESPONDING

Carl Jung once wrote a friend who was responding to a painful tough transition. Here is part of his letter:

> Dear N.,
> I am sorry you are so miserable. . . . I would seek out one or two people who seemed amiable and would make myself useful to them. . . . I would raise animals and plants and find joy in their thriving. I would surround myself with beauty— no matter how primitive and artless—objects, colors, sounds. I would eat and drink well. . . . I would wrestle with the dark angel until he dislocated my hip. For he is also the light and the blue sky which he withholds from me.
>
> Anyway that is what I would do. What others would do is another question, which I cannot answer. But . . . no half-measures or half-heartedness.
> With cordial wishes,
As ever, C. G. Jung

People who have worked through tough transitions are the best source of suggestions for what helps at various points in the process. I've surveyed many individuals to ask how they managed during the disconcerting upheaval of Responding. Here are a few of their strategies.

SLOWING DOWN

Someone described his friend the other day as a person who is so slow that it takes him an hour and a half to watch the television news program 60 *Minutes*. I laughed, and at the same time I thought, "That slow man has a lot of wisdom." People down around where I was born in middle Georgia used to talk about taking life at the speed of a dog-trot. That meant living at a slow but regular pace. Slowing down—taking things at the speed of a jog-trot—is one of the best things we can do for ourselves when emotions are rampant and our inner world echoes in a huge, unfamiliar void.

What alters when we decide deliberately to slow down during a tough transition?

We allow as much time as is appropriate to pass instead of pressing to make a quick decision.

We cut out extraneous activities that take up time and energy we do not want to give.

We loaf, rest, and pamper ourselves at every opportunity.

We use cues like a traffic signal that's red or a phone that's ringing to remind ourselves to breathe deeply.

We pay deliberate attention to our health and well-being.

We ask for time off if we really need it.

We give up all forms of trying to be perfect.

We linger wherever possible to listen to our own voices.

Often solutions to problems related to a tough transition will present themselves if we slow down enough to let our intuition work for us. Certainly by slowing down we redirect our energy. Instead of rushing from this thing to that, we allow time for responding to our emotions and for thinking about what assumptions have disappeared and what assumptions we might still gather—or discover—to stand on.

Part of slowing down is taking care of our health. Illnesses and accidents often increase during the Responding experiences of a tough transition. Studies show: an increase of almost 40 percent in the death rate of widowers over the age of fifty-four during the first six months of grieving . . . 4.8 percent of close relatives died within the first year of bereavement compared with 0.7 percent of a comparable group of nonbereaved people of the same age living in the same area . . . a mortality rate at least seven times greater among a young widowed group, under age forty-five, than a matched young married control group . . . mortality rates may remain high for certain categories of bereft individuals perhaps into the sixth year of the loss.

With loss and unwanted change, there is often an increase in smoking and drinking; use of tranquilizers; antisocial, delinquent, and criminal behavior (stealing, shoplifting, for example); promiscuity; dependency and eating disorders; and replacement, helping, and no-intimacy-required relationships. One researcher from Australia says that when transitions bring great grief, one out of three people may have morbid outcomes or pathological patterns that persist. Another researcher asserts that in his study 5 to 15 percent of the population have ongoing unhealthy grief reactions.

All these indicators suggest that as part of slowing down we need to be aware that some of our physical and mental symptoms may be related to the transition we are going through. This awareness allows us to get the help we need before our health is gone or we establish unhealthy behaviors and patterns for the long haul. Also, we can distinguish between sadness and depression, one researcher reminds us, by understanding that sadness is a healthy response to a shared defining moment of change and loss in our lives. If we can say, "I am grieving," or "I feel discouraged," we are describing normal responses that need to be distinguished from the statement, "I am depressed."

REMEMBERING THAT THE EXPERIENCES OF RESPONDING REQUIRE PATIENCE BUT ARE TEMPORARY

If we are honest about our emotional upheavals (or emotional deadness, as the case may be) and about the emptiness and uncertainty that accompanies the loss of our assumptive worlds, we can count on these experiences to be temporary. This does not mean, of course, that they will not return from time to time, perhaps over many years, but these will not be the predominant modes of experience indefinitely, if we tell the truth about our feelings and allow ourselves to feel them. We choose to endure these periods when it feels as if we are living in a vacuum. We choose to be patient. We recognize that it takes time to rebuild an inner world. We understand that in these Responding experiences we are having to find a way to redefine ourselves and the situation. And until this redefinition is done, we don't know what plans to make for the future. So we are truly betwixt and between. It is almost inevitable that we will feel discouraged, lost, even in despair, in the time between having to discard the old ways we acted, thought, and felt and finding new ways to consider examining and meeting our new situation. For a long time we may find ourselves alternating between the old and the new. We choose to endure with patience, however, knowing that these experiences are an authentic part of a transitions process.

TALKING TO A PROFESSIONAL OR AN EXPERIENCED LISTENER

I admit it. I have a bias. I cannot imagine navigating through difficult times without seeking the wisdom of a professional or the guidance of someone who is experienced in the terrain into which I am now moving. Who are such professionals? Counselors, therapists, and analysts, certainly. What would we do without grief counselors when we lose someone central to our lives? What would we do without therapists and analysts when a tough transition causes us to realize that for all the new opportunities in front of us something we can't name or locate keeps us from stepping into a great future? Pastoral professionals at a synagogue, temple, mosque, or church can provide wisdom and care because they know us well and have a long-term relationship with us.

But there are also the experts who may not be professional health providers or caregivers but who can be invaluable listeners and coaches. They know from their own experience the kinds of challenges we are facing. The person who sits in the cube next to you at work may have been divorced four years ago and would be the perfect person to talk about how to help the kids weather your own current separation. A volunteer at a local senior center may be the perfect pair of ears to listen to your questions about negotiating health care or budgeting your monthly social security. I read in the *Wall Street Journal* a couple of years ago about Hallmark, the greeting card company, setting up a mentoring program to match employee volunteers who had already weathered a particular kind of difficult time with other employees who were going through a similar tough transition now. The creators of this company program recognized how valuable the shared experience of just a "regular person" can be to someone going through a difficult time. We can, likewise, take the initiative to ask someone around us to share wisdom and experience with us.

HARMONY AND MUSIC

Recently a phenomenal man died, and his obituary appeared in the *Economist* magazine. At age 100 William Sunderman had been named by the United States Congress as the oldest person still at work. When he died at age 104, in addition to being lauded for his pioneering work in medicine and science, Sunderman's response to a personal "tough transition" was especially noted. Coming down with tuberculosis in 1937, before antibiotics provided a cure, Sunderman had survived, "helped by music," he said. The obituary reveals that Dr. Sunderman had traveled to Germany most summers in recent years to play his Stradivarius violin with a professional group there. He gave a violin recital at his alma mater on his hundredth birthday. "Music," he said, "helped balance [my] life." While the challenges and successes of his medical research were sources of enjoyment, what he "looked forward to at the end of his working day was losing himself in chamber music." Dr. Sunderman noted that many doctors make music. And he felt that harmony "is what helps to keep people going."

How does music help? I'm sure we could read all sorts of sophisticated explanations, but I settle for something quite simple, which I learned from one of my early music teachers: When you press down a key on the piano, you think you are hearing one note, but you are really hearing the key you have pressed plus all its overtones. These overtones—higher and higher pitches above the note, produce the timbre you hear just as all the colors in the spectrum produce the color white you are seeing when you look at a cloud. And what was so amazing that I remember it to this day was my teacher's assertion that the overtones of a note in music are mathematical, that they occur in specific ratios, that they always occur in the same progression, and that they never change because they are a part of the physical universe. What the ancients called the "music of the spheres" is related to these set-in-nature harmonics.

> See deep enough and you see musically, the heart of nature being everywhere music, if you can only reach it.
> Thomas Carlyle

So my amateur understanding of why I feel better after I listen to Barber's Adagio for Strings is that I've heard order. I've heard the natural harmonics of notes and overtones. I've heard sound that conforms to a progression of ratios set in the universe. And somehow, in listening to this music, I am returned to balance, to internal order, to a sense of more harmony in my own life.

Music also helps me when I'm spent during times of tough transitions by taking me out of my verbal, rational world into a creative, symbolic experience. Beethoven once said that music is the mediator between the life of the spirit and the life of the senses. So when I am trying to figure out how to get my aged parents to pick up meals at the community senior center, and I sit down to listen to Beethoven's Ninth, I am transported to another realm of experience. The music lifts my spirits. I am in this moment cavorting with my imagination, my intuition, my wordless self.

Then there's the power of the emotion in songs I listen to when I'm disconcerted and trying to find solid earth to stand on. When Emmylou Harris sings, "I would walk . . . from Boulder to Birmingham . . . if I . . . could see your face," and I'm grieving for a relationship that can be no more, there's a correspondence, a fit. When I'm despairing over the challenges of a career change and listen to Elvis sing "I Believe," I am quickened by hope; and when

Barbra Streisand sings "We Are Standing on Holy Ground," I am touched by grace. I find a place for my emotions in these singers' emotions. I experience recognition, relationship, and a deep sense of release.

National Geographic magazine recently wrote about a new documentary called *The Story of the Weeping Camel.* In this film, nomadic Mongolians who have a camel that has rejected her newborn bring in a musician. This musician plays a song that brings tears to the mother camel's eyes and results in her taking care of her new calf. One of the filmmakers says, "The nomads have ways of communicating with their animals by singing and playing instruments. Music can convey emotions and show affection, things an animal can sense." Animals, human beings—we are all touched and changed by music.

SPECIFIC MUSIC SUGGESTIONS

I asked my friend Ann Rachlin, famed teacher of music in London and a thriver who has met the challengers of many tough transitions, what music she would recommend during the experiences of Responding. Ann suggests these:

Rachmaninoff's *Vocalise* (piano or orchestral version), and Symphony no. 2, third movement

Massenet's Meditation from *Thaïs*

Chopin's Prelude no. 4 in E Minor, op. 28

Mozart's Piano Concerto K. 491, second movement

Barber's Adagio for Strings

Brahms's Intermezzo in E-flat, op. 117 no. 1

Schubert's Impromptu no. 3 in G-flat Major, Andante

I would add my own "harmony" suggestions for the times of Responding, when emotions are strong, when we're dealing with changes in our world as we knew it:

Anything by the gospel singer Mahalia Jackson or the legendary country singer Patsy Cline

Gregorian chants recorded by the monks at Glenstal Abbey in County Limerick, Ireland

The calming piano music of Kelly Yost on her *Quiet Colors* CD.

A compilation called *Classic Weepies* that includes Samuel Barber, Franz Schmidt, Pietro Mascagni, Tomaso Albinoni, Johann Pachelbel, and Maurice Ravel, if you can manage to get past the silly title

Pianist Carol Rosenberger's beautiful CD called *Perchance to Dream: A Lullaby Album for Children and Adults*, with selections by Brahms, Schubert, Haydn, Fauré, Tchaikovsky, and Beethoven, among others

Any of Dan Gibson's superb *Solitudes* series, where he combines nature sounds with good music. My favorite is *Great Lakes Suite.*

"Wanting Memories," by Keali'i Reichel on the CD *Pick a Hit Hawaii*

Don't forget Emmylou Harris's early work ("Boulder to Birmingham," for example)

There's the group Sweet Honey in the Rock, especially their song "No Mirrors in My Nana's House"

And the wonderful hymns such as, "Great Is Thy Faithfulness"; "Amazing Grace"; "There Is a Place of Quiet Rest"

There are, of course, so many more possibilities. You will have many suggestions of your own.

Other Things That Help

THE COMPANY OF OTHERS

During the immediate experiences of Responding, don't forgo the company of others who care about you. During the emotional, disconcerting times in a tough transition, we do often feel like crawling in a hole. Sometimes we don't want to see anybody. That's understandable. But it is important to spend as much time as you possibly can with people who express their love and concern for you in healthy, supportive ways.

I was privileged to know my great-grandmother Emma Biles—she didn't die until I was ten years old—and heard her story often: When her husband died after having a stroke in the cotton field, she, the mother of fourteen children, received a pittance of insurance money. Much to the chagrin of certain members of the family, Grandma Emma took the insurance money and bought a brand-new 1908 T-model Ford, even though she couldn't drive. "Why in the world?" folks wanted to know. "Because I want to have a way to get to Aunt Sarah's in the next county on Sunday to visit and eat her warm cherry pie." Grandma Biles knew what was most important in her hard time of tough transition.

Also be sure to choose people to be with who are comfortable with anything you want to say and any way you want to be. We don't need folks to push us to find the silver lining that's in every cloud or to remember that the darkest day is right before dawn or to pull ourselves out of it. Such clichés may be true (or not); but when we are in the middle of Responding type of experiences they are irrelevant. What we need our friends to do now is to encourage us to express our feelings and talk about the situation fully, in any way we need or want to. Research shows that those people who talk to at least one other person about any and every thing they are feeling and thinking are healthier and more progressive in moving through the transition process than people who hold back and keep everything to themselves.

I was just speaking to a friend of mine who feels lost and lonely in a new city where she has moved. She talked about how different the people were there, how less likely they are to cut you slack than the folks in the place she moved from, how strange their behavior is compared to what she is used to. I could have stopped her and reminded her of all the successes she's had in the past in moving to different cultures and meeting new people. I could have reminded her of how intelligent she is and suggested a dozen things she might start doing to get to know the city better. But all I did was listen. I know my friend. I know she will adapt. I know she will not stay where she is for a long period of time. It's very early in her move, however, and she's dealing with all the Responding experiences that come with making a major, difficult change in one's life. What she needed today was not advice or the benefit of what I often laughingly refer to as everyone's "infinite wisdom." She just needed to tell the truth as she was now experiencing it. She needed someone on the other end of the phone who cared about her enough just to be there and listen.

CONVERSATION

One of the best uses of the Internet is the opportunity to connect with people who share your own experience. Through specialized chat rooms, personal blogs, and story Web sites, someone feeling isolated can connect with a kindred spirit far away. The *New York Times* reports that many Web sites are dedicated to collecting true stories. Storyblog (fray.com/storyblog) is a group weblog that links to sites about true stories. Sites like myturningpoint.com and randomaccessmemory.org collect stories about crucial life moments. With stories we come to know our lives in a new way. We come to understand ourselves differently. In the process of telling our stories to others we create a new story. Some new meaning emerges. We recompose our lives.

Online chat rooms provide an opportunity for individuals to tell stories and to come to one another's aid with information, empathy, and comfort. One of my close friends tells a story about her experience, as a new widow, of reaching out for help from a chat room:

The Gift of an Online Chat Group

My husband died on January 21. For two weeks my friend stayed with me to keep me company but eventually had to go back to his work as a pianist in a local hotel. The evenings were desolate. I wandered from room to room deeply aware of their emptiness. I was physically exhausted and a little scared by the horrible heavy feeling in my chest. Suddenly I remembered my computer upstairs. My daughter had taught me how to send e-mails and told me about the forums available at that time on Compuserve. "There must be people out there who have been through this—people who might help me," I thought. But how to reach them? Where would I find them? I ran upstairs to my computer.

Bereavement is like an illness, I thought, so let's take a look at "Health." Then I worked out that seniors would be the most experienced so I went to a forum designed for older people. Scrolling down, I looked at many likely sources of advice and finally decided on a forum called Friend to Friend. I wrote a message to all members—"SOS—I AM A NEW WIDOW"—and described all that happened to me in the past few weeks, my physical pains and emotional distress. I posted the message and, exhausted, went to bed.

The next morning when I switched on my computer, it was flashing "Messages! Messages!" There they were, my faceless friends all over the world, comforting me, advising me, consoling me. I replied to them all; and gradually, over the next few months, the list reduced to two or three stalwarts who were there for me night and day, helping me through the most difficult time in my life.

Sometime later, I decided I wanted to put back what I had taken from them. I saw a message, "My Mom needs a friend," and that is how I met Joy, a new widow who needed my assistance.

Today, almost ten years later, I still remain in touch with my online friends, both those who rescued me and those who, in my turn, I have been able to help through bereavement. Those were the early days of online friendships. I remem-

> Your friendship is better than chocolate! Well, anyway, it's right up there.
>
> Julie Sutton

ber how we all "met" in a chat room on New Year's Eve, all bereaved spouses, and we drank virtual champagne and ate virtual smoked salmon. We laughed together and toasted in the New Year with friends. Our loneliness was gone for those brief minutes that we were all united online. There was a future after all.

There are a lot of places we can go to have conversation and share our stories. Support groups in the community. Card games with others who are making or have made the same transition we are currently engaged in. Group counseling opportunities. Walks with a compatible neighbor. Participation in the training programs of organizations, such as Community of Hope or Stephen Ministry or Listening Ministry, that focus on educating volunteers about change and loss before these volunteers serve others. The important thing is to connect with others in useful conversations.

ART

Then there's art. I remember during one awful transition in my life I spent hours sitting in that big upstairs room at the Museum of Modern Art in New York looking at the Monet water lily paintings. And there was a painting at the Metropolitan Museum that mesmerized me during this same time period, which I would go stand in front of again and again. It was a picture by Jules Bastien-Lepage that contained images of Joan of Arc at different times in her life—as a baby, a child, a young woman, a military leader. Looking back, I think this piece of art spoke to me because it depicted growth and change in the life of one woman. Perhaps, even without realizing it, I was comforted by the possibility that I, too, would move through different stages in my own life.

Lately it's been color that's spoken to me most strongly as I moved through new transitions. I've gone to art exhibits based on color. Bought books about color. Sought out artists who build their creations around color. Whole new universes are opening to me that somehow and some way affect the way I think about my own transitions. Don't ask me to explain this in some kind of one-to-one relationship, for I can't. I just know that color and art are now nurturing subjects that I'm drawn to during times of upheaval and change.

At the Museum of Fine Arts in Houston I bought a little book called *Colors*. The left-hand page shows the color of, say, Parma violet. The right-hand page shows a painting, *Evening in New York*, by Childe Hassam, in which Parma violet is a predominant color. On another left-hand page you can see the color green-blue, and on the right Paul Signac's *The Bonaventure Pine, 1893*, where the tree is that color. There's cobalt blue and salmon pink and Sienna earth and carmine red and meadow green . . . each color showing up in a scene or a portrait an artist painted. I've asked myself a dozen times why I love this little book so. Why did I look at it almost every day when I was dealing recently with a really tough transition? I don't know, except to say my eyes were always opened more, my mind stimulated, my imagination stirred when I put the book down. Perhaps the last page of the book gives a hint to why I find looking at and learning about color so satisfying when I'm in a difficult time. The author, Caroline Desnoettes, writes:

> Color, like painting, is a source of beauty and pleasure. By mixing the primary colors of yellow, red, and blue the painter obtains new, complementary ones—orange, violet, green. The painter organizes his [or her] palette with cold colors—violet, blue, and green—and warm colors—yellow, orange, and red. Then he [or she] adds white and black for light and shade. And so, the painter can make an infinite number of color combinations and give life to his [or her] paintings as light reveals the color.

Cold, warm, white, black . . . infinite number of combinations . . . give life . . . light . . . color: perhaps at some level I'm making an analogy to possibility in my own life. Who can say?

I know I am so excited when I come across a line like the following in a book called *Color: A Natural History of the Palette*: "The first challenge in writing about colors is that they don't really exist. Or rather they do exist, but only because our minds create them as an interpretation of vibrations that are happening around us." Yep, I say to myself, there's something there for me to relate to my current life situation! I learn to understand color when Victoria Finlay, the author, compares it to "a soprano singing a high C and shattering a wineglass, because she catches its natural vibration." When light catches the natural vibrations of electrons, the expert tells us, it shoots them to another energy level where that portion of light is used up. What's left is reflected out, and our brains read it as color.

She goes on to explain:

> The best way I've found of understanding this is to think not so much of something "being" a color but of it "doing" a color. The atoms in a ripe tomato are busy shivering—or dancing or singing; the metaphors can be as joyful as the colors they describe—in such a way that when white light falls on them they absorb most of the blue and yellow light and they reject the red—meaning paradoxically that the "red" tomato is actually one that contains every wavelength except red. A week before, those atoms would have been doing a slightly different dance—absorbing the red light and rejecting the rest, to give the appearance of a green tomato instead.

Ask me why this kind of information pulls at me when I'm in a tough transition, and I don't have a clear answer. All I can tell you is that I'm enthralled by what I don't know! By what I can't see with my normal sight. I light up when I think of the turnips I have today in a dish on my countertop "doing" purple and white instead of "being" purple and white. Perhaps somehow this attention to color is enlarging my way of thinking about the world around me and making it less pat and solid and rigid. If the world's full of vibrations that make music and create color, perhaps the "vibrations" of my own life might make something interesting or something useful. And further, if everything is always changing so that this week a berry on a bush is red when next week it will be black and ready for me to put in a cobbler . . . well, why do I try to hold on so tightly to the shape of my life as I have known it? But these suppositions are all in hindsight. Don't believe for one minute that I think this way all the time. I'm just focusing my thoughts in a way that I've come to notice helps me when I'm in the kinds of Responding experiences we've talked about earlier.

MISCELLANY

What else do people say helped them when life was in turmoil? Massages, rest, baths, treats. Journaling, painting, gardening, building a birdhouse. Exercising, taking nature walks, getting a medical checkup. Eating good food. Slowing down. Playing with the dog.

A SCIENTIST NOTES ASPIRIN, MEDITATION, THOUGHTS OF HOPE AND SALVATION, CEREMONIAL RITES, AND SHARED ASSEMBLY

I'm a fan of the writings of Antonio Damasio, Van Allen Distinguished Professor and head of the department of neurology at the University of Iowa Medical Center. Dr. Damasio is also an adjunct professor at the Salk Institute in La Jolla, California, who writes science that a layperson can understand. He shows how the mind and the body are amazingly connected, and he includes the spiritual in solid and useful ways. When writing about joy, sorrow, and the feeling brain, Dr. Damasio says, "The spiritual is an index of the organizing scheme behind a life that is well-balanced, well-tempered, and well-intended . . . spiritual feelings form the basis for an intuition of the life process . . . spiritual experiences are humanly nourishing." (He also, echoing the discussion of music above, lauds the value of "an intense experience of harmony," and asserts that "listening to Bach, Mozart, Schubert, or Mahler can take us there, almost easily.")

So when Dr. Damasio talks about ways to "make our way to a happy ending in a universe where even the cheerful, sunny souls can so easily see human suffering," I listen.

As I read on, I find his recommendation of aspirin, in light of the assault on our health and well-being, easy enough to understand. But what about his discussion of thoughts of meditation, hope and salvation, ceremonial rites, and shared assembly?

Ceremonial rites . . . I understood the importance of such events more fully a few weeks ago when I was talking to a friend about one of my relationships that had recently ended. Even though I understood that it was appropriate for me not to continue to strain to be friends with a particular woman whom I had known since high school—we had, over the years, found very different interests and grown in very different ways—I still was having trouble with the transition. I realized in talking about this situation that I somehow felt that the connection I had with this woman so many years ago, when she and I were such different people, should be enough now to maintain the friendship.

My friend to whom I was speaking—trained in and wise about the challenges of relationship—suggested a ceremonial rite to mark the end of the friendship. She suggested that I write this person's name on a piece of paper, make a kind of little boat out of the piece of paper, and find a stream of running water to put the piece of boat in. "The clear, running water," she said, "will carry your old friend symbolically down the stream to live her own life and you will turn from the stream, moving along the path of your own life."

One of the best parts of this ceremonial rite was looking for a clear, running stream. I live in a city that has a lot of water, but I needed a flowing stream I could easily get down to. I tried a place or two but the bank was too steep or the ground too crumbly. Finally, one day, not even thinking about the ritual, I took the walking trail at my health club and came upon a lovely stream that was moving rapidly among the rocks.

So the next time I went to the health club I took the piece of paper with the woman's name on it, folded it, and put it on the stream. I stood and watched as her name floated away. She was symbolically free to go her way while I went mine. It wasn't until today's experience of writing about that little ceremony that I realized that from that moment I never had another thought of regret or confusion or doubt. This is one meaning, then, of a ceremonial rite that assists in moving me across a threshold.

Shared assembly . . . We can probably all recall a time when we were with other people as a rite was commemorated or a passage noted. A vivid experience comes to mind for me. It was September 14, 2001, three days after the attack on the World Trade Center in New York City. I was traveling on a train, going from London to Paris. In the car where I was sitting were members of an orchestra en route to their next concert location. The musicians chatted, moved around the train car, called to each other down the aisle. I wished several times that I spoke their language so that I could know what they were laughing and talking about. But those few of us in the car who weren't part of the orchestra and who didn't understand their language were a bit of an island unto ourselves as the group who knew one another so well chatted back and forth.

Suddenly the train manager's voice could be heard on the intercom. We were told that all over Europe at this moment—the stroke of 11 a.m. for us on the train—people were being invited to sit in silence for five minutes to honor the victims and their families harmed by the terrorist attack. Everyone in our car sat down and total silence prevailed. As one minute passed, two minutes, three . . . not a sound. Four minutes, five. It was as if the silence were a Presence, an honoring, witnessing Presence among us. Even after the train manager thanked everyone for observing the quiet, no one moved for several more minutes. And when people did begin to talk or move about again, I noticed a difference. Strangers smiled at me and I smiled at them. There was less noise when someone got down an instrument from storage overhead. A kind of gentleness seemed to have settled over the entire car that did not dissipate for the entire rest of our journey. The minutes we had spent in shared assembly had created an intimacy that went beyond all languages and needed no words.

Meditation, thoughts of hope and salvation . . . How can these serve as antidotes to being knocked off center by our emotions and their aftermath during a tough transition? The famed spiritual writer Thomas Merton asserts that we experience God in the same place that we experience music and poetry, only more so. Many of us find enormous strength from sitting in quiet or praying to a Source higher than we are or quoting a sacred scripture or a line of uplifting poetry. Hildegard of Bingen, that brilliant medieval scholar, composer, artist, poet, medical authority, preacher, and advisor to kings and popes, writes about the effects of our spirits being touched by Spirit. She puts it this way:

> It is this vigor that hugs the world, warming, moistening, firming, greening.
> This is so that all creatures might germinate and grow.
> The Spirit is Life, movement, color, radiance, restorative stillness in the din.
> The Spirit's power makes all withered sticks and souls green again with the juice of life.
> The Spirit plays music in the soul . . . gathers the perplexed, strengthens and heals.
> The Spirit awakens mighty hope, blowing everywhere the winds of renewal in creation.
> And this is the Mystery of God in whom we live and move and have our being.

One form of meditation, of course, is prayer. The philosopher Peter Kreeft, who teaches at Boston University, says this: "I strongly suspect that if we saw all the differences even the tiniest of our prayers make, and all the people those little prayers were destined to affect, and all the consequences of those prayers down through the centuries, we would be so paralyzed with awe at the power of prayer that we could be unable to get up off our knees for the rest of our lives."

How many prayers do we need? Check and see if these don't cover just about every situation.
Help, help, help.
Sorry, sorry, sorry.
Thanks, thanks, thanks.
Wonderful, Wonderful, Wonderful.

Elizabeth Harper Neeld

Mahalia Jackson must have been thinking much the same when she belted out that wonderful song "Prayer Changes Things." It was this refrain from Mahalia's song—*prayer changes things*—that first caused me many years ago to begin to give serious thought to the complexities of prayer. What does prayer change? Yes, sometimes the difficulty clears up, the fever goes down, the crime rate in Wichita Falls decreases—all situations about which people are specifically praying. But many times we pray and we do not get the result for which we are asking. Years later—like Garth Brooks singing about the guy who said "Thank God for unanswered prayers" after he saw his high school girlfriend, whom as a teenager he had been dying to marry, at a class reunion twenty-five years later—we may be relieved that some prayers were not answered the way we prayed them. More often, though, our prayers were for the good, for ourselves, for others; and we may be able to see no one-to-one correspondence between what we prayed for and what happened.

For myself, I've come to hold the prayers I pray when I'm in tough transitions this way. Prayer, to quote Richard Foster, is always ongoing research. Prayer, even if it doesn't have a recognized outcome, may lead to the gift of a new question. Prayer may not change something "out there," but prayer changes me. In Mahalia's words, I'm the "thing" that prayer changes. And, most important of all, there is the bedrock truth of that ancient psalm from the Old Testament: "On the day I called, God did answer me. Strength of soul God gave me." This I have come to know over the years can always be counted on when I pray: I am given strength of soul. I am sustained to continue my movement through the tough transition.

There's a verse that was often spoken as a word of encouragement to travelers in ancient Celtic lands. It goes like this:

> Slow is the step of the going,
> Of the riding, or the rowing
> To the glens and bens that are strange,
> Or the exile's isles of exchange,
>   The horizons of unknowing.
>
> Swift is the step of returning
> With a heart brimming of burning
> To the door and floor that is known,
> Where the firelight brightness is shown,
>   Where the loving needs no learning.

In the experiences of Responding, in this time of surprise and upheaval during a tough transition, the steps of our going do seem slow and the horizons full of unknowing. But people who have worked through tough transitions tell us that there is somewhere and at some time a door and floor that we know and a firelight that's burning. Getting there, they say, is all in the traveling.

In Summary: RESPONDING

WHAT

Responding experiences that are normal in a tough transition include:

Emotions that go haywire
Emotions that go numb
Primary emotions like fear, anger, and sadness, as well as social
emotions like pride, shame, and guilt, all swirling together
Our assumptive world disappearing; no firm foundation on which
to stand
Having to deal with transitions that we didn't instigate
Everyone going on a merry way

WHEN

Responding experiences usually happen early in a tough transition. If
the brain has closed down upon first news of the transition, however,
a person might not fully respond for weeks or months (or even years).
Responding experiences can also recur throughout the time we are
dealing with a tough transition. This means that a person might simultaneously be doing Reviewing actions or Reorganizing activities
while re-experiencing Responding feelings and emotions.

WHERE

The Terrain of Tough Transitions is not linear. No one starts with Re-
sponding experiences, completes those, moves on to Reviewing, then
Reorganizing, and, finally, Renewing in some kind of lockstep order.
What the map does is orient and identify four different types of expe-

riences that are normal during a tough transition. When and in what manner and for how long a person has any set of these experiences is an individual matter. There is often a kind of *sequence* in people's experiences—particularly in the predominant set of experiences they have at any particular time. Usually, for instance, people don't Review before they Respond, and they don't experience Renewing before some part of Reviewing and Reorganizing has been done. But the fact that there may be a *sequence* does not preclude back-and-forth, overlapping, recursive, simultaneous experiences. The map does not suggest a 1–2–3–4 clear and clean movement forward. Rather, it describes four sets of experiences that come with a tough transition. How each of us moves from one to another is a personal matter.

HOW

What helps when we have Responding experiences?

Slowing down
Remembering that these experiences are temporary
Visiting with a professional or an experienced person who knows how to listen
Harmony and music
The company of others
Conversation
Art
A miscellany of things like massages, gardening, building a birdhouse, exercising, eating good food, playing with the dog
Aspirin
Meditation, thoughts of hope and salvation, prayer
Ceremonial rites
Shared assembly

2

Reviewing

The wheel turns round and round,
but the vehicle is moving forward.

JOHN S. DUNNE

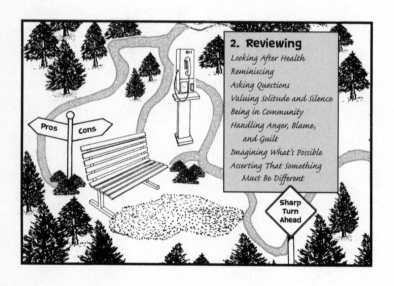

2. Reviewing

Looking After Health
Reminiscing
Asking Questions
Valuing Solitude and Silence
Being in Community
Handling Anger, Blame,
and Guilt
Imagining What's Possible
Asserting That Something
Must Be Different

At some point, if we're lucky, it becomes intolerable to be at the mercy of our situation all day, every day, as we deal with a tough transition. We know we aren't doing our best work. We know we can't make our best decisions. We know we're whirling like a stick caught in an eddy. We know things cannot go on the way they are going.

But what to do?

Perhaps it's time to take a second look. To reconsider, rethink, and reflect on how this tough transition is affecting our lives. To ask, "What do I need to see? What reassessment can I make? What might I do differently?" Perhaps it's time to begin Reviewing.

Aristotle told us a long time ago that to be conscious that we are perceiving or thinking is to be conscious of our own existence. A few hundred years later the philosopher Montaigne modeled excellent advice for us when we begin the experiencing of Reviewing: *I do not understand; I pause; I examine.* We now start to pay attention more deliberately because we know that once we notice what we're doing, we have the power to change it.

Orhan Pamuk, the Turkish novelist, says this about himself:

As soon as I observed myself from outside myself, I recognized and understood that I had a long-standing habit of keeping an eye on myself. That's how I managed to pull myself together, over the years, checking myself from the outside.

In the act of Reviewing ourselves and our situation, we are checking ourselves from the outside. And what we notice will make all the difference.

First Things First: Health and Well-Being

Where do we begin our Reviewing? First, with our health and well-being. Illness and accidents increase when we feel lost in limbo at this point in the transition process. When a person feels out of balance, she has a greater chance of falling and breaking an ankle. When someone is angry and stirred up, he is more likely to run a red light and hit another car. Cancer, heart trouble, autoimmune diseases, diabetes, hypertension, pneumonia, glaucoma: These are just a few of the illnesses that doctors warn often correlate with feelings of loss when we are in a tough transition. And then there are our self-destructive behaviors—smoking, drinking, taking drugs, hanging out with the wrong people, promiscuous behavior, shoplifting—that may look enticing somehow as ways to fill the hole left by what we lost in the transition. Knowing that these detrimental situations do occur helps us to understand how important it is to avoid them.

Because of the churn of basic emotions like surprise, sadness, anger, and fear (and even happiness), and because of the dust-devil swirl of social emotions like embarrassment, pride, guilt, and indignation, we are already operating far beneath our usual capabilities, having less and less of our balanced self available to us. Add to that the disappearance of our internal foundation—our assumptive world—and is it any wonder than we find it difficult just to do the day-by-day? It is only insult added to injury, then, if we have an accident or become ill. There's more research than any of us want to read about the impact of tough transitions on our health. But with all the body reactions that accompany the eruption of emotions—all those internal systems that go haywire, T cells that refuse to do what they used to do, biorhythms that can't tell the difference between night and day—it is amazing that we manage to maintain much of any level of good health at all.

I've noticed these physical responses in myself and the people around me, as I'm sure you have. When she lost her job during a company consolidation, my fifty-five-year-old aunt had her first heart attack. While my mother was caring for my aunt, she had her first automobile wreck. While I was frantic with worry about a major change in my brother's life, I fell on a brick sidewalk in the backyard and smashed my face badly. When my cousin changed her career from practicing surgery to creating and running a nonprofit foundation, she had a host of unexpected illnesses. The week of the first anniversary of my mother's death, I had my first experience of catching pneumonia. When I quit my job as a tenured, full professor to become a full-time writer, within weeks my face broke out in welts and splotches. And all of us in the family had been blessed to be healthy and accident-free before these tough transitions! Such health problems and accidents happen. Perhaps we won't be able to prevent them by Reviewing our situation, but we can associate them with the stress situations we are experiencing and perhaps get a leg up on becoming free from them sooner. And in some cases, through checking ourselves from the outside, as Orhan Pamuk said he did, we may even be able to prevent them.

Then, too, there is the physical and mental cost of the kind of chronic stress that lingers or becomes our way of life. Elevated cortisol levels can cause bone loss, increase abdominal fat, damage memory cells in the hippocampus part of the brain or stop production of new hippocampal neurons, and interfere with immune function. Too much adrenaline keeps blood pressure elevated and can damage vessels in the heart and brain and lead to hardening of the arteries. And chronic stress has been tied, directly or indirectly, to diabetes, rheumatoid arthritis, fibromyalgia, severe depression, and other mental disorders.

> Measure your health
> by your sympathy
> with morning and
> Spring.
>
> Henry David Thoreau

Chronic stress also is linked with short-term memory loss and a lack of focus and clarity that leads to poor decision-making. "Your brain is scrambled, your thinking process doesn't work well, your judgment is clouded. It's very difficult to think clearly," is the way one researcher puts it. Chronic stress also weakens the immune system, strains the heart, damages memory cells in the brain, and deposits fat at the waist rather than the hips and buttocks (a risk factor for heart disease, cancer, and other illnesses). Chronic stress is implicated, too, in aging.

While doctors and scientists don't assert that this illness or that is caused by the experience of, say, losing a job or having a partner walk out on you, they do say that there seems to be correlation between certain diseases (and perhaps our propensity toward those diseases) and emotional experiences of change and loss.

What are some of these specific diseases?

Cardiovascular disorders and heart disease; cancer; pernicious anemia; ulcerative colitis; leukemia; lymphoma; lupus; hyperthyroidism; pneumonia; rheumatoid arthritis; diabetes; tuberculosis; influenza; cirrhosis of the liver; glaucoma; skin rashes and eruptions; chronic depression; alcoholism and other drug dependencies; malnutrition; electrolyte disorders; headaches; lower back pain; frequent bouts with colds and flu; excessive fatigue; impotence; significant sleep disturbances.

Just reading about all this can make us feel sick! Of course, the existence of a collection of medical conditions does not mean that all people who face tough transitions are going to get such diseases and suffer dire effects from stress.

Think of the list as a yellow light in heavy traffic—you don't have to stop, but barreling through full speed ahead may not be your wisest course of action. Research does show that people in tough transitions may experience the onset and/or the aggravation of a condition like the ones we've been talking about. It's a good idea to get a physical checkup, perhaps sooner than you otherwise might, if you are working through a tough transition. Watch, too, for accidents that often increase when your life is out of balance: Avoid physically risky tasks like cleaning your gutters or take extra care when changing an overhead light bulb. Be conscious of ways that you can consciously reduce stress. Perhaps it's getting exercise. Visiting friends. Gardening. Relishing silence. And most of all, pay attention. Pay attention to how you feel, how you look, how much energy you have. Take notice of your health and well-being. If awareness is half the battle won, then just realizing that such things could pop up or develop provides a valuable measure of protection.

> During difficult times, we all do different things to help us heal. I found that in my own life, during my darkest, worst days, my therapy was to bake.
> Ellen Rose

This Is What I Remember: The Importance of Reminiscing

One thing that might seem to be a complete waste of time during a tough transition is to think about the past: The house you loved that you had to move from to accept a new job in another city. The camping trips in Yosemite with the person who just left you. The retirement account you had before the company's debacle of bad business. *Put the past behind you; focus on the future.* We've all been so instructed by someone who considered that he was speaking wisdom.

But such dictums are wrong at times like this. It is very important to remember. To hark back. To recollect. This is one of the most productive ac-

> Memories are the key not to the past, but to the future.
> Corrie ten Boom

tions we can take as part of our Reviewing experiences during a tough transition. When you reminisce, your memories bring to life the *person you were* before the tough transition, uniting that person with the *person you are now*. In memory we can recognize and recall a self we were earlier in our life. Perhaps this self got left behind somehow as we made choices that led us further and further from who we know we truly are. We can reassemble lost parts of ourselves. We actually retain a relationship with these past images of ourself by deliberately remembering them.

By reminiscing, we can shy away from some possible undesirable futures and create other positive ones. Within the quiet of our spirits, we may see with increasing clarity the meaning of past experiences. We may see connections between disparate events in the past that give us a clue to what we may want in the future. We can find meaning in the present by reinterpreting the past. We can collect images of ourselves from the past and see what thread of continuity, running from the past to the present, we might want to extend into the future.

I think of my wonderful cousin Ernestine. The first woman board-certified colorectal surgeon in America, she has given decades of service to her patients and colleagues. She has served both as a surgeon and as the creator of a nonprofit foundation that focuses on providing the public with the critical information that colon cancer is totally preventable. Much too soon in her life cycle, Ernestine has discovered that she has a life-threatening heart malady. She is not shriveling, however, and she is not pining away. Instead, she has reminisced. She has asked herself questions like these: What did the person I was earlier say she wanted to do that, in spite of my medical condition, I could still do now? What part of who I was did I have to put aside to accomplish everything I did in my active life as a surgeon?

Reminiscing about the past is shaping Ernestine's future. She has rediscovered her love and talent for photography: shooting underwater in the Dead Sea, capturing the beauty of ancient faces in China. She is bringing the old photographer self forth from the past to shape her immediate future. Recently she told me that since she doesn't know how long she will be able to travel because of her illness, she is headed for Botswana, Namibia, and Zambia in a couple of weeks on a photography adventure. Not too long ago she went to Sicily on the spur of the moment to see a volcano that had begun erupting again. One of her dreams had been to see an active volcano. She brought this dream of herself from the past into the present.

Reminiscing also allows us to discover that the past has not disappeared but is still available and serviceable. "Serviceable?" someone might ask. "How can a past we can never return to be serviceable?" Because through reviewing our past accomplishments as well as our failures, we can better set goals for the future. Reminiscing works a bit like trial action. When we remember the values and ideals and dreams we held in the past, these memories can guide and direct us as we consider the future.

I experienced the value of this kind of reminiscing when I was trying to establish myself as a writer after leaving a lifetime secure position at the university. On days when I felt incompetent and unsuccessful in just about everything I was trying to do in this new occupation, I would go back and reminisce about achievements from those earlier years. I never wanted to go back to that time; this was not regret or a wish to remake an earlier decision. It was just remembering. Thinking about the challenges I had then and how I had been able to meet them. Remembering this person's advice and that person's suggestions and imagining retooling those comments to use in my current situations.

I remembered the first year I ever taught school. One day the principal came in to observe my work at the very moment one of the seventh graders had climbed up on the windowsill, grabbed a steel girder in the ceiling, and proceeded to hang like a monkey. What had pulled me through that? Laughter. First the principal, then the students, then I, had broken up in guffaws. I reminisced about the person I had been when I worked in a hardware store mixing paint to pay my tuition bills in college. Couldn't I be just as inventive now as I was then? I saw the person I was when I risked my academic career by writing a college textbook that contained what were then iconoclastic statements such as, "Good writing begins in chaos," and "Outlines are at best a rescue operation." I said, "You're the same person who took that earlier risk." (One that paid off, I gratefully reminded myself.) "You're just dealing now with a different kind of challenge." Through this kind of reminiscing, I made my past serviceable in the present. The memories of what I had done in the past gave me encouragement that I could do what I was working on now for my new future.

Reminiscing can help us have more energy and can even help combat depression. When we remember—*this event happened, that person was good to me, those times were hard but I survived*—these memories can comfort and encourage us. Through this way of thinking we find that our minds are "peopled." The figures of the past are not just "memories" or mere abstractions but are still present and available to us in certain ways: as sources of awareness, learning, and wisdom; as reminders of goals and ideals; as part of the context we have for making decisions in the present. Reminiscing also allows the past to take on new meaning in response to present questions and needs. We may come upon something we have known all our lives but now understand in a new way. In the process of remembering we create a new story. Some fresh pattern or meaning emerges. By memory and narration we rebuild our world.

Reminiscing, remembering, thinking about the past can also be downright utilitarian and useful. After my husband and I returned from living in London, we realized how much we missed the coziness of the tiny cottage that had been our home for two years. Because we had only one sitting area in that small space, everything was there: the fireplace, the stereo, the television, our books, magazines, my embroidery, our treasures from home that we had brought with us, my husband's jigsaw puzzles, our journals and books for quiet time and prayer. This one sitting area contained the only

> It's a poor sort of memory that only works backward.
>
> Lewis Carroll

seats in the house and was the only place to entertain ourselves in the entire cottage.

When we returned to our home in the United States, our first response was to rejoice in having a lot of space again. We roamed from room to room—the library, the family room off the kitchen, the living room. It felt so luxurious to be able to spread out all over! But over the next couple of months we both sensed that something was missing. My husband might be in the library watching a golf match; I might be in the family room reading the *New York Times*. Our books might be in any number of three or four places. The CDs were scattered all over because there were places to play them in different rooms.

I kept finding myself remembering the coziness and the intimacy Pond Lodge provided . . . and missing that. So one day I set out to re-create that cozy space in one room in our house. I moved a rug to the library, dragged a sofa out, bought new reading lamps, organized the CDs all in one place, and made an inviting place for my husband and me to sit together for a little while every night when he got home from work. Remembering what had been special about the past let me re-create a form of that in the present. The past, then, was not "just memories" or "mere abstractions," as the researchers say. That memory was still present and available to my husband and me in certain ways: as sources of awareness, learning, and wisdom; as reminders of goals and ideals; as part of the context we had for making decisions in the present.

What Matters Now: Asking Ourselves Questions

I was talking with a friend who has a mysterious illness that, even after two major surgeries, still defies her doctors and specialists. No one can say definitively what is wrong. For more than a year she hardly had the strength to walk to her kitchen to make a pot of tea. Gradually, she has become able to move out into life, even to walk by the lake for exercise, attend classes, and cook for her family.

She told me about a luncheon she had attended recently. "I was so looking forward to spending time with these women whom I have been friends with for many years but whom I had not seen all this summer." But she realized almost as soon as she sat down at the table that in this past year and longer of her illness she had profoundly changed and didn't even know it.

"I realized about five minutes into that luncheon," my friend confided, "that some things which were 'normal' in the past are now just intolerable." The conversation she found inane: losing and gaining five pounds with Jenny Craig or LA Weight Loss; what colleges the kids had gotten into. "They were all consumed with these things. I can't stand that now. I know I've done it myself in the past. But I just can't take it now. I am thoroughly intolerant of people's pettiness. 'Please give it a rest,' I said to myself over and over during that long, long lunch," she said, finishing her story. Clearly, my friend's experience of this tough transition of a major illness has changed her preferences and clarified her values.

One of the opportunities of the set of experiences we call Reviewing is to start to build a new assumptive world. We see the "positive illusions" we unconsciously lived by before this change occurred. We reexamine. We decide what we believe now. If we assumed before that a job was secure or that hard work would be recognized . . . if we assumed that our being as good a person as possible would be rewarded . . . if we assumed that any problems that might be present in a relationship would get worked out— now we know we can no longer live under the protection of those assumptions. We begin to examine what we can stand on now.

We engage with questions like, "Well, if what I thought or expected before this transition event isn't true or accurate, what is?" We know we will never be able to be so trusting or so naïve or so firmly convinced as we were before our life changes brought us such rude awakenings. We now have to do the kind of inquiry that finds its home in complexities, contradictions, paradoxes, and continued examination. Although it is challenging, it's this ongoing questioning that saves us. The alternative is to be angry that life wasn't the way we thought it was or should be. Or to be bitter that a bad thing did happen to a good person. Or to become despondent because our floor of assumptions has fallen out from under us.

Immanuel Kant, the German philosopher, provides direction for this kind of inquiry about our assumptions with his three famous questions: *What can I know? What should I do? What may I hope?* Answering these questions can begin a process of identifying the new assumptions with which we can build our inner world.

A friend recently was laid off at work one morning and then found out that afternoon that she could move to another division of the company because she had enough seniority to request such a transfer. She was elated—until she moved to her new office and began the new job. Everything was unfamiliar; business, though this was the same company, was not done the same way where she now was; people did not welcome her. And she felt like a heel for being unhappy. Why couldn't she feel gratitude—after all, she did have a job!—instead of resentment?

Kant's Three Questions:
What can I know?
What should I do?
What may I hope?

She quizzed herself: *What did I assume before? That a transfer would be a wonderful answer to my problem. That any job in this company would be a good one for me, given my track record. That I would be so happy I had a job that any little irritations would be just that—little.*

Clearly these assumptions had proven not to be true. So, to Kant's questions:

What can I know?
  I know that job change can be difficult, even in the same company.
  I know that I will learn how to do the new job.

I know that I don't have to stay here forever.

What should I do?
I should keep my job search outside the company active.
I should go to a professional to get help handling my resentment if I keep on spilling my anger onto my husband and family.
I should cut myself slack and give this new job time to work out.

What may I hope?
I may hope that my abilities and past experience will stand me in good stead in my work.
I may hope that as long as I can breathe there is a chance something will change for the better.
I may hope that I can grow from this situation and become wiser.
I may hope that I will be sustained by my Creator through this time.

What happens when we stop to question our assumptions the way this woman did? We get the benefit of stepping back. We begin to get some distance from the immediacy, the raw emotion, the grittiness of upset and frustration. Options can now come to mind; clarity about priorities can emerge. The big picture begins to form where before there were only swirls of chaos. I think of an analogy in art: a scene painted in the pointillist style where the artist has used thousands of tiny dots to make the picture. Imagine standing right up at the canvas. All you can see are messy dots. But step back a few feet and you see the scene: a sailboat on the lake; two women sitting at a waterside table drinking tea, the ribbons of their hats flying in the breeze; people milling about in the warm summer afternoon. In the case of this woman whose job change turned out to be a disappointment, she identifies—through the act of questioning her assumptions—actions she can take and hopes she can stand on. From what were only messy dots she can now see a bigger picture.

Can this act of questioning of assumptions also be of value in a transition over which we have no control? Here are the answers from an active, successful businesswoman who has learned that she has an inherited disease for which no cure has yet been found.

What can I know?
> I know that what I face with this disease is a tough road ahead with difficult choices.
>
> I also know that I will make the appropriate decision for myself, just as I have for all the years that I've endured living with it.
>
> I know that I've lived longer thus far than anyone in my family who has had the disease, with the exception of my father who lived to age fifty-seven. And I know that technology is on my side, with options that didn't exist for him or the rest.
>
> I know that I have a network of caring friends and family who are here to support me and the decision path I follow.
>
> I know that quality is much more important to me than quantity, and I will not make the possibility of death an enemy.

What should I do?
> I am looking at the possibility of a new doctor with new technology and a different perspective. I know I'll find her.
>
> I continue to want more time to myself and am finding that—the quiet time to be restful and peaceful that's important to sustaining me.
>
> I continue to see possibilities in the "what's next" steps and to keep an open mind to what's presented.

What may I hope?

> I hope that the time is longer than what's predicted about the course of the tough decisions before me.
>
> I hope that the path will be clear and that I will have the wisdom and fortitude to make wise choices.
>
> I hope that I'll be surrounded by friends who will help when I need them.
>
> I hope that my friends will support the decisions I make and understand that I make them for myself—not for their comfort.
>
> I hope that my faith will endure in the difficult times.
>
> I hope for peacefulness in my choices.

Here a professional woman, wife, and mother who is in multiple tough transitions—marriage difficulties, children moving into teenage years, an extended family in legal difficulties—asks what assumptions she can stand on now:

What can I know?

> I can know who I still am, what matters most to me, what motivates and nourishes me. I can know what is true and clear on the inside even though the outside circumstances are fuzzy and sometimes frightening. I can also know, by reviewing the reality of my own history, that I have lived—and even grown—through transitions before, that I am not alone, that time will pass.

What should I do?

> Listen very carefully to what I'm hearing inside and outside. Try hard to keep things in perspective and maintain hope. Take care of myself—time to rest and think. Have a group of good friends who can give me supportive and objective feedback—and make myself available to that help. Keep saying out loud what I know.

What may I hope?
> First, that there always is hope; that God has bestowed on each of us a future and a hope. That all shall be well and, in fact, that things might actually turn out better than imagined. That I will be a better, wiser, more joyful person on the other side of this transition. That I will see the way clear.

I am struck by the outcome of this woman's questioning of her assumptions, particularly when she examined "What should I do?" The looking she did produced a list of positive steps she can take, even while she's in the middle of the messiness of several tough transitions. *Maintain hope . . . take care of myself . . . get supportive and objective feedback . . . keep saying out loud what I know.* Paralysis often hits us when we are dealing with major changes in our lives: We simply can't think of anything to do. Something as basic as examining our assumptions can enable us to see where and how we might take action.

Here Kant's questions are answered by a daughter whose mother is in a nursing home with severe Alzheimer's:

What can I know?
> Perhaps before I identify what I can know (meaning possibility) I might visit what I do know or seem to know (my reality). I know death is an inevitability. I know that watching my mother die a painfully slow death, a death that diminishes her both mentally and physically on a daily basis, is difficult to witness. I know that this death is not one that either she or I would have chosen for her but that there is learning for both of us in this anguishing process. I know that nursing homes are problematic and even the best leave much to be desired. I know that angels come in the form of uneducated women with limited choices in their lives who take care of the aged, feeble, cranky, or comatose residents with patience, steadfastness, tenderness, and compassion.

I know that I am not the same person I was before beginning this final piece of my mother's journey almost two years ago. I am much more humble and aware that the present moment is a gift to graciously be received. I know that it has been my wish for many years to be able to see the whole of my mother's life from a vantage point more spacious than only that of a daughter and I am so grateful this desire has been fulfilled beyond any vision I imagined.

What should I do?

This is the paradox. What I should do is *to be* more and *do* less, for out of my being comes the doing. It is also the key for me to unlock the "What I can know." My most lucid moments come riding on the sounds of silence. It is then that I awake from fear and separateness and am able to let go of the judgment I put on my mom's circumstances. It is only then that I can even entertain the notion that we are given circumstances required for our awakening; that things that seem so unfair can eventually make sense or not. Most of the time I vacillate between positions of darkness and light minute by minute, struggling to pay attention to all of the synchronistic patterns that continue to appear.

What can I hope?

I babysat with my grandsons this weekend; and, as I fed, diapered, and frolicked with them, I thought about my parents and what they thought of me as their child. I had such a keen sense of the wonder of family, of former generations, of the contribution that each of us makes. I recalled a fond memory of my dad serving as Sunday school superintendent for many years and his delight in that role. I looked forward to Sunday morning and particularly to the songs we sang. My favorite was, "This little light of mine, I want to make it shine." That is what I hope for all of us. That our light can and will shine.

A woman, recently retired, and living in the chaos of temporary housing while her new cottage is being finished, answers Kant's three questions this way:

What can I know?
Out of chaos will come order. That my partner's laughter and ability to joke through the chaos is a lifesaver.

What can I do?
Try to sort out the clutter and plan the final home. When the spring comes and the flowers bloom and people emerge from the warmth of their hearths and walk again in the lane and stop for a chat, then I will begin to put out feelers and start to build on the social structure we know and expand it. There are lots of things to do down here and places to go and artistic things to do. Above all, there will be time to do these things, and that will be a joy.

What can I hope?
I hope that I will stay strong and well and be able to enjoy this next decade. In ten years I will be eighty and I would like to be able to look back with satisfaction on this new adventure of retirement that began with my seventieth birthday, knowing I fulfilled my creative tasks and learnt more and kept my mind active. I hope for a good clear mind that allows me to look back and describe the wonderful full and colorful life I have had, and permits me to go on looking forward to always being interested in things new and creative.

It takes much Reviewing to identify our previous assumptions and build a new world based on reconsidered assumptions. And much time. In the between and betwixt, we often feel as if we are living in the dark at the bottom of a well. Sadness, loneliness, anger at life, even depression may be present as we work to create a new floor of assumptions and beliefs on which we feel we can firmly stand. What is amazing is how often that floor is a floor of hard-won but lifelong wisdom when we might have, but for the work we have done, found ourselves in a perpetual quicksand of bitterness, resentment, and regret.

Where Is God in Tough Transitions: Thinking About Eternal Verities

One thing we find ourselves thinking about when we are Reviewing, especially if the tough transition has a sense of enormous loss connected to it, is, where was God when all this was happening? *How could a Being that loves and cares for us human beings let such a thing happen? What about the prayers I prayed? I believed. I trusted. And I feel that God let me down.* It's with questions like these that we have do some our most difficult grappling when we are Reviewing. We find ourselves examining some of our most cherished beliefs.

> Sometimes we are blessed with the gift of a new question.
> Richard Foster

People tell me that an inquiry that was particularly helpful when they were faced with the quandary of belief was to identify first what they had, what before this transition they "naturally assumed." Did I assume that good people were protected by God? Did I assume that prayers were always answered as I wished them to be? Did I assume that God watches over innocent (young, well-meaning, kind, decent, hardworking, etc., etc.) people? Well, if God doesn't do these things, what does God do? How am I to think about why God lets these painful things happen? What do I believe now?

Maybe it's a matter, one wise woman suggests, of sharing power. The Reverend Barbara Brown Taylor, Episcopal priest, gives this perspective:

> From the very beginning, God has shared power with us, giving us power to name, to create, to choose, to act. We

have done wonderful things with that privilege. We have also abused it. We tend to dilute that fact by believing our rebellions are more or less benign, like two-year-olds pounding their parents' knees. God allows us the temporary illusion of power, we tell ourselves, but God is really in charge, and when things get bad enough God will come back into the room and set everything right.

Only what if that is not how things work? What if God has settled for limited power in order to be in partnership with us and we really can mess things up? What if God lets us? This is a different world from the first one. In the first, everything that happens, happens by the will of an all-powerful God. In this one, God's power is limited by our power to resist. What happens, happens in a world of clashing wills, so that even God is sometimes surprised. We prefer a God who prevents suffering, only that is not the God we got. . . . God's power is not the power to force human choices and end human pain. It is, instead, the power to pick up the shattered pieces and make something holy out of them—not from a distance but right close up.

People who have suffered some of the worst atrocities ever experienced by human beings do find a new way to think about God and God's relationship with human beings. The following words were found on a basement wall in Cologne, Germany, during the Holocaust (they have since been set to beautiful liturgical music by Michael Horvit):

I believe in the sun even when it is not shining.
I believe in love even when feeling it not.
I believe in God even when God is silent.

Elie Wiesel, some fifty years after he survived a German concentration camp, wrote a "Letter to God" that illumines new questions he came to ask about the presence of the Divine in the darkest of times:

What about my faith in you, Master of the Universe? I now realize I never lost it, not even over there, during the darkest time of my life. I don't know why I kept on whispering my daily prayers and the ones reserved for the Sabbath, and for the holidays, but I did recite them. . . . But my faith was no longer pure. How could it be?

At one point, I began wondering whether I was not unfair to you. After all, Auschwitz was not something that came down ready-made from heaven. It was conceived by men, implemented by men, staffed by men. And their aim was to destroy not only us but you as well. Ought we not to think of your pain, too? Watching your children suffer at the hands of your other children, haven't you also suffered?

What these voices say to me is that our relationship with God doesn't result in the Creator's exercising *power over* things. But that relationship does bring us a deep sense of *power with*—God is with us in the pains and problems. This *power with* is the shape of love against the very forces of death and nonbeing. Even when we are driven to the depths of defeat and despair, we can and do experience, in the words of Peter Hodgson, the "miraculous ability to start over, to build afresh, to maintain a struggle and a vision. A future is opened up through even the most negative experience . . . the victory arrives through the living communion of love."

Rabbi Marc Gellman and Father Tom Hartman remind us that God allows human beings to make a difference in their own and others' lives. "Life is a journey," they say, "in which we learn how to take care of ourselves, help others and turn bad things to our advantage." Yes, these clerics say, God could eliminate evil but such an action would eliminate the free will that causes evil. "If you're forced to do good because God says so," they say, "it is impossible to love God or serve God freely." And moral wrongs are "a direct consequence of free will."

Just because people suffer, Gellman and Hartman say, that doesn't mean God has abandoned them. Rather, we are empowered to protect and help ourselves and others when disaster strikes. We also have the ability to use turmoil and even tragedy to find goodness in our lives—"be it in the form of natural beauty, good deeds done, or lessons learned from parents, friends, and elders. Goodness occurs every day, but you need to train your eyes to see it. What seems limiting can really be an opportunity to do good."

All well and good for thinkers and theologians and philosophers, we might say, but how does such ways of thinking play out in "real life"? Thinking about this, I talked with a friend whose teenage son had been killed in a car accident. She spoke first about a conversation she had with a neighbor. This neighbor had always explicitly said to her own teenage children, "I will care for you when you are under my eye. God will protect you when you are away from me." My friend telling me the story said, "When our son was killed, this neighbor was rattled to her toenails. She stopped going to church and even now attends only occasionally, 'just to hear the music.' She's lost her faith in the universe. Now, more than a decade later, she still hasn't put anything back together yet."

I couldn't help but contrast this with the words of my friend who was sitting across from me. She talked about her own beliefs before her son died. "We were taught if we crossed all t's, dotted all i's, kept our nose clean, did right thinking, stayed out of trouble, we would be okay. Good things would come to us. That was a lie. And when Thomas died I had such anger that this was a lie." My friend went on to talk about how she had to find new, empowering things to believe that could include the senseless death of her beautiful son as well as a profound appreciation of the beauty and wonder of this mystery we call life.

"I realized," my friend told me, "that the principles I held before had been made out of smoke. I had to now find new principles— or rather the Principle under all principles, since the other ones were an illusion."

I ventured to ask, "What is that Principle that you have found?"

"That there is only one Truth. As trite as it may sound, Love is all there is." We sat in a sacred pause for several seconds. Then my friend added, "I'm no longer going for getting better and better. My goal is to live close to the fulcrum, in balance with the positive and negative, with hurt and joy. At this fulcrum much energy is there, peace, and transcendence. And while I cannot always stay at the center, I do manage most of the time to live in the shade of it."

Alone: Valuing Solitude

Recently I finished reading David McCullough's biography of John Adams. What a story! What a man! Two entries John Adams made in his diary pop into my head when I think about solitude. He wrote in the diary one day this simple line: "At home. Thinking." Later, at Christmas, he wrote another similar line in his journal: "At home with family. Thinking."

Solitude becomes an ally in the process of dealing with a tough transition. Pascal, the French mathematician and philosopher, once said that all our miseries "derive from not being able to sit in a quiet room alone."

> I feel the same way about solitude as some people feel about the blessing of the church. It's the light of grace for me. I never close my door behind me without the awareness that I am carrying out an act of mercy toward myself.
>
> Peter Hoeg, novelist

Why solitude? Especially in light of the fact that one of the things we need the most when we are in tough transitions is the companionship of others. The last thing we need to do is to shut ourselves off from others and live in isolation. To talk with others, to go to a movie with our friends, to get out and about in active exchange with life—we shrivel without these interactions with others.

Solitude does not require us to cease contact with the outside world; to be in solitude does not mean to wall ourselves off. Think of the ebb and flow of the tides. Or the sprint and rest at a track meet. Or a quiet weekend after a busy week. Solitude is what alternates with our outside life. Victor Frankl once said that each of us is questioned by life and that we "can only answer life by *answering for*" our own lives. It is in solitude that we have the opportunity to begin this *answering for* our own lives.

Authorities tell us that even babies need solitude. When babies first learn to be alone when someone else is in the room—when they can amuse themselves or be with themselves without needing others who may be present—they have taken the first step to personhood. Then, when they can be alone with no one in the room with them and be content and satisfied, they are learning how to have experiences that feel real. The more of these real experiences babies have, the greater foundation they have for sensing that life is not futile but real. This building up of real experiences by being able to be alone is linked to children's self-discovery and self-realization and to their ability to become aware of their deepest desires, impulses, and feelings.

And for us adults much the same holds. When we can solace ourselves alone, we also develop the ability to be more generous, forgiving, joyful, and in awe of the miracle of life all around us. Communing with ourselves in solitude helps us to become aware of our deepest feelings and needs. The discoveries we make when we are thinking alone can help us change what we do and how we think. When we can be private and find value in this privacy, we can comfort ourselves and even help lift ourselves out of depression by the things we do alone that bring us contentment and pleasure.

What are some of the things we can do in solitude? Sit and stare at the fire or out the window; read; write; cook; paint; garden; make collages; knit; whittle; make scrapbooks; rock; listen to music; pray; declutter; dust. We can organize photographs, sort through recipes, arrange stamps, walk a trail, tie flies, sail a boat. Whatever makes us feel at home within ourselves. Whatever draws from us our own resources and our own wisdom.

Wholeness: Valuing Silence

Dag Hammarskjöld, in the journal he kept when he was secretary-general of the United Nations, wrote these words: "We all have within us a center of stillness surrounded by silence." Silence is the ultimate province of trust. Silence is not an absence but a presence. It can be restful and rejuvenating at a time when we desperately need energy. "How good it is to center down," Howard Thurman reminds us, "to sit quietly and see one's self pass by!"

> "Don't just do something; stand there," are words attributed to the Buddha. From Judaism and Christianity, there's the famous psalm: "Be still, and know that I am God."

The Jewish mystical writings, as the Kabbalah tells us, name solitude as the domain of the soul, and the soul is a portion of God that resides in our bodies. It is in silence, the Kabbalah suggests, that the soul has its greatest chance to grow. The value of silence has been held in many cultures for many centuries around the globe. An anonymous monk in the Egyptian desert in the seventh century AD wrote:

> Unless there is a still center in the middle of the storm, unless individuals in the midst of all their activities preserve a secret room in their hearts where they sit alone before God, unless we do this, we will lose all sense of spiritual direction and be torn to pieces.

The Chinese philosopher Lao Tzu reminded, "There is no need to run outside for better seeing. Nor to peer from a window. Rather abide at the center of your being; for the more you leave it, the less you learn. Search your heart and see if he is wise who takes each turn; the way to do is to be. The answer was always quietly there; only our questions drowned it out." It has been suggested that God keeps a layer of silence between human beings and the Mystery and that we must also keep a silence in which to approach that Mystery. The Divine is a self-giving Silence, pouring into us. That Silence, in turn, makes us articulate to ourselves and to the world.

There's a wonderful true story told by Dr. Anthony Bloom of a woman living in a senior citizen home sitting in silence in her room knitting. Here are her words:

> Oh, how nice. I have fifteen minutes during which I can do nothing without feeling guilty! . . . I felt so quiet because the room was so peaceful. There was a clock ticking but it didn't disturb the silence; its ticking just underlined the fact that everything was so still. . . . I began to knit. . . . Then I perceived that this silence was not simply an absence of noise, but that the silence had substance. It was not absence of something but presence of something. The silence had a density, a richness, and it began to pervade me. The silence around began to come and meet the silence in me. All of a sudden I perceived that the silence was a presence. At the heart of the silence was One who is all stillness, all peace, all poise.

Joseph Campbell talks this way about the sacredness we can experience in silence: "You must have a room or a certain hour of the day or so where you do not know what was in the morning papers, where you do not know who your friends are, you don't know what you owe anybody, or what they owe you—but a place where you can simply experience and bring forth what you are, and what you might be. . . . At first you may find nothing's happening. . . . But if you have a sacred place and use it, take advantage of it, something will happen." Our communion with this silence creates strength, depth, and wisdom that both contain and expand us as we work through our tough transitions.

Community: Valuing Others

While solitude and silence can be healing and instructive during a tough transition, being with others is also essential. But what kind of people do we need to be with? Those who are wise and who wait to be asked to share their wisdom. Those who understand that there is a natural process and progress through the terrain of a tough transition and who believe we are strong enough to move through this terrain at our own pace. Those who don't try to "jolly us along" inappropriately but who also don't sit with us in sackcloth and ashes as some kind of memorial to the past.

We need people who ask us to go to the movies (and don't mind whether we answer yes or no). People who cook up a pot of spaghetti on the spur of the moment and say, "Come over and eat with us." People who read about a seminar or a support group in the newspaper and cut out the notice to give to us in case we are interested. People who are comfortable when we want to explore philosophical and spiritual issues. People who are comfortable just sitting in silence with us. People who thoughtfully leave us alone when we need to be alone.

> How to pick the right friends? The key is to keep company only with people who uplift you, whose presence calls forth your best.
>
> Epictetus

What we don't need are people who know all the answers; people who are always right; people who want to tell us how to live our lives. We don't need people who pry or poke or prod. We don't need people who need us to stay helpless so they can feel useful. We don't need people who themselves have chosen to stay stuck in old transitions. The important thing to pay attention to is to be aware of the kind of people with whom we are surrounding ourselves. And to choose to be with those whose way of being truly helps us create new community.

One of my friends who was recently divorced discovered she had to become deliberate about the people with whom she remained friends. One day in the grocery store she ran into a high school girlfriend who gushed, "Sally, you haven't called me in weeks now. I'm dying to know the news." My friend decided to answer her straight on. "No, Meg, I haven't called you because when I do you keep saying things like, 'Are the kids taking drugs yet? You know, teenagers whose parents divorce usually start using drugs.'" Meg replied, "Oh, I know, it's just too painful." And my friend retorted, "No, Meg, it's not too painful to talk to you. It's just too boring."

A man dealing with the loss of a son told me last week about several unsatisfactory exchanges he had with one of his oldest friends. This old friend talked and acted as if no loss of any significance had ever occurred. "Perhaps it is his way of trying to make things better," the man told me, "but by refusing to engage with how much my life has changed and how much pain I experience every day he is ignoring the single most important thing in my life right now." After making several efforts to let his old friend know how he felt, the grieving man finally took a stand. "I'm going to take off some time from talking with you," he told him, "because things are so different for me now. I'm such a different person." Then the grieving father said to me, "My friend acts as if what has happened is no more significant than if I had lost a cat."

On the other hand, I think of a friend I had when I was a young widow. Emma would listen to me interminably, even if I were telling the same story over and over. She would watch home movies with me, never reminding me that we had just looked at these same films last Tuesday. She included me every Friday afternoon when she and her husband met friends after work; and soon those people were my friends, too, giving me a group of new companions. Emma was also the same friend who came to my house one day and confronted me. "You know," she said, "I am your friend and you can count on me. However, if you continue to do this self-destructive behavior that you have started doing, I will not continue to be your friend. I will not be party to your acting in ways that can only hurt you." What a friend! This is the kind of support and the kind of honesty we need when we are navigating our way through a tough transition.

Achieving Freedom: Working Through Anger, Blame, and Guilt

In an interview Jay Leno said that if he were ever angry with anyone for anything, before he went onstage or on his show, he made a point of talking to the person to work out whatever was between them. "As a comedian," he said, "you cannot hit the stage with any malice in your heart, or it won't work. There's nothing funny. If I have a problem with someone it's resolved before showtime—win or lose." If we think about what Leno is saying, we see the control that anger holds over us. If his emotions are tied up in anger, he cannot be funny. He can't fake it. Some resource that he needs to do his job well is just not available to him if he stays ticked off at someone with whom he's had a problem. What is true for a comedian who does his job onstage is the same for us who do our jobs in an office, a classroom, outside, or at home.

> For every minute you are angry, you lose sixty seconds of happiness.
> Ralph Waldo Emerson

At some point each of us realizes that it is costing us a lot to stay angry. I remember what one man told me about his anger for his ex-wife:

For a long time after the divorce it was so easy for me to get angry. All I had to do was see her red pickup truck just parked on the street. One night when I was in my house by myself I realized that my anger toward her was my enemy and that when I didn't have anger, life went on in so much better a fashion. Finally, I realized that my bad feelings toward my ex-wife gave her control of my life. That was the hook she still had *in me. It was like a cable running from her house to mine. All the way across town—from Oak Street to Hilton Drive. That cable of anger connected her to me, and I permitted that connection. It even determined whether or not I'd fix anything to eat or how much I accomplished at work. How stupid can you be!*

So I began to make a conscious effort; it was not something you do like slice a piece of cake, or at least for me it wasn't. I'd have to repeat over and over: "Don't let that anger keep you connected." I'd say, "Look, anger is anger; it's an emotion, and it's just stored in a closet in your mind; and you let it out, and it does all kinds of cruel and mean things to you. Anger doesn't necessarily come in kinds—anger toward your wife, anger toward yourself—it's just anger."

When worse comes to worst, and I can't get rid of the anger any other way, I go out to the flowerbeds and start digging up the weeds. The ground is really dry, and there are lots of clods. I have this brick wall around my backyard. So, if I'm so angry that I can't talk myself out of it, I go out there and pick up those clods and swing them as hard as I can. They just explode when they hit that wall. I confess, sometimes I even get to talking to those weeds and clods of dirt. "Okay, you so-and-so," I'll say, "you're going next—just hold on, you're going next!" I tell you, I am killing weeds! I am breaking clods! And what worked out so well was that when I threw the clods against the brick wall they fell back into the flowerbeds as soil!

I've also found a category to put my ex-wife in: people that I don't like. I'm not talking about enemies; I'm not talking about people I fear. I'm just talking about people that I don't like. You know, they just don't appeal to you. Well, that's the category my ex-wife is in now, and it works.

It's imperative that, like this man, we find a way to work through our anger so that we are not crippled by it as we attempt to move on through a tough transition. Anger twists us, atrophies our strengths, and absorbs the very energy that we need to build a new and appropriate shape for the life we now have.

Then there's blame and guilt. Philosophers tell us that people often hold on to blame and guilt because they don't want to face

> The only thing guilt is good for is to move us to change. If it does not do that, then it's just a sorry substitute for new life.
>
> Barbara Brown Taylor

how ultimately powerless we all are. Better to be a bad person who caused this thing to happen than to be a person living in a world over which we have no control. Better to accuse someone else perpetually than accept the complexity of human actions and the inevitablity of human error and mistake. So blame and guilt are preferable to vulnerability. We either use our blame and guilt as a place to hide out in a past of what we did or didn't do or we use our blame and guilt as a stimulus to review what we did and how we can change now and behave in another way.

I remember that when my young husband dropped dead while jogging, I blamed myself, even though the coroner told me Greg's death would have occurred that night even if he had been sitting in a rocking chair. But I kept lacerating myself: *I was the one who wanted us to take up jogging in the first place. I jogged only two miles that day instead of six, so I wasn't with him when he died. I should have gone to look for him sooner.* And on and on.

Later I read some insightful words: "A world that can be explained, even with bad reasons, is a familiar world." I knew when I read this that I was using bad reasons to avoid the truth that life was unpredictable and that things happened for no reason that I could personally account for or prevent. Another writer whose message got through to me said, "The tendency to go over the events leading up to the situation and to find someone to blame even if it means blaming oneself is a less disturbing alternative than accepting that life is uncertain." Yes, I would blame myself, even with ridiculous logic, before I would accept that I could not control what happened in my life and the lives of those I loved.

One day I was telling my grief counselor—probably for the umpteenth time—about the guilt I felt for getting mad at Greg when he was alive and saying mean things. I told him about standing in front of the kitchen cabinet, throwing silverware into the drawer, one day after Greg and I had had an argument, saying to myself, "I wish I'd never married him! I wish I'd stayed a single woman in New York City." I told my grief counselor that I felt so guilty about this . . . perhaps God had heard me and that was the reason that Greg died. My wise advisor looked at me and said, "Well, Elizabeth, if you said something that killed Greg, why don't you say something and bring him back?" Finally, I got his point—I wasn't *that* powerful and my guilt was just a way not to let the past go and move forward.

Anger, blame, and guilt chain us; acknowledging this, we do the work, no matter how difficult, to get released. We work with a professional; we pray for Divine assistance; we look square in the face at the cost of continuing to live these emotions instead of beginning to live the possibility of the next phase of our lives.

Possibility: Asking What I Can Imagine

The philosopher Kierkegaard once wrote:

> Take the pupil of possibility, set him [or her] in the midst of the Jutland heath where nothing happens, where the greatest event is that a partridge flies up noisily; still that pupil of possibility out in the empty heath experiences everything more perfectly, more precisely, more profoundly, than the person who is applauded upon the stage of universal history but who is not educated by possibility.

What I hear Kierkegaard saying here is that the person who is alive to possibility—who can imagine, who knows that the future does not have to be a replica of the past—that person is luckier than some person who is famous on the world stage but who lives as if things must stay the way they are or have been in the past.

Nelson Mandela was a pupil of possibility even while he was in solitary confinement on Robben Island. Granny D.—aka Doris Haddock of New Hampshire, age ninety—was a pupil of possibility

when she walked from Los Angeles to Washington, D.C., to promote the cause of campaign finance reform. Ron Reagan and the
late Christopher Reeve were pupils of possibility when they spoke
out in support of scientific research that can make life better for
millions in the future. My niece Ashley, age
fourteen, who lives in a small town in north-
ern Michigan, is a pupil of possibility when
she talks excitedly about a city she has never
visited—Boston, Massachusetts—and plans
to go there to live when she is an adult. My
friend Claudio, who just got his green card
after years of working and waiting, is a stu-
dent of possibility when he writes to ask for the name of an employment recruiter who might assist him in finding a better job
now that his work permit is secure.

Are you one of
Kierkegaard's
"pupils of
possibility"?

How do we become a pupil of possibility? Perhaps possibility
looks like our thinking back to the occupations we rattled off joyfully when someone asked us as a child, "What do you want to be
when you grow up?" Perhaps it's doing an inventory of what has
meaning for us at this point in our lives. Perhaps it's making a list
of the things we have said we wanted to do for years but haven't
yet gotten around to doing: *Will I go back to school? Will I downsize
and use the money to travel? Will I teach children instead of run a company? Will I reorder my priorities for real? Will I offer to others what I
have learned in this painful time?*

My research shows that people do interesting things when they
let themselves loose to imagine new possibilities for their lives. "I
make collages," one woman told me. "I collect and then tape on
cardboard images of the kind of life I want to have or the specific
kind of work/living environment/activities I am drawn to. I put
these collages all around my house to remind me of what is possible, operating on the principle that if I can think of it and if I can
desire it, then it is possible." Another person told me about putting together a "Master Life Group," friends each of whom was superb in some area that she admired or wanted to emulate. "We
would meet once a month for potluck," she said, "and afterwards

discuss the crossroads I was at in my life and what options and possibilities were in front of me to be taken advantage of." She went on to add, "One of the greatest contributions of this group was to keep me from falling back or hiding when things I tried didn't work out or when I was afraid of the risk."

Others report working with a professional to clarify goals, affirm values, and loosen crusty chains from the past. Some talk about the wisdom and clarity and strength that come from daily meditation or from attending spiritual retreats. Many say that prayer has created amazing openings in their lives. People read books, go for career counseling, explore on the Internet, take courses to check out the depth of an interest, volunteer in an area in which they think they might be interested.

Emily Dickinson said in one of her poems, "I dwell in possibility." That's where we find ourselves now during this time of Reviewing. We are now anticipating beginning a process of redesign.

Replanning: Asserting That I Need to Do Some Things Differently Now

The experiences of Reviewing require each of us to consider: What are the things I must change in order to live consistently with the circumstances in which I now find myself? We've all seen people who haven't done this. The man who, while going further and further in debt, still drives a luxury car and lives in a posh high-rise even though he lost his high-tech job eighteen months ago and, in spite of his efforts to find another position, is still unemployed. The widow who, though she is in excellent health, refuses to become self-sufficient, instead demanding that her adult children center their lives around her desires and requests. The employee who doesn't get an expected promotion and remains stuck in anger and recrimination six months after the disappointment. People like this—people who will not replan their lives to include the new situation in which they find themselves—end up

> In preparing for battle I have always found that plans are useless, but planning is indispensable.
>
> Dwight Eisenhower

living life on a false basis, a kind of fantasy. Or they end up living life with no plan at all so that everything about them is in disarray.

At this point we don't have to know the answers, and usually won't know the answers. We don't even have to prepare a plan. We just have to make an assertion: *I must and I will replan my life because things have changed.* The how of it all, we will work out over time, but at this point we have to admit that we cannot keep doing things we did in the past because now those things no longer fit. We realize that if we do not replan our life, we will live as a person, in the words of the old French saying, whose clock has stopped.

PEOPLE TELL THEIR STORIES OF REVIEWING

The wonderful *cantadora* storyteller, Clarissa Pinkola Estes, reminds us, "Stories are medicine. They have such power. They do not require that we do, be, or act anything. We need only listen." Here people like you and me tell us how they are Reviewing as they navigate their way through many different kinds of tough transitions.

REVIEWING: A CEO AND FORCED RETIREMENT

There's a movie I've thought of often since I took forced retirement. In Tender Mercies, *Robert Duval plays a down-and-out country-and-western singer whom people stop on the sidewalk and ask, "Didn't you used to be Mac Sledge?" I feel that way now. I held a position that had national visibility. If people didn't know me personally they knew the or-*

ganization I was head of. So I expect people any day now to stop me on the street and say, "Didn't you used to be Carlton Sullivan?"

I don't know what the future holds. I don't think I would be willing to take on another full-time position. I might go into a company that needs an interim chief executive or I might do consulting. I have agreed with my wife that I will make no decisions about the future for the remainder of this year. We're going to travel most of the next two months. Fortunately, I don't need additional income; we have enough to live on comfortably. But I know I will want to get involved in something substantive.

Being identified with the role and the job is even more severe in high-profile positions where you are remembered by what you did and where you worked, not for who you are. I prepared myself as best as I could because I don't think I ever got so ego-involved in a position that I saw it as all I was. I've maintained close friends over the years who have remained friends no matter what my job was. These people are still there and the outpouring of love and respect is making this current hard transition easier. I've also kept multiple interests: sports, reading, plays and movies, church.

But my whole life has been achievement-oriented, goal-driven. I've been very successful in taking a position in a company that was in turmoil and unrest and bringing about positive change. This sense of satisfaction has been a primary motivating factor for me, rarely money or ego. But the ability to take on a leadership role and achieve a level of success that usually exceeded what was there before was what energized me. That will be the most difficult thing to replace. I don't know how I will. But can I give it up?

Right now I'm holding those questions in abeyance, just as I am the future. Now I can kick back and enjoy life for a little bit. Do things I've missed. Read, reflect. Wash everything out of my system before finding something that requires day-to-day commitment.

This whole change has caused me to reflect on my spiritual life. I have been reading, trying to sort out and get down to the core of what I believe. I'm trying to reconcile the way I was raised with a new understanding of the life of the spirit. It's a challenge and a struggle but certainly one worth doing.

REVIEWING: THE BETWIXT AND BETWEEN OF A PENDING DIVORCE

My husband of eighteen years went to his high school graduating class's fortieth reunion and came back to tell me he had fallen in love with a classmate who had been his teenage first love. He wanted a divorce immediately. He said he realized when he saw this old flame again that she had been his true love all this time. I was stunned; felt kicked in the stomach. When he would say things like, "I can't get her out of my mind," or "Her mother and my mother are the best of friends," or "She loves my stories and she loves me unconditionally," I would think, "I can't be hearing this." I couldn't sleep at night and cried for two months straight.

He asked for a structured separation while the divorce papers were being drawn up. Everything was hurried because he did not want to be committing adultery, he said. He wanted to be free. I asked him what he thought his life would be like with her, and he said, "Oh, I'll have a lot less money because she's not a professional; she's just a shopkeeper. But we'll get by." This, from the man who loves to travel to London on a regular basis. The psychiatrist who saw both of us together and separately told me to breathe deeply because my husband was set on this. That he was able to compartmentalize his life in such a way that he was cut off from his feelings related to our marriage and life together. I knew that was the case when he moved out and said, "I hope we can still be friends and go to lunch." I retorted, "Oh, as you do with your first wife?" He and his first wife have nothing to do with each other.

Three months into this situation my parents had their sixtieth wedding anniversary. It was so painful for me to see the contrast of my life with theirs . . . my father taking care of my mother with such devotion . . . their long years together through thick and thin. To see these sixty years together for them was so profound and so painful.

I do take responsibility and see my part in this. I have always known my husband and I did not meet emotionally. We had a good life; we loved traveling together; we created a beautiful living environment. But we did not connect in any deep way with our emotions. I tried to change that with courses I would ask him to go to, counseling, talking to him.

But since I'm a resister of change, I just let things slide along because it wasn't awful . . . in fact, in a lot of ways, our marriage was good . . . but at some level I knew we didn't connect in the very ways we most needed to. I would say to myself, "That's just how men are." I chose security because I was afraid. I didn't want to get old and die alone. What I concentrated on was finding meaning in my work—changing careers, finding great places to work—instead of finding meaning in my marriage. Or getting out of my marriage.

I'm determined not to be a bitter and angry woman. Just because I didn't have the courage to choose this situation doesn't mean I don't have the courage to deal with it. I do have that courage. I've returned to Jungian analysis, which is life-giving. My analyst said something the other day that released such a sense of freedom in me: "The old contract is up," the analyst said. I can feel that this is true.

REVIEWING: PONDERING CAREER CHANGE

It was the best job I had ever had, in circumstances I had dreamed of since I was ten years old. As a work situation goes, things could not have been any better. I had global executive responsibilities. I was challenged. I wasn't underutilized. I hadn't had a bad day. I wasn't headed to a useless meeting. Yet, as I was getting up from my desk, picking up my materials, and walking away to go to a meeting, I looked out the window. Suddenly I had a moment of knowing: I am bored with this job. In that knowing that I was bored I knew I would leave that kind of work. I didn't spend a lot of time thinking about it then or later, but looking back now I know that was a moment when I knew I was finished with that kind of work, that it was complete for me, that "it was over."

Sometime later a second event happened. I took a new job and six months later it was discontinued. I was without a job then, looking for a job. That provoked my thinking: Should I look for the same type of work? Or should I look for something else? I answered the question out of survival, since it was a tight job market, and found a great job like the one I had, a new job that used my credentials. But the questioning

*of what kind of work I should look for started me on an inquiry that is
still active today.*

*A third development occurred in my spiritual life. I began to question
my priorities. I had oriented my life and thinking underneath the hier-
archy of values of work, career success, company benefits (monetary
and otherwise). Now I ask, "What should be my priorities? What do I
want to reorient around?" The conclusion is that I want to reorient my
life around work that truly gives me meaning and purpose. I get enough
calls from headhunters to allow me to keep checking where I want my
priorities to be. But so far no big offer for work similar to what I'm
doing now has interested me.*

*For now I am just in not knowing. I don't know what kind of work
I want to do. It's a question I can't answer right now. I hold the question that way. When I was younger I obsessed about questions about
my life. I would worry the questions, play out scenarios, try to figure it
out, feel anxious about not having an answer. Now the question about
changing to another kind of work is simply a question that I just let be.
I do wonder. I imagine myself in different situations. If an interest
emerges, I go talk to someone in that field. But I'm not anxious about
the question. I know it will be answered in time.*

*I do believe that I will make a change and I believe what that change
will be will become clear. Therefore there is no reason to push or rush.
None of that will make it come any quicker. No striving will make it
come faster. It's like the season—fall, winter, spring, summer. They
come on their own terms. I am comfortable waiting. What else am I
going to do in the meantime but live? I'm not asleep at the switch but
I'm also not pushing. I'm active in waiting.*

REVIEWING: A WIDOWER IN LIMBO

*I live with a rambling dialogue in my head. I'm just making my way
through the fog. For sixteen years every decision I made was filtered
through my happy marriage: Where are we going on vacation? What do
we want to do about the swimming pool? What is Sarah doing tonight?
It is very disorienting now not to have a we in my life. I am having to*

learn to rethink everything. My life right now lacks structure. And I've lost the comfort of being in a happy, committed marriage and relationship. Suddenly there is no form to my existence. I'm just a person out there.

I have gotten clear on one thing. I am not going to focus on getting anywhere. I am staying in the process, dealing with today. I hope someday the process will allow something that feels like peace. But for now I'm just focusing on what is right in front of me today. Right after my wife died, people said things like, "You've got to stay in the moment. Take one day at a time." That seemed platitudinous, an easy thing to say. I wasn't taking it in, wasn't hearing it well. Then working with a therapist I came to understand how that really was. It became less a token of speech and more a real piece of advice.

At first I tried to gobble up information. I ordered ten or fifteen books on the Internet. I wanted to steer my grief, force it on down the road. Which is understandable. I've always been a planner, analyzer, building a business, managing my life very well until this. Now I have to suddenly surrender, letting things be. This is quite different for me. I did read one book that gave me my first glimmer of what my life might be like in the future as I find a real possibility of living with this loss in my life. That was a very hopeful message and that book was a gift to me. But for now I'm just staying in today, not worrying about what the future will look like. It's the only way for me to have any peace of mind.

I observed a major turn recently. It was the simplest of moments. I had come home from playing tennis and a World Series game was on, in extra innings. I was interested in watching. But then I had the thought: You need to go upstairs and have your usual time of quiet at the end of the day and write in your journal about this grief process you are in. I was torn between the two, wondering which would be more helpful. I should go still my mind and write . . . no, I want to relax and enjoy the last innings of this game. I knew I could force myself to write. I could try to "manage" my grief.

I watched the game. This, I saw later, was an example of my allowing the natural healing process to occur. So now I try to find little bits of pleasure. Maybe dinner with friends. I used to come right home from tennis league on Thursday nights for the still/writing time. But now I'm *staying out there for about an hour and joining the conversation. This brings some pleasure. Not on the scale of being with my wife, of course, but some pleasure in this bleak world I live in.*

I catch myself asking questions like, "How am I going to find happiness? Will I ever find a person again where I have love and sense of belonging? And if I do, how will Sarah's memory fit into any other story of a mate? At age forty-four now, will I ever have children? What about this house we built that is so big and so beautiful and that held the vision of our future?" These questions bring me despair. So I now have stopped asking the questions. It isn't time. I believe as I progress in my grieving, I will have natural movement about these issues. For now I am making no decisions.

REVIEWING: GO FOR THE GLASS CEILING OR WHAT

I had a therapist who told me one time that I was the kind of person who wouldn't make a change until I was up against the wall. It's almost like I have to be propelled by a trampoline jump or experience something like an internal car crash. That was the case when I made a major change the year my mother died; I left our family business in New York and moved down to Houston. This was so unplanned. I knew I was unhappy in New York, bored with my job, and exhausted after ending a relationship. It was a set of circumstances that just happened, and I went with it. Moved to a city I had never even seen before and where I had no resources.

But without internal upheaval I find myself wanting to make changes but being complacent. I have a good job in a global concern, but I haven't reached the level of success I want to. So I can go for breaking through the glass ceiling, and I know I stand a good chance of making it. I put a lot of pressure on myself to perform better and better. But do I want to stay in the corporate world? What about my dream to have a yoga studio with a Japanese tearoom attached? What about the idea I've had for years of going to cooking school and then creating a new restaurant guide for America?

Turning fifty was a big shift. I could no longer check off the 25-to-

49 age group. And when a friend was talking about introducing me to someone new, I dreaded that she would have to say I was fifty. That sounded so old. The age thing may turn out to be the internal car crash I need. I have decided I cannot just put my life on hold indefinitely. I cannot keep waiting for things to accelerate at work. I'm much more in touch with my mortality. And I know I still have a lot of time. So the question I started asking myself was, "How am I going to live the rest of my life?" This question was so profound that I immediately took to my bed!

The intensity of the question comes and goes. For now I'm following the advice of an author I read a long time ago: If you don't like what you do, love why you are doing it. I love my clients. I love the stimulation of my work. And I love the money and what it allows me to do. So for now I'm just on hold as far as work goes.

But I have decided to move on one thing at least. I'm going to buy a new house. I've given myself three months to find one. So that's movement in one area. And I'm going to travel a lot this year, including going to Washington, D.C., for the Women's March in April. I have never been to a march in my life. But I am so upset about the direction of our government that I'm becoming an activist. I want that march to be a statement that reminds everybody in Washington: We are women and we vote, too! I'm amazed I'm doing this but I am excited and thrilled. It feels right to go, and I feel great that I have decided to do it.

REVIEWING: THE WONDERFUL AND THE HARD CHANGES THAT COME WITH THE BIRTH OF A BABY

My husband and I had our first child six months ago. The joy of having this child exceeds anything we have ever experienced. There is nothing like it. And it is amazing that something so wonderful can be so hard. I am in many ways a completely different person than I was before Pete was born. My lifestyle is different both at home and away from home; my schedule, no matter whether I'm with him or not with him, centers on his needs. I have always taken the time to read, to write, to sew. These things are really important to my emotional and spiritual health.

But now this is something I just can't do until Pete goes to bed around eight o'clock. Then there are the dishes to do, bills to pay . . . things my husband and I share the responsibility for but which still are in my consciousness. Often, too, I'm just exhausted and only want to fall into bed. I think, though, that anything that we are passionate about is something we really need, something our emotional and spiritual health depends on. We must be mindful of these things. So thoughts of reading, writing, and sewing nag at me. I did start a sewing project for the first time the other day, and I'm at peace that the project is going to take me much longer than in the past, that I'll just work on it regularly and it's okay whatever time it takes.

My career path is different from what I thought it would be. I took two months off when Pete was born and have been back working for four months part-time. Before Pete was born, I planned to return to my work full-time when he was one. But now I know I will not do this. Even though I had just received full certification in my profession right before the baby came and could move into a beckoning career path now, I do not want to work full-time in the immediate future. This, of course, has ramifications. There are immediate financial burdens and long-term costs. Since I am working part-time, the contributions to my pension fund are halved. One advantage I knew I had by being as young as I was when I started in my profession was that I could get to the retirement point of thirty years' service while I was still fairly young. The longer I work part-time, the longer I draw out that thirty years of service. So I'll probably end up working until I'm elderly. This is something I will look at year by year. I do consider myself now bivocational. My professional work is a vocation; and motherhood is a vocation.

Our marriage is another area that requires attention and intention. We didn't realize this for a while but Stan and I now see how important it is that we be more attentive than ever before. We recently committed to going on a once-a-month date, saving the money to hire a babysitter and to go out. We never had to plan that way in the past; now we have to be much more organized. We have the idea; now we have to implement it, which is taking longer than we thought it would.

Marriage is both a safe place when you have a baby and a place that takes the punishment. It can catch all the stress. I see my husband as a safe haven, so it's easy for me to vent my stress with him. But that is alienating. The spouse doesn't need to be the lightning rod for everything that's going on. I'm having to learn about that. Also it's clear to me that at this point in Pete's life our roles are different—I'm the one breast-feeding and spending every afternoon with Pete. So we have to be intentional in our conversations about the stresses of life with this little person we are both in love with, and support each other more than ever. We have said more than once that this time is one of the hardest things we'll ever go through and one of the most wonderful.

REVIEWING: EVALUATING WHO I AM AFTER A DIVORCE

I became clear over time that I was married to someone who was unwilling to change. I had thought our issues could be contained, but more and more his anger—and violence—became directed at me.

Do I stay? The strong part of me said you can deal with it.

If I left? Things that at age thirty-eight I had planned for, like children, would probably now be precluded. And I had given up a lot, leaving graduate school in the Northeast to follow his career. But this deal was now broken.

What turned the situation was my realizing that I had bankrupted myself. I had traded off for a future that was no longer there. My credit cards were maxed out. I had stopped spending time with family because my husband was uncomfortable around them since he was unemployed. I was not with friends because he felt inferior around them. I had made all these trades on the idea of a future that was good. But now when I looked at what was in front of me, everything looked really bleak. I had married for love, and love was gone.

So I had to weigh these things: alcohol, violence, anger. I was doing fieldwork abroad by this time, and in the emptiness of living by myself I did the accounting. I made the decision to get a divorce. It was a safety issue, if nothing else. And it was also a lot more.

I've returned now to live with friends in the town where I grew up. At first I couldn't even pay them rent, so we bartered. I would help with the children and the cooking and they would provide me space and a sense of daily purpose. And I was smarter than I thought when I signed up for a Centering Prayer workshop at a local church. I really only went because it was something inexpensive and healthy that I could do on Friday night and Saturday. As a result of beginning that simple practice of sitting in silence in the Presence of the Divine twenty minutes in the morning and twenty minutes in the afternoon, I look at my life in a whole new way. Nothing has changed, but everything has changed.

It has taken a year of grieving the loss of my marriage to get to the place where I can say my heart isn't broken. I was grieving the loss of all those futures I thought I would have that are now empty. I've started dating again, and this time I'm choosing men who are adult. Who don't need fixing. This is strange and new not to pick people who are needy. I'm realizing that I had low standards for myself in the past. I didn't know myself, so I couldn't say what was right for me.

It's hard to reconcile. In many aspects of my life—like getting my doctorate—I've done so well. Yet I've always felt misplaced. Not feeling at home. Now I am beginning to have glimpses of another way where I feel healed and whole when thinking of the future.

REVIEWING: ANGER AT AN ELDERLY MOTHER

The anger burned in my gut like a white-hot iron. How could she have been so stupidly stubborn? How could I have been so stupidly cowed into letting her get away with not going immediately to the emergency room that evening before Christmas Eve? After all, when she finally let me be the medical doctor that I am rather than just her daughter, I had diagnosed peritonitis. But the old games had won out. She would rather hurt than do something I recommended.

So here I was heading back to Sun City. I listened to my brother's message on the answering machine within half an hour of getting home. Our mother had instructed him to take her to the emergency room on the way back from taking me to the airport! And she had been rushed immediately to the operating room where a perforated ulcer had been patched. Oh, yes, she was doing fine; and she expected me to return to Arizona ASAP.

After talking to my brother from my home in Chicago, I was so mad after hanging up the phone that I spent a good two to three minutes swearing, screaming, and banging my fist on the desk. I had just taken a week off from my practice to spend it with my mother. I had office hours filled to overflowing to cover. I had surgeries and colonoscopies scheduled to do every day for the next two weeks. I had my life to live. And now she expected me to turn right around and fly back out there. What for was unclear to me except to prove she was the mother and she was demanding this. She had survived the surgery for the perforated ulcer. She had really great neighbors more than willing to fetch her home from the hospital and help during her recovery. Her son was even there with her for the moment. So why the hell did she expect me to come back and be there?

But . . . I got back on a plane and headed west. Franklin met me at the airport. I don't remember what we talked about. Probably because I have repressed how I vented my anger and rage. He was always a patient listener. He was wise enough not to try to make it better. I do remember walking into my mother's hospital room. There she was, all chipper and victorious. God, I could have screamed at her such hatred and pent-up hurt and resentment and disappointment. Instead I looked at her and felt a great sadness.

For suddenly I saw the full picture: It all had to do with power and control and proving she was the mother and I was the daughter and daughters did what their mothers told them to do. Not that she necessarily did so with her own mother. Ah, but this was different. This was she and I. This would be another victory for her in her ongoing war of competition and dominance. It had become so a part of our relationship that I'm not at all sure she even realized it was happening much of the time. And I had taken the position of acquiescing to avoid her anger and blame when I didn't. Until that moment I was susceptible to feeling guilty the moment I displeased my mother. After all, isn't one of the Ten Commandments, "Thou shalt honor thy father and mother"? Anger . . . guilt . . . guilt . . . anger. A cycle that until the experience of the perforated ulcer I was never able to see and, therefore, never able to break.

But here, in this hospital room where my mother now lay in all her queenly splendor, I knew I had learned a powerful lesson. I realized that I could look outside myself and use what I saw to influence how I chose to be. I learned that as malignant and powerful as my anger and rage was, I was very capable of controlling it rather than it controlling me. I also had an epiphany: This person—this woman who was my mother—had a totally pervasive need to be in control. And I saw that when I became angry and showed my anger, when I felt guilty and did what I, as a fully functioning adult, knew was a stupid thing to do but did it anyway because Mother said so—in these situations I played right into my mother's game, just as she always intended.

I became free when I understood about the anger, the guilt, and the control. Until the day she died, I took care of my mother—through her illnesses, through her grief after my brother's death, through her immobility, through her long years in a nursing home. She had the best of everything that could be provided for her. I visited her frequently. And I never again felt guilt for making a decision that was not exactly what my mother dictated should be done. This was a powerful internal freedom, though the circumstances outside remained much the same until the end of my mother's life.

REVIEWING: BECOMING A STEPMOTHER

I was naïve about what it would mean to become a stepmother to two preteen daughters. I had no children myself, and in previous relationships I was used to it being just me and whomever I was with. We could pick up and go. After Matt and I married, I realized that I had no understanding of the responsibility of being a stepparent. No longer was it just me and the person; two more young lives were involved. If they got colds on the weekends they were with us, we were concerned: Should we take them to the doctor? What is best to do?

It hit me totally. We have to build a life together. I began to review what we could do to build a history together. The girls and their father had a history together that went back ten years—what they did last Christmas; what last Valentine's was like. I had known my husband less than a year when we married, so I had no history with him or the girls. One thing I thought of was photograph albums. So I started taking pictures and making albums so that the girls, Matt, and I could look at our history, almost as we were making it. I think this idea of building a history together is something that is helping tremendously.

I'm also having to understand the girls' dilemma about how close they can get to me without it being a betrayal of their mother. That's push-pull, progressive but not steady. It takes a while to find a balance, I'm sure. There's a sense of disloyalty that the girls deal with.

I do not reprimand the girls; I leave that up to their father. But there has been one time when I took a stand about a situation in which I sensed an absence of safety for the girls that my husband didn't see that way. He finally agreed with me. This is something I will have to look at all along . . . knowing when to be a role model but hands-off and loving, and when to take a stand about something about which I feel strongly.

As I work this out, I'm counting on my girlfriends. When I get really frustrated, I talk to them. If I say something about the girls' behavior, for instance, my husband will come to their defense immediately. I use my girlfriends as a sounding board. Also, Matt and I go for couples counseling related to the girls. We're learning how important it is for a husband and wife to be allied together in their beliefs and to hold boundaries together.

Every now and then I get a flickering of being odd person out. But this is happening less and less frequently. As the girls get older, they are going to be less interested in being around parents. I can already see signs of this, and can see that this is going to be hard for my husband. There's lot of criticism of Disneyland Dads. But we ask ourselves, "What else we can do?" We envy the girls' mother the routine life with the girls. And she envies our taking them places on trips and vacations. The situation is hard on the mother as well as the stepmother.

I still think how naïve I was. I had no idea how different it could be. How hard. One day I mentioned to the girls that sometime we would take them to Boston. "If you're still around," the ten-year-old said. I had to swallow hard, just as I did when she tried to continue to sit in the front seat after her dad and I married. They can be horrible little creatures. I keep looking for ways to create family. And it is becoming more comfortable and more fun but not easy.

REVIEWING: THE LEGACY OF A LOST CHILD

In this time of reflecting following the death of our child, I have gotten clear at least on this much. There are two things I can do something about—his legacy and my life. I am determined that his legacy will not be the black hole I see out there now, a slide into nothingness. I won't have people saying, "Oh, look at what happened to that little family after that boy died." No, how we live after his death will be a tribute to how he lived his life. To do anything less would be to have his life be wrong because his death is wrong. And that is just not going to happen. I also have control over my life and my future. These two things—his legacy and my life—give me focus. I am not a victim anymore. I don't feel like a victim. There's also something to be said for surviving the worst thing you could ever imagine. I have said many times after our children were born that the worst thing I could even start to imagine would be for one of them to die. Now that has happened, and I am surviving. That within itself gives me some kind of strength and courage.

REVIEWING: LIFE WITH A PARENT WHO HAS DEMENTIA

Even though my mother has had dementia for fifteen years, I still have to make the decision almost on a daily basis on how I will deal with this. I have to look at the situation and say, "What is needed at this time? What am I required to do?" Her condition has deteriorated over the years. The first ten years my father was still alive; and, while my mother had dementia (which in those years showed up as rage), she survived with Dad. Then there were three years in a personal care home where a different level of involvement for me was required. A broken hip two years ago put her in a nursing home where she is today. And by now she is completely without memory.

Sometimes I go daily, as last week when she had such serious respiratory problems that the hospice nurse said she thought this would be it. But then yesterday my mother was playing bingo in the recreational hall. There are periods when I go only twice a week. Then there will be another crisis, and I'll be in paralysis again. It can be overwhelming and certainly unrelenting. And wearisome. Oh, so wearisome.

And then there's the brother who lives away and doesn't help. I called him when our mother was near death last week and he said, "Oh, I've got to go to Geneva, Switzerland, on business." When our father died on Friday, I called and he said he had guests flying in for the weekend. So he arrived on Sunday night in time for the funeral Monday morning. And then left Monday afternoon. He never says, "Thank you," or "You're doing a good job taking care of Mother." His wife says he says it to her, but he never says it to me. I feel anger at him most of the time. I'd like to be a bigger person, but I'm just not.

A friend asked me the other day how I take care of myself, and I said, "Not well, my dear." Actually, it is cyclical. I take care of myself better at some times than others. Last week when there was the health crisis with Mother, I just had a meltdown. Canceled all appointments for the afternoon. I knew I couldn't be helpful to my clients in the shape I was in. So I cleared the calendar and went home.

There are things I do on a daily basis that help. I sit in silence thirty minutes a day on most days. And I surround myself with love. Husband, family, friends. And our dog, Shannon, nurtures me. Gives me hope, comfort. The love she expresses is enduring.

REVIEWING: THE FUTURE AFTER A MISCARRIAGE

It is a sad time, and I am still working through my grief. The grief counselor I am seeing is kind and compassionate. She had a miscarriage years ago and she lost a son to a drug overdose in 1985. I feel she understands my pain, and she knows how to work through loss.

Which so many of my well-meaning friends do not.

They tell me that I should consider myself lucky because I've had only two miscarriages and not seven. That I should feel fortunate I did not give birth and then lose the child. Well, I do not feel particularly "lucky," since this is a long, painful process.

And this grief is so intertwined with the loss of innocence, an understanding of God, and an awareness of the hardships of life. Perhaps the hardest question to answer is, "What's it all for?" I mean, why are we even alive if we do everything we feel guided to do with an open, trusting heart, and no matter what we do it does not bring us what we felt we were guided to have? This is the most frustrating thing for me. And the main reason I have no confidence in myself or a higher power at this time. Life feels so random and futile. And the irony is I have such faith in myself and a higher power that I ask the question so I can go on. And not only live this time, but love life and appreciate it. More than anything I am tired. I could curl up like a big ball in the bed. I really don't want to do that because I do have the strength and desire to go about my day and do the things I love.

I am seeking the advice of a new doctor who has me taking a baby aspirin every day to thin my blood, and he plans to put me on progesterone supplements later. Visiting his office was hard because it meant I had not only to face the loss one more time but I had to evaluate it as well. The doctor did give me hope. He still considers me normal since the majority of women have at least one or two miscarriages. And he sees no reason why we shouldn't try again. We'll see. This is something we have to review and reflect on.

These stories illustrate to me very courageous acts: The act of waiting. The act of reflecting. The act of checking oneself from the outside. These kinds of acts are active, not passive. They are not a flopped-back-on-the-couch zoning out of life. Instead, they are intentional questions and purposeful noticing, but toward learning, seeing, realizing. Not toward rushing pell-mell ahead to do something, anything, no matter whether such movement would be useful or not. I suspect that each of these individuals would like for the future to be clear to them. Some would like to know exactly what to do next and when to do it. Some would like to be able to see how past events will integrate into their future lives. Some would like to know what they need to know but don't yet. Some would desperately like to know how things are

> Mango trees take seven years to grow fruit.
>
> *Tropical Book of Gardening*

going to turn out. But such answers are not now available. What are these individuals doing in the meantime? They are actively— and courageously—waiting. Reflecting. Checking themselves from the outside. It is much more comfortable, of course, to know an answer; but these people understand that struggling for a definitive answer often brings premature closure that cuts off the very solution or outcome or revelation that would bring the greatest satisfaction.

What Helps During Reviewing

The poet Rilke once wrote about having the courage, when one is in a quandary, to "live the question" rather than grasp for a quick solution.

> Have patience with everything that remains unsolved in your heart. Try to love the questions themselves, like locked rooms and like books written in a foreign language. Do not now look for the answers. . . . At present you need to live the question. Perhaps you will gradually, without even noticing it, find yourself experiencing the answer, some distant day.

This is marvelous advice for us when we are in the experiences of Reviewing.

REDUCING STRESS

Time-Honored Advice. When Reviewing reveals that we are still at the effect of emotions that trigger unhealthy stress, what specific advice is available to us? Dr. Bruce McEwen of Rockefeller University offers "the time-honored ones: eat sensibly, get plenty of sleep, exercise regularly, stop at one martini and stay away from cigarettes. 'It's a matter of making choices in your life,'" he says.

HeartMath. The Institute of HeartMath, whose work has been featured in the *Wall Street Journal* and the *Harvard Business Review*, and is used by thousands of companies and individuals, offers a unique and effective approach to reducing stress. The people at HeartMath are committed that the techniques they offer for reducing stress will result in people being able to use "all the pieces of their intelligence—intellectual, emotional, organizational, behavioral and intuitive—in making decisions." One technique for which they are most known is called "The Five Steps of Freeze-Frame."

These steps go like this:

1. Recognize the stressful feeling and FREEZE-FRAME IT! Take a time-out.
2. Make a sincere effort to shift your focus away from the racing mind or disturbed emotions to the area around your heart. Pretend you're breathing through your heart to help focus your energy in this area. Keep your focus there for ten seconds or more.
3. Recall a positive, fun feeling or time you've had in life and try to re-experience it.
4. Now, using your intuition, common sense, and sincerity, ask your heart, What would be a more efficient response to the situation, one that would minimize future stress?
5. Listen to what your heart says in answer to your question. (It's an effective way to put your reactive mind and emotions in check and an in-house source of commonsense solutions!)

Three Questions. Another way to defuse emotions: When everything is taxing and we have exceeded our resources, we can ask these three questions:

1. How do I understand and evaluate the situation?

2. What can I do about the problem represented by the situation?
3. What can I do about my reaction to the situation?

What we are trying to do here is to "maneuver ourselves into states of optimal survival." Some degree of happiness, scientists tell us, comes quite simply from acting in conformity with our self-preserving tendency, as needed but not more.

CREATIVE ACTIVITIES

Engaging with Art. A study of postsurgery patients in Sweden who regularly saw a painting of calm water and trees showed that they exhibited less anxiety and required fewer strong pain drugs than patients who saw no art. Dr. Andrew Weil, citing this study, offers these suggestions:

Take time to admire works of art you find beautiful and inspiring, whether paintings, buildings, or statues.
Make your living and working spaces visually attractive.
Doodle.
Keep a visual journal, using imagery to express your feelings.
Learn more from *The Art Therapy Sourcebook* by Cathy Malchiodi (Lowell House, 1998).

Writing. James Pennebaker, PhD, has shown that people who write about stressful experiences visit doctors less often and have stronger immune responses. Here is what Professor Pennebaker has to say on his Web site about writing about emotional upheavals. You might also look for his book on this subject, *Writing to Heal: A Guided Journal for Recovering from Trauma and Emotional Upheaval.*

Writing about emotional upheavals in our lives can improve physical and mental health. Although the scientific research surrounding the value of expressive writing is still in the early phases, there are some approaches to writing that have been found to be helpful. Keep in mind that there are probably a thousand ways to write that may be beneficial to you. Think of these as rough guidelines rather than Truth. Indeed, in your own writing, experiment on your own and see what works best.

Getting Ready to Write

Find a time and place where you won't be disturbed. Ideally, pick a time at the end of your workday or before you go to bed.

Promise yourself that you will write for a minimum of 15 minutes a day for at least 3 or 4 consecutive days.

Once you begin writing, write continuously. Don't worry about spelling or grammar. If you run out of things to write about, just repeat what you have already written.

You can write longhand or you can type on a computer. If you are unable to write, you can also talk into a tape recorder.

You can write about the same thing on all 3–4 days of writing or you can write about something different each day. It is entirely up to you.

What to Write About

Something that you are thinking or worrying about too much

Something that you are dreaming about

Something that you feel is affecting your life in an unhealthy way

Something that you have been avoiding for days, weeks, or years

In our research, we generally give people the following instructions for writing: *Over the next four days, I want you to write about your deepest emotions and thoughts about the most upsetting experience in your life. Really let go and explore your feelings and thoughts about it. In your writing, you might tie this experience to your childhood, your relationship with your parents, people you have loved or love now, or even your career. How is this experience related to who you would like to become, who you have been in the past, or who you are now?*

Many people have not had a single traumatic experience but all of us have had major conflicts or stressors in our lives and you can write about them as well. You can write about the same issue every day or a series of different issues. Whatever you choose to write about, however, it is critical that you really let go and explore your very deepest emotions and thoughts.

Warning: Many people report that after writing, they sometimes feel somewhat sad or depressed. Like seeing a sad movie, this typically goes away in a couple of hours. If you find that you are getting extremely upset about a writing topic, simply stop writing or change topics.

What to Do with Your Writing Samples

The writing is for you and for you only. Their purpose is for you to be completely honest with yourself. When writing, secretly plan to throw away your writing when you are finished. Whether you keep it or save it is really up to you.

Some people keep their samples and edit them. That is, they gradually change their writing from day to day. Others simply keep them and return to them over and over again to see how they have changed.

Here are some other options:

Burn them. Erase them. Shred them. Flush them. Tear them into little pieces and toss them into the ocean or let the wind take them away. Eat them (not recommended).

There are other forms of writing that are valuable also. Journaling can serve as a receptacle, a mirror, and an alternate voice as we weigh our current situation. People write letters to God, to dead people, to mythical people, to real people (deciding only later whether or not to send them). Poem-making speaks to many people as they say yea to this and nay to that during a Reviewing time of their lives.

Listening to Music. We saw in Responding how music and harmony can center, relax, and restore us. During Reviewing we might want to choose music for specific purposes.

Music for Prayer. If you want to hear music that promotes a sense of being in a sacred space, you might select:

Andrea Bocelli's *Sacred Arias*
Prayers by Sumi Jo
Mahalia Jackson's spirituals
Chant by the Benedictine Monks of Santo Domingo de Silos
Agnus Dei: Music of Inner Harmony by the choir of New College, Oxford
Anne Murray's *What a Wonderful World*
Musical Book of Hours by Pomerium
Richard Paul Fink's *I Love to Tell the Story*
Domine Deus Taizé chants with English verses
Tibetan Singing Bowls and *The Sound of Om*
Barbra Streisand's *Higher Ground*

Music for Supporting Yourself. If you want music to help you think straight, feel creative, boost vitality, and gain equilibrium, you might listen to:

Songs of the Auvergne, First Series, no.2, "Baïlèro," by Marie-Joseph de Calaret Canteloube
Brahms's Violin Concerto in D Major, second movement

Dvořák's *Serenade for Strings*; Symphony no. 9 in E Minor (*New World* Symphony)

Beethoven's Symphony no. 6 in F, op. (*Pastoral*)

Mozart (check out the CD *Music for the Mozart Effect, vol. 3: Unlock the Creative Spirit* by Springhill Music)

Doc Childre's *Heart Zones: Music Proven to Boost Vitality*

Henry Mancini's "Meggie's Theme" and "The Thorn Birds Theme" from *Ultimate Mancini*

César Franck's *Psyche*

Bizet's Symphony in C.

Putumayo's *Cover the World*

Beth Neilson Chapman's CDs *Deeper Still* and *Hymns*

Music for Solitude. If you want music that gives you pleasure when you are alone, you might select:

Kitaro's *Silk Road Suite*

Bach's motets

Pablo Casals's "Song of the Birds"

von Gluck's "Dance of the Blessed Spirits"

Paul Horn's *Inside the Powers of Nature*

Ralph Vaughan Williams's "Sine Nomine (For All the Saints)"

Michael Jones's *Wind and Whispers*

Eternal Light: Music of Inner Peace by Priory of the Resurrection

IMAGINING POSSIBILITY

Exploring.

Make collages using pictures from magazines that reflect the life you want now, goals that interest you, problems you want to solve.

Keep a Future Box into which you put everything you come across that speaks somehow to the future you want: articles, pictures, advertisements, whatever.

Talk to a life coach and begin to formulate the directions you
would like to explore.

Play around with a Life Plan for yourself—nothing tight and
finished but full of imaginings and possibility.

Making Lists. The act of making a list is deceptively simple—after
all, we've been making lists since we first went to the store to get
our school supplies. But list making, in this time of Reviewing, can
be something so much more than a mundane activity done to jog
our minds. The ancient meaning of *list* came from the Old English
word *hylsnan*, which means *to listen to*. So when we make lists
during Reviewing whom are we listening to? We are listening to
ourselves. We are eavesdropping on our own conversation. List
making works like dropping a bucket down into a deep well, a well
of memory, desires, experiences. Lists we make reveal things to us,
surprise us, remind us. When we make lists, we can explore the unexamined interior of ourselves and discover things about ourselves
that we didn't even know we didn't know.

Once I was in a meeting where the leader asked us to list all the
telephone numbers we knew from memory. Our home telephone
number was the first I put on my list. Then my husband's mobile,
my office number, our fax number, my sister's number in Tennessee, my aunt's number in Georgia. First of all, I was surprised at
how few numbers I knew. Then I realized that the one person in
my immediate family whose number I did not have memorized
was the number of my brother Frank. This amazed me, given that
I have only two people in my family of origin who are still alive—
my sister and my brother—and I didn't know his number. Oh, we
e-mailed almost every day and talked on the telephone occasionally. But what the list making revealed to me was that I don't talk
to my brother enough on the phone to have memorized his number. And I wanted to change that. So when I got home, I copied
his number out of my database and taped it under the telephone
where it could stay until I had committed it to memory. This is the
power of the simple act of list making.

Ilene Segalove and Paul Bob Velick have written a very good

book called *List Your Self: Listmaking as the Way to Self-Discovery*. Here are a few lists they suggest that I think might be useful when we are experiencing Reviewing while navigating a tough transition:

List the things you think you can't live without.
List the components of your perfect day.
List the heroic feats you've performed.
List what you hear when you get very quiet.
List all the times you knew something but didn't trust your intuition.
List all the prayers, sayings, and chants you've been taught that make you feel better.

Think of your own lists . . . a good/bad list about a time in the past; a list of those things in the past that you'd like to bring forth in the future in a new form; a list of things you assumed before this tough transition happened. Make these lists and see what you discover.

Learning Just to Be. Jockey, the briefs company, recently ran an eye-catching ad. A full-page image shows a forest, with moss-covered trees, ferns, ancient rocks making a wall, clear sky in the far background. The words on this ad? "Are you comfortable being?" Study after study shows that learning "just to be" brings a decrease in stress, plus access to wisdom, peace, and tranquillity. Consider mindfulness, centering prayer, or any other form of "just being" that appeals to you.

Mindfulness, to choose just one possible approach among many you could take to learn just to be, is based on seven attitudes, according to Jon Kabat-Zinn of the University of Massachusetts Medical Center.

Non-judging: Watch all your thoughts but suspend making a judgment.
Patience: Understand that things unfold in their own time.

Beginner's Mind: Try to see things a fresh way, not as you "know" them to be.

Trust: Develop a basic trust in yourself and your feelings.

Non-striving: Pay attention to what is happening without striving to get something.

Acceptance: Focus on the present and be willing to see things as they are.

Letting go: Watch and be nonattached.

These attitudes support a meditation practice and a way of living that reduce stress and increase enjoyment.

Practicing Active Waiting. Be alert the way a birdwatcher is alert. Not doing anything, simply paying attention. Noticing. (I'm always encouraged when I remember that noticing is categorized as a creative act.) Pay attention to what shows up and how you respond to it. Be willing to be in sync with whatever process of change is going on without having to know what you are going to do about it.

Thomas Merton's story of being in a cabin in the woods during a heavy rain catches the essence of Reviewing for me. He writes:

> The rain . . . fills the woods with an immense and confused sound. It covers the flat roof of the cabin and its porch with insistent and controlled rhythms. And I listen, because it reminds me again and again that the whole world runs by rhythms I have not yet learned to recognize. . . .
>
> I came up here from the monastery last night, sloshing through the cornfield, said Vespers, and put some oatmeal on the Coleman stove for supper. It boiled over while I was listening to the rain and toasting a piece of bread at the log fire. The night became very dark. The rain surrounded the whole cabin with its enormous virginal myth, a whole world

of meaning, of secrecy, of silence, of rumor. Think of it: all that speech pouring down, selling nothing, judging nobody, drenching the thick mulch of dead leaves, soaking the trees, filling the gullies and crannies of the wood with water. . . . What a thing it is to sit absolutely alone, in the forest, at night, cherished by this wonderful, unintelligible, perfectly innocent speech, the most comforting speech in the world, the talk that rain makes by itself all over the ridges, and the talk of the watercourses everywhere in the hollows!

Nobody started it, nobody is going to stop it. It will talk as long as it wants, this rain. As long as it talks, I am going to listen.

Reviewing is receptive, if nothing else. We are noticing, weighing, questioning, sifting, balancing, wondering. And perhaps most of all we are listening. Listening, as Thomas Merton did, to the "whole world of meaning . . . of silence . . . cherished by the talk that rain makes." Since the rain will talk as long as it wants, our job is to say, "I am going to listen."

In Summary: REVIEWING

Reviewing experiences that are useful in a tough transition include:

Looking after health and well-being
Reminiscing
Asking questions
    Kant's three questions: What can I know? What should I do?
    What may I hope?
Thinking about eternal verities
Valuing solitude
Valuing silence
Valuing others
Working through anger, blame, and guilt
Asking what can I imagine
Asserting that I need to do some things differently now

Reviewing often begins when we recognize that we need to get released from the grip of our emotions or want relief from our despair. Sometimes an illness triggers the acts of Reviewing. Sometimes a wise word from a friend starts us asking questions and considering how we might move forward in dealing with a tough transition. It may be a raucous upset that lets us know enough is enough and we must work through our anger, blame, or guilt. Or we may just find ourselves wanting to be alone in the quiet, led to this act by our own inner wisdom. We don't do all our Reviewing at once. The very nature of Reviewing means that insights and realizations come often over time and certainly not on a called-up schedule.

WHERE

Reviewing does not begin and end with a sharp delineation. Therefore, we will probably find ourselves, once we begin these experiences, doing acts of Reviewing off and on for the duration of our engagement with the tough transition. This being so, we will nevertheless probably be able to look back later and see that there was a distinct period of time during the challenge of the transition where what we did was mostly Reviewing. In the natural sequence of our movement through the difficult time, there will perhaps have been a period when we did a lot of reminiscing or made a concentrated commitment with a therapist to deal with anger or guilt. But since the Terrain of Tough Transitions is not linear, we don't "do Reviewing," check it off, and be done with it. Reviewing is the kind of experiences that prove valuable long after we have begun to concentrate on Reorganizing or enjoying the gifts of Renewing.

HOW

What assists us when we are Reviewing?

Reducing stress
Creative activities
    Engaging with art
    Writing
    Listening to music: for prayer, for supporting ourselves, for solitude
    Imagining possibility
        Exploring
        Making lists
        Learning just to be
        Practicing active waiting

3

Reorganizing

A path is a marvelous thing.

ANCIENT RUSSIAN PROVERB

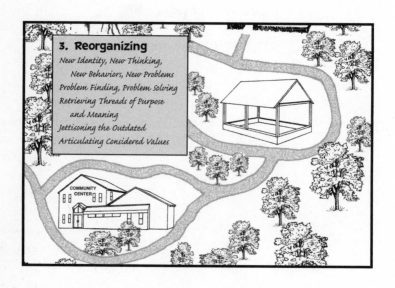

3. Reorganizing

New Identity, New Thinking,
*   New Behaviors, New Problems*
Problem Finding, Problem Solving
Retrieving Threads of Purpose
*   and Meaning*
Jettisoning the Outdated
Articulating Considered Values

COMMUNITY
CENTER

My friend the late poet William Stafford once entitled a book he wrote, *You Must Revise Your Life*. There have been long transition periods in my life when I have kept Bill's book propped up on my desk, title facing out, just to remind me of the job at hand. Bill believed that each of us is constantly being shaped by our encounters with experiences, people, and events. These encounters and our converging with life outside are our ongoing story, he said, sometimes moving forward with little impediment but more often in need of redirection. And it is amazing, Bill said, what small acts might signal that redirection. "Something as natural as choosing a color one likes," he wrote, "becomes like a banner for the life force."

When we are Reorganizing ourselves and our lives during a tough transition, we must use everything we can find that will help us redirect, everything that might be a banner for the life force. When we start to create our new identity, get the new skills we need, change what has to be changed to shape a life appropriate to where we are now, we are experiencing having to revise our lives. Instead of feeling defeated by the twists and turns of life, we have to find some way, in Bill Stafford's words, to "treat experiences as a set of surprises on which to exercise our quirky selves."

I think about an experience I had recently in the wild far west of China. East Turkistan is the correct name of the country I was traveling in, once an ancient kingdom of the Uighur peoples with

> Why isn't this the way it is?
> A little health,
> A little wealth,
> A little house and freedom,
> And at the end
> A little friend
> And little cause to need him.
>
> anonymous poet

thousands of years of its own history, language, dances, food, and rulers, but now occupied and controlled by China. (Think of the ravages of Tibet but with no Dalai Lama to educate us about the atrocities of domination, and you'll have a sense of the lives of the Uighurs in East Turkistan.) As our group drove through the Xinjiang area, as the Chinese call it, now and then we came upon nomads from other Central Asian areas traveling about the country to find grazing lands for their animals. These groups live in round white yurts. When it's time to find a new place for the animals to graze or a new place to winter where the winds are less fierce, the yurts are just folded up and moved. It was amazing to find that when these mobile homes are unfolded in the new location, everything that felt like home is right there, full and complete.

One late afternoon we were invited into one of these yurts for tea, which included spicy soup and grilled kabobs. Even though the tribe, which travels all over Central Asia, had just arrived at this location in East Turkistan, the first thing I spotted inside the yurt was a colorful hand-woven rug on the floor. The walls were lined with big pillows of red, blue, white, and yellow. In the center of the space was a small brazier on which the soup was heating, while the kabobs were cooking on the fire outside. Hanging from hooks in different parts of the yurt were hand-woven bags containing the family's clothes and possessions. Everything was there. Home had been carried from one location to another and could just as easily be picked up and carried somewhere else when need be.

That yurt experience has become a tantalizing metaphor for me: If only, as I am required to revise my life, as I am required by life's changes to transition from one place to another, I could pack up "home"—familiarity, comfort, safety—and take it with me, having only to unfold and set it up when I get there. In spite of the fact that I do experience that possibility in my *inner* life—knowing that I carry safety and confidence and faith within myself—my *external* life is something else. There's never a colorful patterned rug on the floor or cushions of red with gold spangles when I arrive in a new place in my external world. There's never anybody cooking savory pepper soup over a little brazier in the middle of the floor. Instead, at the new place, it's empty space, innumerable boxes to unpack, things to pitch or patch that broke in transit. It's change, reshape, risk, redirect, and transform, over and over again, as I reorganize my life. The consolation is knowing that, as chaotic and uncharted as this time of Reorganization is, there are things I can do that will make these experiences of reorganizing shorter rather than longer. There are ways of thinking and acting that make this time of Reorganizing productive rather than defeating.

New Identity, New Thinking, New Behaviors

First there is discarding. We are discarding old patterns: how we think; how we feel; how we act. These patterns, of course, fit our previous circumstance, but they no longer serve in the new place of this transition. While we are discarding and before we have had time and the opportunity to design new patterns, it is natural that we feel low and lack energy. But gradually the old patterns start to alternate with new trials of action and we begin to examine what can be kept from the past and what has to be created to work in this new situation. We are beginning to redefine who we are.

A newly single man once gave me a very homey example of turning a corner to establish a new identity, with new ways of thinking—and acting.

One day I decided, "Hey, I'm sick and tired of eating in restaurants. I'm not willing to keep on running away from myself and from learning how to do things on my own. Tonight I'm going to fix round steak and cream gravy!"

So I stopped by Kroger's and I picked up a beautiful piece of round steak—a little expensive and far too much for one person. I'd just eat the leftovers, I decided. "I'll have parsley boiled potatoes that you can put gravy over, a fresh loaf of bread, and a little salad—lettuce, tomato, some mayonnaise on it," I said to myself.

I started preparing all of this as soon as I got home. I was really anxious. I cooked the steak, cut up the salad, got the potatoes to boiling. Then I thought, "Oh my God, I don't know how to make gravy." I'd tried when Laura was still here, and it always came out in one lump instead of liquid. "Well," I thought, "it's time for you to learn. If you're going to have gravy, that's what you got to do. What you gonna do, otherwise—invite Mama down from Oklahoma to cook it for you?"

I began. "Settle down and think about it. If you do this first and this second, it's probably going to turn out all right. Do it carefully, do it slowly, take your time, learn how to do it." I ended up making the most beautiful pot of cream gravy you've ever seen. The only thing was that I made way too much, but I saved it and put it on my toast the next morning.

You know, I found myself to some extent—I found this independence, this ability to live on my own—through cooking that cream gravy. After I made the gravy, I took on an even bigger project—doing my own washing. I had always divided everything into man's work and woman's work. Now it was all my work. Riding the crest of the wave of gravy success, I said, "I'm going to do some hot-water washing with some bleach. I'm going to get my things really white."

So I read the instructions on the washing machine and the instructions on the bleach bottle. I put all that information together, and I did a wash and then I did a dry. I remember that when I took those things out of the dryer it was dark. I reached in and bundled them all up and took them to the living room, where I had been listening to music, and put them on the sofa to fold them.

This was another mark of success—success at taking responsibility *for finding a new identity and doing new things. You know, all the king's horses and all the king's men couldn't do it, so how can you? You don't think that finding out how to put yourself together again consists of things like washing clothes and making cream gravy!*

Clearly this courageous man had begun to acknowledge his new situation and to find ways to act appropriate to that situation.

We may, like the gravy maker, discover as we work to create a new identity appropriate to our new circumstances that we face a developmental crisis. Skills must be developed that we don't already have. We have to learn things that we wish we'd learned a long time ago: balancing a bank account, going into a crowded room alone, being really good at problem solving. We have to be a beginner, at the very time in our lives that we most need to feel confident and assured. The things we did in the past, the ways we looked at the world, the future we had set for ourselves by our goals and dreams . . . these must now all be augmented so that we can take on the roles and tasks our current situation demands of us.

> Beginnings are always messy.
> John Galsworthy

Learning new skills and new ways of being can be exhilarating and fulfilling, but being forced to learn can also engender resentment. I'm thinking of a woman I know whose job was eliminated but who managed to find another position in the same company. However, instead of her former managerial position, the woman is now only a "worker bee." Used to leading, having enjoyed helping to develop and mentor employees who reported to her, the woman now holds a position where she is asked only to execute what someone else says needs to be done. "Most days I can handle the situation pretty well—after all, it's far better than not having a job," she says, "but there are times when I know from my experience that doing x instead of y will solve the problem. Or I see a colleague who's struggling and who, in my previous job, I'd have trained and mentored; but now I'm not that employee's manager. I'm just another person on the team. It feels like regression . . .

having to do the kind of work I did years ago. Some days I say to myself, 'I've already been here, already done that.' But this is an accommodation I have to make, a person I have to be until I can do otherwise." This woman, because of the transition in which she finds herself, is doing a kind of learning that she would have preferred not to do.

As difficult as forging these new roles, identities, and behaviors can be, the situation can be satisfactorily worked through. When that happens, our new identity may be more stable and secure and more closely linked to the core of who we are than the identity we had before. I asked a divorced friend about this: Did he feel, now that he had created a new identity—built on the foundation of who he'd always been and added to by what he needs to be now— that he was more stable and secure and more linked to the core of his being? He answered by saying, "Yes, I've had to become another person because of my divorce. I've had to become someone who can cook, at least grilled cheese sandwiches and spaghetti; someone who can sit alone at night after work in an empty apartment and not go crazy but, instead, find interesting things to do; someone who thinks consciously about how to bring up a little boy and girl to be good people, resulting in my taking continuing education courses in parenting and in religion. I'm stronger and more confident now, even though the impetus for doing all this work on myself started out as a negative. I do think that I've uncovered and developed more of the person I am capable of being."

So there could be good news lying *in potentia* when we do the work of Reorganizing: In working to act, think, and be the person we now need to be, we forge new strengths and discover resources, desires, and directions that are new and expanding.

Three Strategies for Exploring Who I Need to Be Now

There are at least three strategies that people say have helped as they created the new identity necessary for the life in which they now find themselves. They say:

1. I look at others to gain information that will help me make the transition easier. When I see a colleague or a friend or a family member who is in a similar transition and seems to be headed toward a satisfactory outcome, I ask myself (and sometimes them), "What is that person doing that works? What abilities are they putting into play that I could also use in my own transition?"

2. I work to know what I want to change by asking, "What, from my current vantage point, would I do differently from the past, if I could?" This isn't a self-blaming exercise; it's a learning exercise. Now that I'm redirecting my life in a tough transition, what can I see in my own past behaviors and ways of thinking that I can learn from? That will lead me to do things differently in the future?

3. I find legitimate ways to think about my situation that lead me to feel grateful. For instance, I see or hear of people who have let a tough transition do them in—maybe they're drinking too much or have become so bitter and angry that life has little meaning—and I'm thankful that somehow I've escaped that outcome. "It could be worse," I tell myself, words that I experience not as a cliché but as powerful and true and, therefore, very helpful.

What works? What would I do differently? For what can I be grateful? These are three questions that can bring perspective. These strategies help elevate us above the grind and bump of the difficult changes that Reorganizing our lives brings.

> We are called to be architects of the future, not its victims.
>
> Buckminster Fuller

This past month I've seen an inspiring illustration: My sister Barbara has been required to create a new identity for herself as she changed jobs, changed her city of employment, and changed the habits and routine of her daily life. After several years of being a high school librarian, she resigned to become librarian of an elementary school in a city thirty miles from where she lives. She's had to retool her skill set. What an eleventh grader in a biology class needs from the school librarian is a world apart from what a first grader needs who is just learning to read. To do this, she's participated in a faculty retreat, visited other schools, searched for resource materials. She's sought specific advice and asked for direction from people who are working as elementary school librarians. Even her computing skills had to be upgraded because the new school uses an entirely different database system and method for inventory and checking out books. She's had to alter her getting-up time and going-to-bed time to accommodate travel to the new job location. She's had to find ways to see her friends whom she would previously have seen at the school where she had been working.

One thing I noticed was that, even before she chose her new job (she was fortunate to have more than one job offer to choose from), Barbara was setting up criteria based on what she wanted to be different from her previous position: fair and equally divided work, professional attitudes and approaches to problem solving, a work environment nurtured by support of administrators. She was using the past proactively, to help shape the future she intended to move into. She insisted that any job she took would have, as far as she could discern in interviews and through investigation, the potential for fairness, professionalism, and administrative acumen.

And is she grateful? She brimming with thanksgiving, so happy to be a part of this highly professional staff at a highly recognized school making the news—and history—in student accomplishments and staff recognition.

> The winds of grace are always blowing; but you have to raise the sail.
>
> Sri Ramakrishna

She is thrilled with the quiet time her drive back and forth to school provides her. And she is feeling very good about herself for being proactive and stepping out of a situation that was becoming more and more untenable. She is creating a new identity and is invigorated by the challenge of the transition.

New Problems Present Themselves

As we Reorganize our lives during a tough transition, often new problems arise as a result of our taking new action. And, of course, we have all the regular problems that were there even before the transition. Life, then, can knot up into something of a double thread. It's clear that there is no way we can solve all the new—and the old—problems quickly or easily. So we inch along in some cases and grow in bits and spurts in others. Nothing seems quick and straightforward. On some days we feel like that title of a country-and-western song: "I need a vacation from my life."

One of the most important things is to distinguish the problems related to the specific transition we're in from the problems that occur in normal day-to-day living. "Why make that distinction?" someone might say. "Problems are problems." One advantage of separating the "new" problems—for example, *How can I stay fit now that I have a chronic illness?*—from the ordinary ones—for example, *What is the right thing to do when my mother calls every night during dinner?*—is that we can set priorities. *Which of these problems must be tackled now?* We can put problems in order of their difficulty or simplicity to solve. *Cleaning out one drawer in my late husband's desk I can do today, but I won't decide whether to sell the house this morning.* We can avoid putting a lot of freight on top of the tough transition by relating everything that's wrong to the transition, thereby keeping the situation to its appropriate size.

A friend told me about the day she realized she was mushing everything together and associating all her problems to the transition she was in. She put Beethoven's "Moonlight Sonata" on the

CD player and found herself bursting into tears when she heard the first few bars of the music. "I thought I was crying about being alone, about my husband being gone," she said, "so I decided that I just couldn't listen to any more classical music." But then a memory became so real that she said she could almost see it in front of her eyes. "I was sitting in a movie house in Waxahachie, Texas, watching Kathryn Grayson up on the screen. Oh, that world on the screen looked so beautiful, so inviting, to a little fourteen-year-old girl growing up in a tiny town who had little to lift her horizons. I had such longing for a bigger life, for something different from what I knew. A longing so strong that it was almost painful." Then my friend told me what she realized next: The music being played in the background of that movie had been "Moonlight Sonata"! So she wasn't crying because her husband was gone. She was crying for that fourteen-year-old girl she'd been who had wanted a more meaningful life. "And that's a situation I can do something about," my friend said. "I can take advantage of the open-endedness my life has now and fulfill that little girl's longing for bigger horizons." A powerful outcome, isn't it, to realizing that some problems are about our transitions and some are about our lives in general?

Another new problem that arises when we start to Reorganize our lives during a tough transition is the continuing questions that plague us. These questions interfere with our achieving any sense of stability and normalcy in the new situation. For instance, a man told me that even though he'd found a good job to replace the one he'd lost and was enjoying the work, he was still unsettled by all the questioning he'd begun in the months when his life was in limbo:

I'd never taken the opportunity to wonder whether I was doing what I wanted to do in my life. As long as I had a good job and was on an upward trajectory in my career path, I just moved along with little, if any, reflection. But in the months when I was looking for a job, I really started to engage with the question of what I want my life to be all about. And this new job hasn't provided a clear answer at all.

This questioning about life's purpose and meaning, the man told me, has upset the equilibrium of his home life. His wife had thought that once her husband had a good job again, all would return to normal. But now, because of the introspection that began during the time of his previous job loss, this man realizes that he might want to change careers completely. He may move into a field where the work is more meaningful but less well-paying. And he may begin this move soon. This possibility has created a whole new problem, not only for his wife but for the entire family.

Unbelievably Useful Tools: Problem Space and Problem Finding

PROBLEM SPACE

What to do in the face of these new and old problems? One could decide that all is hopeless and that things are never going to get any better. One could become a pessimist. Just forget the whole thing. But researchers have done a lot of work on how to approach solving problems that threaten to keep us sucked into the mire of defeat and apathy. One of the most powerful concepts about solving problems that I have ever read is something called "problem space" and "problem finding."

What is a *problem space*? The academic definition reads like this: *a conceptual space of alternatives*. But put in everyday terms, I think about a problem space this way: Imagine that the problem is located in a certain place, say, a circle of open ground in the middle of a forest. You're going along on a trail through trees, and then you come upon a large open place like a camping spot. Right in the middle of this spot sits your problem. And in the large open space all around the problem are zillions of possible answers to the problem. More answers than you will ever need. All these answers are just sitting there, awaiting discovery. Multiple approaches and multiple solutions abound. You don't have to search, head down, fists clenched, for the one and only right answer. The "space" of the problem holds such a variety of good answers and good ways to go about solving the problem that you would never need them all.

When I consider a problem I'm trying to solve as being in a "space" like this—where many, many good answers exist and where I can go and find first this possible solution and then that equally acceptable one—I have energy and verve. If, however, I don't think "problem space" but instead act as if there's only one right answer, I struggle until I find that answer and then I think I have to hang on to it tenaciously.

I had an experience of shifting from the find-the-one-solution approach to the problem-space-full-of-possibilities approach when I was attempting to come up with a title for this book. I struggled for weeks to think of a good title when I began the rough draft. Finally, after a long struggle, I got it! I thought of the one title that was perfect! All was well. Then many months later, when I began the collaboration process with my editor, the design team, the sales staff, and others, my perfect title no longer seemed so perfect. I was just about to start back on the there's-only-one-solution search when I thought, "Problem space!" I remembered that there were lots of titles out there that would work great for this book. More titles than I could ever use. All I had to do was roam around among all these possible answers to find one that everybody agreed would work. How did that look, as far as my actions were concerned? I started asking people, "What title would you suggest?" From friends, family, and acquaintances, I got in one weekend more than a dozen excellent titles. How did I decide? When three individuals came up with the same title independently, I said, "That's the one"; and I sent it in. A bit of collaboration on a subtitle with the professionals at the publishing house and the problem was solved. The problem space had contained more answers than I would ever need, and I felt refreshed at the end rather than depleted by a struggle to hunt for the one right thing.

PROBLEM FINDING

Problem finding is another powerful distinction to remember when we are faced with the plethora of problems that occur when we engage in Reorganizing during a tough transition. We might compare problem finding to experimenting, trying something out, doing a dry or a trial run, practicing and rehearsing. You look for an answer to your problem by checking things out this way, then that way, staying tentative and open to new ideas for as long as you possibly can before choosing a solution.

A while back someone did an experiment to see what difference taking the problem-finding approach makes to the quality and satisfaction of the final solution. A group of student artists were convened and given the problem of painting a still life in a prescribed amount of time using only the objects on a nearby table. Imagine a table: bowls of fruit, picture frame, drapes and table covers, a tall vase here, a short vase there, blue bottles, green vines, a lone yellow lemon, a long string of pearls.

The students were told only to begin painting and to finish by a certain time. Then their pieces were rated by professional judges. The winners all had one thing in common: They had picked up more objects—tried them out, taken them back, gotten new ones—and had looked at the objects more closely—opening the top of this small box, examining the hinge on that miniature cabinet—than the other students. The winners had rearranged or substituted objects, changed paper or switched media, and even added something new to the picture right near the end. The young artists who were most successful tended not to have a definite, fixed idea early on but remained open to change right up to the end. What is amazing is that when all the students who participated in the experiment were surveyed seven years later, the ones who had been winners on the day the still life was painted continued to be ahead of their peers in recognized accomplishment in their field.

How would this apply to us as we look at the problems we face during tough transitions? If we took the problem-finding approach, we wouldn't be upset if the perfect solution or best idea didn't present itself immediately. We would try out more solutions in a kind of exploration; we would be willing to make changes well into the process. We would accept unconventional thoughts and suspend judgment until far along in the problem-solving process.

What does it look like when someone with problems explores many alternatives freely and only gradually decides on a specific course of action, allowing that even that specific course will be flexible and revisable until very near the time to make a final decision? Imagine a businessman working in the banking industry, successful in his field, who is attempting to solve the problem of finding more meaning in his life by changing the kind of work he does. Teaching geography or economics is something that appeals to him, perhaps in a boys' private school. The man first remembers the idea of *problem space*: More answers exist than he could ever need or use. Then he chooses to act in a *problem-finding* modality. He starts by exploring any and all avenues, by having this meeting and that, by reading all different kinds of books, and by writing not one but multiple job plans. One friend introduces him to a financial planner who is skilled at helping people transition from one level of finances to another, and they talk about what it will mean to take a huge cut in salary and how best to plan for such a reduction. There is an alumni gathering in his town for the private school he himself attended, and the man talks there to employees of the school who have come for the meeting: What is the job market like in private schools right now? Is geography even taught nowadays? What kind of economics programs does the school now have? The man signs up to tutor a young man one night a week at the public library just to see how "teaching" feels to him, at least in that setting. He talks to his wife and family often about how they would feel about his making this kind of change. And he sends off for catalogs from master's programs that offer quality studies in the two fields he is interested in.

There's no angst about having to make up his mind. There is no deadline set, although the man knows he'll have to make a decision in some kind of timely fashion. There's exploration. There's discovery. There's activity and action. But no push to closure. No demand that he has to know today. He is *problem finding* with something a bit akin, perhaps, to what the philosopher Kant once called "purposeless purpose." Serious, moving forward, working, yet everything is tentative. This open trying out, considering this and then considering that problem-finding approach, allows for new ideas to surface, connections to suggest themselves, and the most fitting possibility for the man and his family to emerge.

When *problem space* and *problem finding* are put together, we are even more empowered as we look for solutions to our problems. Let's imagine that a woman is getting divorced and must find another place to live. First of all, when she thinks about problem space, she remembers that possibilities are teeming; there are many solutions to her problem, more than she will ever need. Then she moves to take problem-finding action. Assume she's living in the home she and her husband owned, which must be sold now for property settlement. When she begins to *problem find*, she won't automatically assume that she must move to an apartment. Neither will she automatically assume she must have a single-family house. She will explore widely, even going to see places that she thinks she can't afford and places that don't match her history or places that are too small/big/distant—whatever. She talks to many people and asks all kinds of questions: What about foreclosures; should I consider looking at these? What are the challenges for a single woman if she buys rather than leases? What time of year are the best bargains likely to be on the market? She leaves open all possibilities as long as she possibly can. She closes no avenues of investigation prematurely. Gathering information, gaining experience in shopping for a new home, watching her own preferences evolve, change, or clarify—these are important to her. Only when a timeline gets close or she realizes she has found the perfect spot does she close down the looking and move toward ending her search.

Specific Problem-Solving Approaches

Dr. Martin Seligman is a seminal thinker and leader in identifying the positive responses we can make when we are looking straight in the face of what seem like intractable problems. One of his suggestions has to do with what he calls "flexible optimism," otherwise known as watching your ABCs—with A being the situation, B being what we think about the event, and C being how we feel.

Let's say you have retired and, instead of enjoying it as you thought you would, you find yourself staring out into a big blank nothingness. You feel slack. There's nothing that really excites you, nothing you want to do. Your ABCs might go like this:

A. The clock goes off, but there is nowhere for me to go and nothing I have to do.
B. I think, "This situation is the pits."
C. I feel empty and lost.

Now, Professor Seligman says, it's time to argue with yourself:

A. What's the evidence for this belief? *Is there nowhere for me to go and nothing for me to do?*
B. Is there any less destructive way to look at this situation? *Perhaps it's early in my retirement; I might want to do something or think of something to do later.*

C. Even if what I think and feel are true, what are the implications? What is the worst-case scenario? *In this case, I know the belief isn't ultimately true.*
D. Is it useful for me to continue to think this way? Is

> Am I rebutting my ABCs?
> What is the evidence?
> Can I look at this in a less destructive way?
> Even if true, what are the implications?
> How can I change the situation?

the situation changeable? How can I go about changing it? *Sure, the situation is changeable. Maybe I don't want to do anything now, but I know I could if I decided to.*

Another useful problem-solving tool is related to the explanations we give for the problems we have. It's almost impossible to be a good problem solver when we explain the situation by making the problem *permanent and pervasive.*

Permanent: It will never change; things will always be this way.

Pervasive: This will ruin my whole life and undermine everything else about it.

On the other hand, people who make explanations for a problem at hand that are *specific and temporary* have much more power to solve the problem in front of them.

Specific: This problem is about my relationship with this one person, not about everything else in my life.

Temporary: There is no place here for words like *always* and *never.* This is a *sometimes* and *lately* situation, not something that has always been there and always will be.

> It is something to be able to paint a particular picture, or to carve a statue, and so to make a few objects beautiful, but it is more glorious to carve and paint the very atmosphere and medium through which we look.
>
> Henry David Thoreau

The problems we encounter when we are Reorganizing during a tough transition don't have to undo us. Tax us, yes. Aggravate us, certainly. But stop us completely and cause us to spin our wheels until we are fender-deep in mud and can't get out? No. Recognizing, categorizing, and solving the problems of this period in our lives are ways that we are changing ourselves, consistent with what the circumstances of life now require of us.

Retrieving Threads of Purpose and Meaning

Nothing has any meaning anymore. Nothing interests me. I don't care about much of anything now. We have all felt, in one way or another, the truth of words like these while working to build a new shape for our life during a tough transition. Those things that gave our life purpose—although they may have been mundane activities or ordinary events—now appear about as interesting as old clothes we've bunched together to give to charity. And no matter how much our well-meaning best friend or our trying-to-be-helpful family members urge us to find new interests or to just do some of the things we loved in the past whether we feel like it or not, we still experience the days as blah and colorless and life as empty and without much meaning. We can't avoid the dissonance by just up and choosing new purposes, as if we were choosing shoes off a rack. Purposes have meaning for us because we have learned over a lifetime of experiences what gives us satisfaction and meaning. What we have to do now is retrieve purposes from the past that still resonate with us, and create new purposes out of the life experiences we are having now.

> Pondering the meaning of life we get not always great revelations but little daily miracles, illuminations, matches struck unexpectedly in the dark.
>
> Kathleen Fischer

As a young widow, I learned how hard this retrieving of purpose was with something as basic as cooking. Ever since I'd had a home of my own, I had loved to cook and have people over. It might be a Betty Crocker cookbook tuna casserole with pinwheel biscuits on top (you made the biscuits out of canned dough so even I, a new cook, could do it); or it might be, as I progressed a bit in skill and ability, a loaf of kneaded cheese caraway bread and a beef stew with burgundy. Then when my husband and I started cooking together, the sky was the limit. We joined a dinner group that believed in trying anything, no matter how hard or exotic! So we made all kinds of dishes together and won a few and lost a good many. But it was great fun.

But after he died I had no interest whatsoever in cooking. None. Nada. Never. And this was a big hole in my life. I wanted to want to cook again, but no matter how much I chided myself I truly could summon forth neither the interest nor the energy to do it. The connection with a lot of my friends at that time centered around food—people in the dinner group, Friday night pop-overs with friends where we took turns making a big pot of soup or a platter of enchiladas. So this wasn't just a hobby kind of thing that I had lost interest in. It was a keystone activity that mattered enormously in my life.

Then one day—I'd probably been a widow for a year and a half by then—I was standing in the produce department of a natural foods store. The scene was beautiful. Yellow, red, and yellow bell peppers, bright green broccoli, purple eggplant, orange apricots, wine-colored beets. I just stood there luxuriating in the environment. Then I saw a row of cookbooks on the ledge above the vegetable and fruit bins. My eye hit on a particular cookbook; *Cooking for One* was the title. I found myself picking up the book, leafing through it, and then taking it to the checkout stand and buying it. That was the beginning of retrieving a thread of meaning and purpose in my life and pulling it forward to tie into the fabric of my life as it was now constituted. I had established continuity with cooking only by separating the act of cooking from the circumstances and person from the past. The thread of purpose was there, if the future I had expected wasn't.

There isn't a quick fix here. Some people attempt to find immediate new purpose and meaning through "practical busyness"— by taking on volunteer projects, signing up for classes, going on trips, joining groups. But this flurry of activity often doesn't bring any sense of coherence to life because the individual is grabbing at anything, often to avoid thinking about the loss of meaning and purpose. This kind of helter-skelter going out and coming in can cause long-term damage because our very identity becomes totally

fragmented. Our task, then, during the time that we are Reorganizing in a tough transition is to abstract what was truly important
from the past and rehabilitate those important things so that they
fit in our current situation.

When this happens, people have stories such as these:

*When you've lost your job and are almost out of savings, you don't
even think of going to a concert, no matter how much you love live per-
formances. Music has always been a family affair for us, and it was a
big loss—on top of so many other losses—for my teenagers and my wife
and me not to be able to go to the summer music festivals we had gone
to in the past. Or to go hear Simon and Garfunkel on their reunion tour
when they came to our city. While it wasn't like having to go without
bread and milk, missing out on music was one more situation that reminded me and my family of everything we had lost the day my job was
eliminated. One day I was standing near a bulletin board in our local
grocery store, waiting on my wife, and I saw a handwritten card that
read, "Drum set for sale. Cheap." On a whim, I decided to call the
number. I ended up buying this used drum set, and the kids and I are
having a lot of fun. I'm not so sure my wife enjoys it as much as we do,
but she's a good sport nevertheless.*

*   *   *

*My wife and I hiked together every year in one of the western states for
our vacation. After the divorce, it was no fun to go alone; and the kinds
of places we always hiked were not locations you were likely to find an
organized group heading off into. Later I saw an advertisement for a
walking trip in the Cotswolds in England, just six or so people. I decided
to do it. Everything about the experience was new and different so there
was no referring back to the past. And it feels so good to be hiking
again.*

*   *   *

*Hunting was the biggest thing in my life outside of my family and work.
The day deer season opened each fall I was like a kid. Get up early, go
out on the lease, move quietly through the woods, get on the stand and
start waiting. But after our son died I had no interest in hunting in any
form or fashion. But what I find myself doing now is reading books*

about woodland animals and learning everything I can about things like habitat, life cycle and patterns, care and feeding. Then I go out in the woods and observe, trying to match what I've read with what I'm seeing. It's a fascinating study and one that has gripped me completely.

Jettisoning the Outdated

Sometimes we find during Reorganizing that things that gave us purpose and meaning in the past no longer interest us. For years climbing to the top in my profession had been an exciting reason for me to get up every morning. It really mattered to me when a talk I gave at a professional conference was well received. I enjoyed the challenge of department meetings where some of my colleagues and I could argue for revamping the curriculum or lowering the faculty/student ratio. But after my husband died, I was uninterested in my career as a source of achievement and accomplishment. Even though I did go on to get tenure and the rank of full professor, such rewards were no longer the stuff of which my dreams were made. In fact, I ended up resigning my professorship in about four years because I had found other interests and commitments that had so much more meaning for me. I jettisoned the outdated.

Sometimes we make changes during Reorganizing because we realize that we had been doing a lot of things out of habit or because others expected us to, not because we really cared about doing them. I remember one friend who had been a tennis doubles partner with an acquaintance for years. As part of her reassessment during her divorce, my friend became clear that for a long time she had continued to play because her partner expected her to and because that was what she had done every other Tuesday for years. She now told herself the truth; she

> Tell me, what is it you plan to do with your one wild and precious life?
> Mary Oliver, poet

didn't even like tennis! After dropping out of the league, my friend signed up for a course in genealogy at the local community college and which met on Tuesday mornings. She found this new course invigorated her in ways that tennis never had.

Jettisoning the outdated reconfigures our daily activities. It redirects our energies. It refreshes us. And it can cause new problems. Friends may say we have changed, their tone revealing that they don't consider this a positive thing. We may feel discombobulated ourselves, even though we were the source of our routine's being altered. Holes may appear in our schedules that, for a while, we don't know how to fill productively. But we can be reassured. When we have been courageous enough to identify those things that are no longer meaningful to us and change them, in time any vacuum that such changes created will be filled with things that authentically matter to us now.

Articulating Our Considered Faith and Values

For many, a tough transition marks the end of an innocent or trusting stance toward faith and values. The difficult event raises questions, destroys confidence, and throws off keel any constancy we might have known in the past. What occurs next can be a long gap of not knowing, of anger and resentment that what we had believed and counted on did not seem to hold. These reactions, however, come to be replaced with a genuine grappling with lost certainties and a genuine groping for new insights and understanding.

Perhaps previously I repeated a creed or quoted ancient prayers in a kind of automatic way, not thinking at all about whether or not I believed what I was saying. Or perhaps I didn't even take note of what I was saying. Now, during the experiences of Reorganizing, I begin to examine. I study; I talk with informed others; I mull over different possible interpretations. Finally, I construct out of all this thinking a considered statement of what I believe and what I value. This statement might be what I espoused before but can now put forth with clarity that comes from deep examination. This statement might be a whole new take on what I believe and what I think is worthwhile in life. Or it might be a different interpretation and understanding that allows old truths to become new for me in the current circumstances of my life.

Tough transitions often bring us up short in front of questions of monumental import: What is life all about? What am I doing here? One writer puts it like this:

> Many human beings require something that involves, at the very least, some clarity about the meaning of one's life. Whether we articulate this need clearly or confusedly, it amounts to a yearning to know where we come from and where we are going. . . . What purposes greater than our immediate existence can life possibly have? And along with the yearning, there comes a response, in sharp focus or soft, and some purpose is either gleaned or desired.

During the experiences of Reorganizing it is this turning toward meaning, this clarifying of purpose and commitment, that start to get refocused and redirected.

I know a lovely woman who is a breast cancer survivor. After her illness—and in response to the serious inquiry about how she wanted to live her life that followed—she sold her successful temp-help business in a large city, trained to become a professional photographer, moved to a smaller community, and began a career focusing on photographing women who had survived cancer. She holds exhibitions and is planning a book, all to raise money for cancer research. I know a man who, after the trauma of losing a high-profile job and working through the aftermath of that transition, has chosen a much quieter life. He works shorter hours, takes more time to be outside, reads more, and nurtures a deep spiritual life. Both of these people do now articulate their considered faith and do live their considered values.

❦

PEOPLE TELL THEIR STORIES OF REORGANIZING

I remember once a ship captain telling me that while, to an observer, it looks as if a cruise liner is moving in a straight line, the ship is actually moving in zigs and zags that only seem straight from a distance. "Zigs and zags" would be a good term to apply to the lives of the women and men who describe below the Reorganizing period of tough transitions in their lives. It will only be from a distance in the future that these zigs and zags will appear as a defined line from there to here. For the present, Reorganizing is experienced as trial and error, course corrections, practice, and ongoing problem solving.

REORGANIZING: FROM BEING A SURGEON TO CREATING A FOUNDATION

My life changed substantially, in lots of way unexpectedly, once I made the decision to resign as chief of surgery at the hospital and leave my private practice. I had planned, with great intention, for at least three years, but once I made the decision public and permanent, a lot of things changed that I had not anticipated.

One of the first things I had to grapple with was my identity. Until I made the change, I had no idea that my identity was centered on illness: that who I was professionally was someone who had a focus on managing illness and people with illness and making that as good as it could be. What I was about was creating circumstances that ensured wellness. And my skills had been honed to a very fine point after twenty-five years of doing the same thing. It wasn't until after I left my practice that I realized this had been the water I had swum in for almost three decades, and, like a fish, I didn't even know I was in that water.

But then I made the change from surgeon to creator of a foundation to educate the public specifically about the prevention of colon cancer. Now I have stepped into an arena where I don't know what I am doing at all. What is needed? How to do it? I have a vision—people not dying of colon cancer—but I have to learn a lot of things to know how to bring this vision into reality through the work of a nonprofit foundation. I find myself saying every now and then, "What did I get myself into? Why am I doing this to myself? What was I thinking, going from being an accomplished surgeon to being a neophyte foundation runner?"

I have to say, it brings on a crisis of confidence. If I didn't have an absolute passion for what I'm doing, I would spend all my time questioning my judgment and second-guessing myself. All I can say right now is that the passion for what I'm doing now has to provide a bridge over which I can walk—stumbling perhaps—because I see now that there is no easy leap from one kind of work to another completely different kind of work.

Everything I'm doing now in starting this nonprofit foundation is a sheer act of creation. I've stepped into everything/nothing and society offers me no structure for this. There are a lot of people who think I'm nuts to give up what I had . . . they can't understand why I would walk away from a lucrative practice and stop making money. But, even then, these people support what I do and acknowledge that their response comes from their not being able to imagine in a million years doing it themselves.

I know now that I'm in a developmental phase. Developing who I am! Imagine that, at near retirement age! I have the fullest opportunity now. But it comes to mind that the Chinese writing character for "crisis" means both danger and opportunity. So I admit I feel the danger, too. Now I have to develop my vision of people not dying from colon cancer into a solid, successful nonprofit foundation . . . and there are days when what this looks like is a vacuum. But that's just part of being in this new developmental phase, just part of being the creator and not the reactor in my wonderful life.

REORGANIZING: ADAPTING TO LIFE WITH AN AGING PARENT

I'm having to learn how to change the way I am with my mother. I find myself now having to tell her something maybe three times, and it's clear that this embarrasses her and also confuses her. So I'm looking for ways to give her information that she can refer back to—some things I put on her little tape recorder, some things I write on a notepad and put on her refrigerator door. The most important change I think I'm making is not to correct her when she says that I haven't told her a specific thing. At first I was upset with her and would correct her. I think I was doing that maybe mostly for me. I hated to see my mother failing, and I wanted her to "snap out of it" and be the way she had always been. But now I'm doing my best to practice tolerance. I've realized I have to have a willingness to deal with an aging parent. That this is a new place in our lives. And that I have to learn new behaviors and new ways of thinking, as well as deal with my own emotional issues about her aging . . . and probably my aging, too.

Mother said the other day that she would like to go on a hot-air balloon ride. Not knowing whether this was a "real" desire or not, I answered as if she were totally serious. I said, "Well, Mom, check it out. Call the number that was in the newspaper and get the details. Then e-mail me, and we'll talk about it." New behavior for me. I'm trying to be respectful.

But then there are some things that are just the way they are. Mom had to stop driving about two years ago—we actually had to take the car away—and she has been so resentful. Talks about it all the time. Angry at my brother and me. Then, the other day, I was at Mom's house when one of her doctors—a lovely woman now retired—dropped by to visit. Mom started complaining to her about losing her car and not being able to drive. The doctor friend said, "What do you miss most about not driving?" "Going to the cemetery to my husband's grave," Mom answered. "I went every day to talk to Hugh, to tell him decisions I was making and what I was thinking about doing next."

This amazed me, because I had no idea that she went to the cemetery every day and no idea that this was at the heart of her being upset about not driving. The doctor friend said to me, "Why don't you work out a schedule where you take your mother to the cemetery, say every Wednesday at three o'clock, leave her while you go on an errand, and then come back and get her?" Just this simple thing—which we have now been doing for a couple of months—seems to have given Mom some of her self back.

So I'm learning: Make specific plans for doing the things she says she wants to do. Don't correct her but find some other way to be sure she has information that she needs to have. Don't show irritation when she repeats herself. Be respectful. Sure, I'm being required to change a lot of things in my life to accommodate her, but won't I want someone to do this for me when I'm that age? I'm seeing more and more clearly that her situation is a mirror for me to look at myself and think about my own future.

REORGANIZING: HAVING TO RETOOL MYSELF TO KEEP MY JOB

Our company, which has been in existence for more than a hundred years, is changing its core orientation from commitment to individual consumers to commitment to grow into a larger, global organization. For those of us who have been here a long time—I've been a manager here for twenty-two years—this is totally discombobulating. In my department we have focused on building up a set of competencies based on service to schools and nonprofit groups, something the company believed was not only a good thing to do but good for the bottom line also. Now, with the new leadership at the top, the emphasis is on "how to play with the big boys." How to have political clout. How to have a huge global reach.

I realize that if I stay here—and with two teenage kids about to go to college what else can I do?—I have to learn to manage a completely different way. Heck, I have to learn to think a different way! I have to find some way to align myself with goals that seem to me to be so cold and hard. All my new boss ever says now is "build it to scale." I get so sick of "build it to scale" that I could puke. I've been deployed to a new area, and I feel deflated. What am I to do with the skills I've built up over twenty-two years . . . oh, I know, I have to "retool" these skills. I've lost my identity because now there's no call for it. And I'm creating a new identity as best I can to match the current focus of the business.

REORGANIZING: LOOKING AT THE FUTURE AFTER A MISCARRIAGE

Tom and I are slowly rebuilding our future. Today was Thanksgiving, a great day with friends and family. Twenty-seven of us ate at my mother's house; and once the meal was over the males went out to the side yard and played football for two hours. My husband, who was too small in high school to play on a team, was the star quarterback. He had a blast.

A week ago I participated in a medical conference as a member of a team where I work. I was nervous about my part on the panel. But I decided to talk about my recent miscarriage and its aftermath because that subject fit into the program topic perfectly. Amazingly, out of the 120 participants, one-third were women who had experienced multiple miscarriages. Several came up afterwards and said they were so glad they had been there to hear what I had to say. I have to say that this felt like a glorious new day for me. Something is brewing . . . something new. Although I do not know what it is, I know that this "something new" is what's next.

And there are numerous questions I have just decided to put aside. Questions like, Why did I have to go through this painful, doubtful time? Did all this have to happen to get me to where I am today? *I've decided my finite mind will never understand certain things. So I've decided to ask those questions when I pass to a higher state of being! (I even feel my humor coming back!) For now I will focus on making this life the best possible life for myself and those around me.*

REORGANIZING: LIFE AFTER RETIREMENT

I was in euphoria the first four or five months of retirement. There was so much to do, so many things to set up. I bought a computer, and that took a lot of shopping, reading, and talking to people. Then I cleaned out a room to put the computer in so I would have a great workspace at home. I bought a sewing machine, in anticipation of finally having the time to do the sewing projects I had wanted to do for so long. It was just a flurry of activity, getting set up to be retired.

Then when all that was done, I suddenly had no specific thing to structure my day. It was like a quote I had read earlier: *Freedom came crashing down on my head.* I kept asking every day, "What do I do now?" I was a woman who had measured her days by how much she got done. Now there were no requirements or demands to measure myself against.

There's a sense of total disorganization. It's like my friend at the office told me when she retired: "You know, those things that were B and C items when you worked; well, they're still B and C items when you're retired." I found this to be true. All those things that I thought I would do when I was working but which weren't priorities weren't priorities now either, even though I had retired.

So I filled my life up with volunteering. I volunteered at the hospital; I volunteered at our local community theater, and then added on another theater where there was some performance going on every night so you could stay as busy as you wanted to; I volunteered at church.

That went on until I realized one day I had to take a good look at what I was doing and make some new decisions. I experienced such stress from one deadline after another that I knew I had over-volunteered. The pendulum had swung too far the other way. So I began to ask, "Which of these activities do I really want to continue to do? And which have served their purpose and can be let go?"

Now I believe I have an organization for my time that is balanced. First of all, finding a good structure for my retired life required me to make a big mind shift: from task accomplishment to just living life. I have certain rules for myself that hold every day: get up at the usual time, read the paper, eat breakfast, get dressed. And I have certain routine things that work like anchors for my week: bowling on Tuesday; volunteering at the hospital on Friday; meeting with a social group every other Monday night; teaching in a grief program on a regular schedule. I am also intentional about having lunch at least once a week with a former colleague or a friend. Around these routine activities I now put in the other projects I want to do.

What I've found interesting as I live this process of grieving and letting go and creating change is this: As the process has continued, I have found myself closer and closer to the center of who I am and finding out what I want to do that genuinely satisfies me. For instance, I'm now clear about how important it is to me to learn more about spirituality. I participate in conferences and workshops and read an enormous number of books. This is now congruent with who I am. I'm also reading about aging and reassessing what is important and what is not as I look at the years ahead.

So, I am no longer bothered by any absence of structure. I'm living the whole ball of life, and my life has meaning and purpose.

REORGANIZING: LIVING WITH A CHRONIC ILLNESS

Here I am, a fifty-year-old woman, with an illness that no one can definitively diagnose but which required two stomach surgeries within six weeks and which, a year later, still baffles a whole team of doctors. I'm also a woman who has a teenage son and daughter and an active husband. With this illness, I am required to live in the moment. I have to exert control in the smallest of ways because there is so much over which I have no control.

This has required a whole new pattern to my life. I've left the corporate world where I was a senior vice president and am planning a new career. I will become a therapist working with adolescents; and to prepare for this I am starting back to school to get a master's degree in counseling. Right now, since I can't plan things as I used to plan them, I volunteer to do things that I can do at home, whether I feel good or not. In the past I was active in the volunteer program at our church for Freeze Night—those times when it's too cold for homeless people to sleep on the street—going to the church and helping set everything up to receive the overnight visitors. Now I can't do that, but I did offer to coordinate the volunteers and call everyone to explain what tasks needed to be done, etc. This I can do from my bed if I need to.

The structure of my day is very different now, as a result of my illness. All the years I was a corporate executive, it was rush out the door. No time to drink a cup of tea and watch the news. Now I really enjoy watching the news and drinking tea. I just asked for what my family thought was a strange birthday gift: gas logs for the fireplace in my husband's and my bedroom, complete with piñon smells and sounds of crackling wood. I cannot tell you how much I enjoy watching the fire.

Before, when I was asked what I would want to do if I had only one year to live, I would say, being the Italian American I am, "Go to La Scala and hear Pavarotti sing." But at one point when that supposition seemed like it might be real, my choice was not to go to La Scala but to savor every moment I could, living normal day-in, day-out life.

I've also stopped trying to please people. If a person doesn't make me feel good, I just don't spend time with that person. Including my own daughter. If she's in a snit of some kind and being negative about everything, I tell her, "I can't do this." I have to conserve every ounce of energy, and I don't feel guilty about it. Actually, I think this behavior of mine is going to have a lasting positive effect on my daughter.

At some level, you know, we are all terminal. When you come upon the truth, all you really can do is ask how you're going to live right now. All of us can do that.

REORGANIZING: FINDING A NEW SHAPE FOR THE FAMILY AFTER THE DEATH OF A CHILD

I have become friends with paradox: There were all the daily adjustments related to our son's death and there was the big cosmic struggle related to the subject of death itself—as in "I'm going to die . . . this person is going to die . . . I'm not going to see her/him again." Two parallel tracks were going on at same time, and I saw them that way. It helped me in times of utter grief to separate them.

In the adjustment things—what cereal you buy, how many napkins you put on the table—I tried to find a way to think about that. I would say to myself that people have to make these kinds of changes when there is a divorce. Or when a spouse goes into a nursing home. When a child goes away to college. It wasn't that this thinking made the adjustments any easier, but I did feel connected to others with their own kinds of losses and I knew that I was just one among many. This was not peculiar just to me and my family.

Then there was the challenge of how to keep our teenager present *while at the same time acknowledging in how we live each day that he is no longer alive. I knew right away one way we were not going to act as we made changes; I learned this from the pain of my childhood. My mother died when I had just turned nine. Within just a few days every evidence of her had been stripped from the house and she was not mentioned. That was just the way you got over these things, was the understanding of the day. I was determined that we would not do that with our son. We would keep him present in all ways that were appropriate: pictures, conversation, offhand references.*

My husband and I have also focused on our daughter. She deserves a chance for a normal life. We're not overly protective or obsessed. But we talk a lot with her, reassuring her, letting her know that she—and we—are going to be okay. We actually made a pact among the three of us that we are going to see this through together. We still call ourselves as a family a four-legged table; it's just that one leg of the table is not here. But a four-legged table can stand with three legs. And we are learning about that balance.

REORGANIZING: DESIGNING LIFE AFTER DIVORCE

We were married more than thirty years. I had been his four children's mother since they were preschoolers; and we had had four children of our own. It had been my heart's delight to run a household, teach and love our eight children, and be my husband's support in his high-profile public position. Then he left for a younger woman, and the world as I knew it was gone.

At the beginning, of course, all I could do was cry. Then I took a next step and went to a support group at my church. I started reading everything I could find related to my predicament. I went to a six-week seminar on loss and cried during every session. But somewhere in those six weeks I internalized some simple but lifesaving information: that I was not the only person this had ever happened to, that this had not happened because I was an unworthy person, that other people felt as rotten as I did, and that there were choices you could make, even in an unwanted circumstance.

A turning point was when I hosted my first party since the divorce was final. I invited to that party every person who had been supportive and kind to me—my dentist, the woman who led the seminar, the people in the support group at church, my children, friends. It was one big thank-you for help given when it was so needed. I also recently accepted an invitation to go to dinner with two new friends, a couple. I was very nervous—it was just the husband, wife, and me. Would I feel like an extra wheel? But the evening was totally delightful. I sat at dinner and thought to myself, "I'm going to be okay. Here is a neat couple who want to be with me!" It was a great confidence builder and they didn't have a clue that was happening. They had never known me when I was married or going through my divorce. They had invited me out because they liked me! I have an image of an empty glass of self-confidence that I am now filling by putting nice experiences into the glass.

There are nights when I still sleep with my rosary beads in my hand. And I read Psalm 143 every night before I go to sleep. Everything is not settled and certainly not easy. But my faith is a bedrock that I'm standing on while I create my new life.

REORGANIZING: A PROFESSIONAL WOMAN BECOMES A STAY-AT-HOME MOM

I made the decision to leave a job I loved working at as a social issues news reporter for a major newspaper to be a stay-at-home mom when our first child was two years old. That decision coincided with our moving so my husband could take a job in another state. The two changes intertwined to create a downward spiral in my spirits. Here I was, an award-winning journalist used to working happily in a big newsroom long hours each week, now at home with a two-year-old in a city where I knew no one and had no network of support of any kind. The isolation and depression bore heavy. The only thing I could compare my situation to was someone in a witness protection program. I had another whole identity from the past that no one now knew about. That person I was had just disappeared. I didn't see myself as a suburban housewife type, but here I was living that life. It felt confusing and like something

I really had to come to terms with. Even though this was my choice, I felt as if I were marooned on an island.

I learned to focus on why I had made this change: because I felt no one could provide the love of learning and creativity for my children better than I could. That commitment took the form of being home with my son and daughter. I also had to learn to let go of control. When my son and I first started playing in the sandbox, I would build my own sand castle which he couldn't touch. And which he could knock down only when I said. That progressed to our building a sand castle together but by my design. He still could not knock it down until I said so. Finally, I reached the point of being relaxed building the sand castle together with him, and he could knock it down anytime he wanted to. This was symbolic of the kind of letting go I had to learn to do in this role I had chosen.

I did find that I needed an artistic outlet. I was not writing at all at first. I was cranky; something was missing. Then one day while the children were asleep I went to the computer and started writing essays. My professional colleagues began to call with things for me to do, one of which is a nationally syndicated column on family television, which I continue to write today. This work brings together my family and my reporting. I also do some writing coaching in newsrooms one or two days a month. I recently planned a writing conference at the children's school bringing in a lot of writers; this was very successful and I felt again that I had blended my identities: journalist and mother. Now that my youngest is in kindergarten, I have begun teaching a journalism course at the local university, and this puts me back in the newspaper world, if on a part-time basis. I've also joined a writers' group and have a couple of drafts of children's books.

I am still working on creating a network of wonderful women. I've met many moms whose main goal seems to be having a spotless floor. I am clear I am not a "vacuum mom"; that isn't the section of camp I signed up for. In fact, I say I'm going to establish the "Association for Lowering Housekeeping Standards" and run for president. It is a balancing act.

REORGANIZING: A LESBIAN FRIEND COMES OUT

We had worked together at the hospital for more than five years. Both of us doctors, both married to doctors. Mary and I often had lunch together to talk about the art each of us did in our free time. We wanted to expand our artwork, be in exhibits, and become a part of the larger arts community. I think we encouraged each other just by acting as if the art each of us did mattered. These lunches led to deeper discussions: about Mary's conflicts with her teenage daughter, about spiritual matters such as silent retreats, books we were reading. Ours was a comfortable, if occasional, connected relationship.

Then there was the morning she called and asked me to meet her in a park nearby. We sat on a bench and she said she had something to tell me. She asked me if I had met the new doctor who had been at the hospital for the past six months on a post-doc research project. It turns out I had met the woman she mentioned at a staff Christmas party but only to say hello. Our paths never crossed in the hospital.

Mary then said that she had left her husband and was moving in with the visiting doctor. I was speechless. I think the first thing I said was, "What about your daughter?"—who, it turned out, was going to stay with her father until she went to college the coming September. I was truly flabbergasted. Surprised totally. I did find words to acknowledge Mary's authenticity and courage and to tell her that this change in her life would do nothing to alter our collegiality and our friendship.

But the situation is very difficult. None of the awkwardness has anything to do for me with the issue of Mary's choosing a lesbian relationship. I meant it when I said her choice would make no difference in our relationship. The awkwardness lies in the social construct of the hospital and the community. Here is Mary, her soon-to-be-ex-husband, and Mary's partner working in the same hospital, with all the political and social machinations that go on in a facility like that. There's the behavior and talk of many people in the community who fault Mary for leaving her teenage daughter, perhaps as a screen for a deeper criticism of her lifestyle. There's just a swirl of gossip, talk, moves, and countermoves that float like fog throughout the hospital and the community.

Recently Mary and her partner had a house blessing for their new liv-

ing space. I and several other of Mary's friends from the hospital went. But it was so uncomfortable. There was the teenage daughter looking morose and refusing to talk to anyone. There was the cheerfulness of Mary and her partner as we moved from room to room, the minister blessing each location. There were the conversations of guests wanting this event to be lovely and normal, but knowing that we were, at best, in a cocoon of acceptance inside these four walls.

I—and many other of Mary's friends—am committed to the reshaping that this new configuration requires. When you think about it, the situation at the hospital and in the community is no different than if two doctors who worked there got divorced and one of them married another doctor on staff. But there's the overcoat of approval or disapproval of a lesbian lifestyle. This is an opportunity to take a stand for a friend's right to choose her partner and her lifestyle. I do wish for everyone's sake that it could be easier.

REORGANIZING: AN ADOPTED DAUGHTER FINDS HER BIRTH MOTHER AND SIBLINGS

A long search came to completion last year when I found my birth mother whom I had been seeking for many years. I actually became quite an accomplished cyber sleuth, as well as a searcher of legal records, during the process. With the aid of the actual files from the adoption agency my parents used when they adopted me, I located an ex-husband of my birth mother and through him her . . . and my eight siblings!

I'm very, very happy that I found my birth mother and half sisters and brothers. I have a lot of love for them and am in contact with some on a regular basis. But the outcome isn't looking like a Norman Rockwell painting. In fact, the first thing my husband said to me privately the night we located my family was, "We have a lot of thanks to give to your mom and dad for adopting you." And he was right.

My birth mother, forty-eight when I found her, had been married seven or eight times and had been in prison for drug possession. She had eight other children after me who live or lived sometimes with her or sometimes with whichever husband was their father. One of my half brothers has also been in prison for drug possession. On the other hand, some of my sisters have made a good life for themselves. One with whom I'm in contact almost on a daily basis is a professional woman with an excellent job who's also a wonderful mother to her own children.

One of the things I'm having to work out is how much to try to help my birth family. My husband and I are both from poor backgrounds and we have worked hard to create a better life for ourselves. When one of my half sisters said recently that she desperately needed a car to be able to go to school and graduate, we bought her a car. I guess we should have expected it, but she did not keep the rules that came along with the car and we had to take it back. It's easy to imagine that someone else will have the values and behavior that you do and that you so want to think they do.

I'm also having to learn how to deal with my birth mother's requests for help. A couple of weeks ago she called late at night and said she was moving to our town. Clearly she expected to move in with us. I had to be firm, not only about that but about her other expectations. That is hard because in my heart I want to help in every way possible and in my head I know this would be enabling, not supporting. And that it also is not what my husband and I should be doing with our resources that we are working so hard to provide for ourselves.

It is also a transition with my mom. At first she was upset that I had looked for my birth family without telling her. But we talked through that and she understood the decisions I had made. I also thanked her deeply for adopting me and said I so wished my dad was still alive so I could thank him. My mom and I are much closer now. Somehow talking about my adoption and birth family made it easier for us to talk about other touchy subjects, like the resentment I had at not getting to be around my father much the three years he was sick and dying. Talking through that cleared my resentment completely and I could think about that earlier situation much more clearly. I saw that my mother, who was quite young at the time, did the best she knew how to do. Our relationship is just much more at ease now. There's no pretense around it.

Clearly my birth mother and many of my siblings have a maturing curve that they are not hitting at a good level. I am very clear now that I'm not going to help anybody. What I will do is support them when the choices they make are positive and forward-moving. I can only support them in what they are committed to doing that is good for their lives. So I feel compassionate without feeling guilty; and, most of all, I'm starting to feel calm.

REORGANIZING: A MOTHER MOVES IN

My husband and I have been married thirty years, and since we have no children, we have always lived alone. Now my ninety-year-old mother has moved in with us, and life is so different. Probably the biggest challenge is in internal one: adjusting to a sense of having no privacy. It is such a different feeling to have someone besides my husband and me in the house.

There are also the forty boxes of items that we moved in with her. She loves quilts and pillows, so everything is covered now with a quilt, and we have her pillows all over everywhere. I've incorporated her things as much as I possibly can, putting mementos she loves all around the living room, cups and dishes in the kitchen. But there are still many things we haven't yet found a place for.

I see now that we made one huge mistake. When we cleared out her apartment, we did that while she was away visiting. She had not objected to our packing while she was away; but now she keeps missing things that she wants. "Where are my hats?" she keeps asking. Unfortunately, her grandson took the hats to the theater department of his university; we didn't dream she would want winter hats in the warm climate to which she was moving. And her linens. She had so many that I knew there was no place we could store them all. So I brought all I thought she would need, but it turned out to be not the right ones. So we had to go out and buy linens and she hasn't forgotten about that yet. I didn't bring her pots and pans, and she complains that mine are too heavy. She cooks her own breakfast every day, so I had to buy a lightweight skillet and pan. She insists on frying her own potatoes, after peeling them with a knife, not a peeler, so I got her a new knife to use. But she still wants the one she had at home. If I could do the packing again, I would have her right there every minute, making each decision about what goes and what stays.

I've had to get used to the way she lives on a schedule. And she doesn't want that schedule interfered with. She comes down at a certain time every morning and makes breakfast. Then she puts the newspaper on the couch and then sits down to read it. Since she now reads the paper every day instead of once a week as she did back in her apartment, she keeps saying, "This state . . . killings every day. Very bad people." She takes a walk every afternoon and then sits on the bench out front. We do our best to honor her set ways and rigid schedule.

I've had to get used to being talked to like a twelve-year-old daughter again. She is always giving advice: Don't go barefoot; put cream on your face at night. She's very didactic. You should stand at the washing machine to put a new load in as soon as the other one is finished. You should never have one thing sitting on the kitchen counter. This used to upset me. Now I genuinely am not bothered. It's like, I've been there, done that. It's not worth it to be upset. What does it hurt for her to tell me to do this or that? Sometimes I do what she says and sometimes I pretend I don't hear. I just feel no need to have conflict with her about these things.

REORGANIZING: BLENDING TWO FAMILIES

I was divorced with a four-year-old son and a seven-year-old daughter when I married my second husband, who had never been married. When we decided to get married, we bought some books on blending families and decided to counsel ourselves. We tossed them out fairly quickly, but I think some of the tips stuck with us.

As we work to get everything organized, looking back I think we did several things right. While we were dating, Joseph never slept with me at our house. We treated him as a guest and he stayed in the guest room. It was important for the children to feel as if their relationship with me wasn't threatened by our new intimacy. And they needed to know Joseph first as a friend and then have him work himself into the family.

I talked to the children a lot before the wedding and let them ask any questions they wanted. I involved my daughter in shopping and choosing things for the wedding and lavished my son with love and attention. Still, my daughter became constipated on the wedding day and remained constipated for a week. The kids loved Joseph but the transition to marriage was more than my daughter was prepared for.

When we first married, Joseph's role in disciplining the children became the biggest challenge. He didn't feel right in that role, but at certain times he was thrust into it. His relationship with them was still vulnerable and disciplining them almost seemed to be a threat to that. Also the change was tough for the kids at school. They had to answer questions about a stepdaddy. For my son, who is very private, these questions put him in a spotlight he didn't want. Another challenge was that all of a sudden the kids were loaded up with grandparents. The kids had grown up with my ex-husband's mother as the closest and most involved grandparent. Now there was a new set of grandparents—Joseph's parents—to come into the family.

Joseph and I now have two sons together. My ex-husband has a new family. And the reshaping of life still goes on. We all work hard at getting over the rough edges so that everyone can do things as a group. Joseph makes a point to talk to my ex-husband on the phone as a friend, asking questions about how things are going in his life and being amiable. Now we're this kooky extended family. We go to basketball games together to cheer the kids on. Everyone goes to communion parties and to all the big events for the kids.

I think the kids' definition of a good marriage is stronger. When Joseph came in and started helping and spending time with the kids, that forced their father to be a better father. He's a competitive guy, and when he saw Joseph giving them attention he didn't want to be left behind or lose out to him. This spilled over to his spending more time with his new children when he had them. I don't want to be Pollyanna about this because you never know how things affect kids until they are much older. But I don't think divorce is necessarily a bad thing. You hear *about how much damage it does to kids, but I think the kids are stronger and we are better as a family—all of us.*

REORGANIZING: REESTABLISHING ONE'S OWN CAREER AFTER MOVING FOR A HUSBAND'S JOB

We moved out of state because my husband got a great offer to be the director of an organization that is committed to the kind of work he most wants to do. I had a statewide job in arts management in the city where we lived before we moved, a job that I enjoyed. But now I'm having to reinvent myself. I'm like Pirandello in search of a play. On one day I'll have a blast of passion to do this, and on another day a blast of passion to do that. In between I go for interviews for jobs that I don't even want.

When we first moved, I took some time off. I assumed this freedom would bring enlightenment. But instead, all I did was sit around "worrying the thing." What do I want to do? Instead of clarity I kept getting the image of a smorgasbord where I could choose anything for my plate . . . but I kept looking for what wasn't there, snow crabs.

I'm in a dilemma. I want someone to walk up, ring my doorbell, and tell me what I want to do. I've taken some time to look at my past work . . . and I've decided that I'm a serial careerist! First I did acting and achieved a real measure of success at that in New York. Then I changed to become a counselor. Then I discovered the arts management field and worked there. But none of these is what I want to do now.

I heard a term the other day: the procrastination of perfectionism. Maybe that's what I'm doing in this limbo time. Waiting for the perfect thing. I guess there is a certain security in chaos. What I've got to do now, though, is go out and create or redefine security.

Clearly, the people telling their stories here are a sturdy lot. They find themselves way out of their comfort zones. The habits and patterns that shaped their lives before the tough transitions now impede as often as they make easy. Problem solving is a daily requirement, as these folk, accomplished as they may have been previously, find that they are beginners in new arenas. They are having to redraw the shape of their lives, ask new questions, practice new behaviors. The past no longer holds and the future isn't firm yet. These individuals courageously tell the truth about what challenges they experience before them.

WHAT HELPS DURING REORGANIZING

Dr. Lewis Thomas was a physician and biologist who wrote fascinating essays about snails and music and language, among many other things. I remember one piece in particular where he talked about how amazing it is that we human beings are even here on the planet. He said that the probability of any of us being here on earth is so small that you'd think that the mere possibility of our existence would keep us all "in a contented dazzlement of surprise." I came across a statement of his the other day that I thought captured the to-and-fro nature of this Reorganizing period of our lives. Dr. Thomas reminds us that we always arrive at our best decisions in oblique and unexpected ways:

> We pass the word around; we ponder how the case is put by different people; we read the poetry; we meditate over the literature; we play music; we change our minds; we reach an understanding. Society evolves this way. Not by shouting each other down, but by the unique capacity of unique, individual human beings to comprehend each other.

Words like these encourage me. Reorganization is not a straight shot from chaos to order. It is a time of trial and error, experimentation, practice, and evolution from where we have been to where we want to go, from who we were to who we are going to be.

IDENTIFYING AND USING OUR SIGNATURE STRENGTHS

All of us have ancient strengths inside of us. We may never know we have these strengths until circumstances in our tough transitions call them forth. Each of us has several signature strengths that are specifically ours. These are strengths about which we can say: *This is the real me. I have enthusiasm when I use this strength. This strength is one I exercise every day.* Martin Seligman lists twenty-four signature strengths in his book *Authentic Happiness*, including: street smarts, love of learning, perseverance, integrity, kindness and generosity, appreciation of beauty, gratitude, open-mindedness, and curiosity about the world.

Some people work to try to correct their weaknesses. Perhaps our time is better spent identifying our signature strengths and using these as often as possible. There is probably no more important an occasion to do this than during the rough-and-tumble life of a tough transition. Our signature strengths are not skills we have acquired or developed. They are strengths we possess innately. These signature strengths are integral to the unique way each of us approaches life. When we use them we are our most authentic. As we make decisions about what shape our life will have that will be congruent with the new circumstance we find ourselves in during a tough transition, it can be our signature strengths that provide us the means to a satisfactory end.

I recently participated in a retreat where we identified our signature strengths. First we were given a list of a variety of qualities to consider. From that list, I pinpointed one of my signature strengths as "storytelling; explaining by painting vivid pictures until others are inspired to act." Another was "collecting information, things, quotations, artifacts, and facts that are interesting; finding the world exciting because of its variety." I thought back on a day a few weeks earlier where at the end of working six hours I felt fresher and more energetic than I had when I had begun. My work that day involved telling stories about my ancestral land of Ireland and sharing ancient Celtic prayers I had collected. I had been using two of my signature strengths; no wonder that day's work had been so joyous.

TALKING YOUR WAY THROUGH A HARD PATCH

Reorganizing can be discouraging at times. As soon as you step out and do something different, old fears return or you find even more ways to be disoriented. In fact, it's not uncommon to find yourself right back in the kinds of Responding experiences we looked at in Chapter 3, with your emotions haywire and your assumptive world unstable. So now you have a double task: to keep moving forward in Reorganizing and to deal with recurring experiences of Responding. *And this is what progress looks like?* you may be prone to ask. Yes, as paradoxical as it may seem, in spite of the setbacks and overlapping sets of experiences, you are moving forward in creating a life consistent with the changes brought by a tough transition.

Albert Einstein once said that some of the most elegant things in the universe are the simplest. I think of his statement when I remember how effective certain things I say can be when I'm going through a hard patch during Reorganizing. What do I mean, "certain things I say"? I mean those truisms, sayings, quoted lines, pieces of poetry that work like buoys when I'm sinking down into discouragement or despair. We all know the negative power of suggestion: *If you say you can't, you can't. I always mess up. There is no way out. Nothing is going to work.* Try saying those kinds of things a time or two and you're ready for a hole in the ground as your permanent residence.

What about the opposite?

Is it possible that by saying something that makes sense and means something to me, I can support myself through a difficult situation? How about that wonderful Gandhi quote, "Full effort is full victory"? How about a mantra like, "You never know when the Divine will break through"? How about, "Hail Mary, full of grace"? Or Scarlett's "Tomorrow is another day"? A friend of mine banks on, "As long as I'm still breathing, I can change." Another keeps asking herself, "What is possible now?" I heard a great speaker a couple of weeks ago say that two questions spur him on as he moves into his sixties: "What do I want to learn now and who can I find to teach it to me?" My Aunt Frances who lives in the country down in Georgia scales back her activities when they get to be too much by quoting the old saying, "If I don't watch out, I'll have a lot of irons in the fire but none of them will get hot."

It doesn't matter what your words are, just as long as they are powerful. Each of us has our own. The important thing during the challenges of Reorganizing is to remember to use them.

CONSTRUCTING A "BIOGRAPHY OF JOY"

There's an old John Denver song that has always been one of my favorites. The main refrain is, "Some days are diamonds, some days are stones." John sings about the inevitability of life's ups and downs; and I always leave off hearing this song thinking, "Why can't I be more philosophical about the mix of good and not-so-good that makes up the lives of all of us?" But I'm so much more inclined to focus on the problems rather than the days of ease. The aggravations and pains and frustrations crowd out thoughts of pleasure and high spirits. That's just the normal way things seem to be.

A few years ago, though, I heard a woman speak at Texas A&M University, where I was a professor at the time, and what she had to say about intervening in the normal thoughts of problems and upsets and irritations has stayed with me ever since. This woman was Dr. Verena Kast, a distinguished professor of psychology who was visiting A&M from the University of Zurich. In a series of lectures that later were published as a book entitled *Joy, Inspiration, and Hope*, Dr. Kast talked about how some people's bodies seem to beam with delight. She talked about the scientific studies that show that it is possible for our lives to be filled with hope rather than despair, for us to be inspired rather than downcast.

One thing that Dr. Kast recommended to all of us in the audience was that we go home and write a "biography of joy." She suggested that we attempt to remember all the moments in our lives when we experienced joy and then write a short vignette describing what those moments were like. This suggestion startled me. By this point, I had told my "life story" a lot of times, always with a big emphasis on what had gone wrong. The danger the Harper women were in during the War between the States when they were the only ones left on the land and Sherman's troops were moving swiftly toward them from Atlanta. The devastation of the Harper family's livelihood when the boll weevils attacked the cotton fields in the early 1900s. The time during the 1940s when our house burned right after Mother had gotten the telegram that Uncle Eliot was missing in action, his plane shot down somewhere over France.

But write a biography of joy? This was a new way to think. I did as Dr. Kast recommended and continue even today adding to this collection of stories about those times in my life when I feel joy. I'd like to recommend the same to you. We all have told our stories from certain perspectives—troubles we have had, stories handed down in the family, relationships we have been involved in—all emphasizing different strands of our lives for different listeners. When we shift perspectives—say, as in constructing a biography of joy—we can see new dimensions of our lives. "Reconstructing a biography of joy removes us from our usual biographical treadmills and habitual conceptualizations," Dr. Kast says in her book, and we "discover a new story about ourselves." I urge you to try it.

You might have a vignette similar to one of mine. It's a fine summer day. I've just passed from the fourth grade to the fifth, and this is the first morning after the school year finished. I'm about to go play jacks on the sidewalk with Judy Crane who lives across the street. On the off chance that she will say yes, I ask Mother if I can go barefooted. When she agrees that it's late enough in the spring to go without shoes, I am exuberant. I skip down the twelve or so concrete steps from our high front porch to the lawn below.

Then my bare feet touch the still-wet grass which hasn't been cut yet this season and I know in that moment pure joy. I'm running across the lawn, soft thick grass under my feet, school is out, the summer lies ahead, and my friend Judy is waiting across the way. When I recall this moment of magic I do remove myself, as Dr. Kast promises, from my usual biographical treadmill and discover a new story about myself.

Questions Dr. Kast recommends we use for our biography of joy:

What in my life has given me joy?
How have I expressed my joy?
How does my joy affect my relationships?
How do I keep control of my joy?
What spoils joy for me?
How is the joy I experience now different from the joy I had as a child?
In the past, in what situations was I really happy?
How did I express my joy then?
And perhaps the most important question of all: What has become of my joy?

Working on a biography of joy helps us identify ourselves as joyful children (when we were) and helps us see what we did with this joy. It also helps us ask valuable questions about our present lives: How can what I have remembered be useful to me today? What can I do differently to hold on to the times of joy I do experience so that they are naturally a part of my everyday experience? In the best of circumstances, this biography of joy that we construct can not only remind us that we have been joyful in the past, it can also awaken that joy in the present.

LAUNCHING A PROJECT

For more than a decade I consulted in the area of organizational change for *Fortune* 500 and 100 companies in the United States and other companies in many countries around the world. I would often begin a conversation with a new client by quoting Niccolò Machiavelli, who said, "There is nothing more difficult to take in hand, more perilous to conduct, or more uncertain in its success than to take the lead in the introduction of a new order of things." With all heads nodding in agreement with that statement, we would then laugh together at another quote, Rita Mae Brown's assertion that "The definition of insanity is doing the same thing over and over again, expecting different results." So Reorganizing during a tough transition can be difficult, perilous and uncertain . . . but we would be foolish not to decide to make changes. Launching a project can be an excellent first step to discovering how you want to redirect your life.

The beauty about launching a project during Reorganizing is that the project can be about anything. It's the practice of creating and following through on the project—any project—that brings value as you decide what focus your life will take at this point, as you work through a tough transition. I love what Herman Melville said: "Life is so short, and so ridiculous and irrational (from a certain point of view) that one knows not what to make of it, unless, well . . . finish the sentence yourself." Choosing a project is a way of finishing the sentence yourself. The sum of individual projects, one philosopher reminds us, is what human reality is about at any particular moment. Recently I read about a conversation Mary Wheelwright, the famous ethnologist, had with a table companion at a dinner party in New York. The man had said to Mary, "What are you working at?" She replied, "How do you know I'm working at something?" He answered, "Because you're happy." So all you have to do for this project is work at something. The work itself will make you happy.

What are some kinds of projects you might launch during Reorganizing?

You do something physical.
You study something.
You produce something.

You complete something.
You go somewhere.
You develop a new skill.
You establish new practices.
You contribute something.
You become an expert in something.
You open up a new area of interest.

Here are some excellent questions to use to create your project:

When will the project begin? When will the project end?
What is the purpose of this project?
What are the goals/objectives of this project?
What are the major milestones of this project and dates for each?
What resources do I need to gather/what actions do I need to take before I begin this project?
What is likely to go wrong with this project? What will make this project fail?
What do I propose to do to prevent these stumbling blocks from interfering with the project?
Who will be a good partner for this project?
How will I know the project is a success?
Why is this project worth doing?
How will I celebrate the completion of this project?

I personally like the idea of launching projects as a way to check out what I really want to do and what I enjoy now that a tough transition has brought me to a different place in life. Every project is useful. Every project moves me forward. It's like the traveler in ancient Greece who lost his way and asked a man by the roadside, "How can I get to Mount Olympus?" "Just make every step you take go in that direction," came the answer. Any project you decide to do—whether it succeeds or fails, whether it turns out to be a lasting interest or a passing fancy—can be a step taken in the direction of finding out what shape your life is going to take now.

LIST MAKING

We explored list making in the Reviewing period of tough transitions. What we might do differently now—during Reorganizing—is change the topics of the lists so that we are jogged to think of solutions, to identify what will give us meaning now. Ilene Segalove and Paul Bob Velick make several suggestions in their book *List Your Self* that are useful when we are Reorganizing. Here are a few examples:

> List how you'd like to change your outer life right now.
> List how you'd like to change your inner life right now.
> List all the times you've fallen flat on your face.
> List the major changes you feel you need to make in your life right now.
> List all the times you've gone off the beaten track.
> List the ways you sabotage yourself from getting what you want.

Or if you just need to amuse yourself as a break from dealing with things, you could make these lists:

> List what's in your glove compartment if you own a car.
> List the fantastic pranks you've successfully pulled off.
> List the names of all your pets from childhood until today.
> List the fads you embraced while growing up.

USING MUSIC INTENTIONALLY

It is easy to find recommendations for music that delights and uplifts during the challenges of Reorganizing. Here are a few selections to consider:

For Getting Up: Starting a New Day
    Grieg's "Morning Mood" from *Peer Gynt Suite*
    Vivaldi's *The Four Seasons*

The Theme from *Rocky*
"The Battle Hymn of the Republic"
Patti Griffin's *1000 Kisses*

For Falling Asleep
    Bach's "Air on a G String"
    Debussy's "Clair de Lune"
    Pachelbel's Canon in D

To Relax and Relieve Stress
    Beethoven's Symphony no. 6
    Mozart's Concerto for Flute and Harp
    Sambodhi Prem's *Reiki Forest*
    Hilary Stagg's *The Edge of Forever*
    Raphael's *Angels of the Deep*
    Josh Groban's *Closer*

To Quiet Your Home
    James Galway (soloist), *The Magic Flute*
    Mendelssohn's *A Midsummer Night's Dream*
    Tchaikovsky's waltzes from *Sleeping Beauty*, *The Nutcracker*,
        and *Swan Lake*
    Doc Childre's *Quiet Joy*
    Tibetan Singing Bowls
    The Sound of Om
    Gregorian chant

For Thinking Clearly
    Bach's Brandenburg Concertos
    Brahams's Violin Concerto in D Major
    Doc Childre's *Heart Zones*
    Music for the Mozart Effect, Vol. 3: Unlock the Creative Spirit
    Strauss's waltzes
    Sweet Honey in the Rock's "No Mirrors in My Nana's
        House"

To Release Anger
   Beethoven's *Egmont* Overture
   Beethoven's Symphony no. 7
   Brahms's Piano Concerto no. 1
   Chumbawumba's "Tubthumping"

To Calm Anger
   Bach's Two Concertos for Two Pianos
   Bearns and Dexter's *The Golden Voyage*
   Handel's Harp Concerto
   Sarah Brightman CDs

To Relieve Sadness
   Beethoven's Piano Concerto no. 5 ("Emperor")
   Mozart's Symphony no. 35 ("Haffner")
   Rachmaninoff's Piano Concerto no. 2 (last movement)
   Jean-Michel Jarre's *Oxygene*
   Romancing the 50's CD
   "How Great Is Thy Faithfulness" (hymn)
   "The Wind Beneath My Wings"
   IZ's *Facing Future* CD, particularly "Somewhere Over
      the Rainbow/What a Wonderful World" (IZ is Israel
      Kamakawiwo'ole)

To Energize Your Day and Help You Focus
   Bach's Brandenburg Concertos
   Beethoven's Symphonies no. 1, 2, and 8
   Smetana's *The Moldau*
   Beth Neilson Chapman's *Deeper Still* and *Hymns*

To Motivate
   Beethoven's Piano Concerto no. 5 ("Emperor")
   Mozart's "Eine Kleine Nachtmusik"
   Wagner's "Ride of the Valkyries"
   Mendelssohn's oratorio *Elijah*, especially "Be Not Afraid"

CONSCIOUSLY CULTIVATING GRATITUDE

I remember one morning walking across the floor in our family room and being swept with gratitude for my computer. This was strange. I wasn't thinking about my computer at the time, but something stirred at an unconscious level and I found myself not just thinking about being thankful but actually feeling grateful to my core that computers had been invented. Recently, I tried an experiment involving gratitude. It was a gray, cold day outside and I didn't have much spark for getting started. In my quiet time I decided to make a list of things I was thankful for, and I ended up with sixty items. My attitude brightened and my energy level rose even before I got the list finished. Being grateful had changed my day.

Here are some characteristics of a person who has gratitude:

You can appreciate the abilities of other people and tell them so.

You notice and appreciate even the ordinary good things that happen.

You never demand or take for granted the good things that happen.

You express awe and wonder.

You know that the source of beauty is not the work of human beings.

You appreciate the things people do for you, even if these are things that people "should" do, e.g., parents, teachers.

You consciously value people who do good for others in whatever field and whatever way.

> If we do not exist under oppression or in famine and yet cannot convince ourselves how lucky we are to be alive, perhaps we are not trying hard enough.
>
> Antonio Damasio, scientist

You can feel gratitude for more than human beings—pets, trees, streams, the Divine, Life.

You honor and recognize the gifts of good health, laughter, and quietness.

You tell others that you are thankful for them.

"Can I see the holiness in things I take for granted, like a paved road or a washing machine?" Rabbi Harold Kushner asks. As we practice noticing and attending, as we cultivate an attitude of wonder, we are not surprised to learn that the root of the word *gratitude* is the Latin *gratia* and that *gratia* means *grace*.

A Final Word: Christopher Alexander Talks About Building

For more than twenty years the work of Christopher Alexander has provided for me not only fascinating reading but life instruction. Strange thing to say about the writings of an architect, isn't it? Life instruction? But when Mr. Alexander writes in chapter 9 of *Timeless Way of Building* about the nature of process, I apply his words to those situations in my life when I can't get to the end all at once, when it's this-leading-to-that, when it's a matter of something's not being able to come clear to me until I have known and seen something else first. When I look through *A Pattern Language* and see the core elements of building that Alexander identifies, I place my own environment against his template and understand why this patio brings so much pleasure but that entranceway feels too tight and narrow. Recently the architect published a new work, written over thirty years, which he calls *The Nature of Order: An Essay on the Art of Building and the Nature of the Universe*. Since this treatise takes up four volumes, I was delighted to find in a recent issue of *Wired* magazine a summary of this work called "15 Rules for Rebuilding the World." As I read these fifteen rules—Alexander's "Elements of Style," as the *Wired* writer Jessica Scanlon called them—I saw statements such as these:

A balanced range of sizes is pleasing and beautiful.

Repeating various elements creates a sense of order and harmony.

Simple forms create an intense, powerful center.

Looping, connected elements promote unity and grace.

Texture and imperfections convey uniqueness and life.

Empty spaces offer calm and contrast.

Use only essentials; avoid extraneous elements.

Designs should be connected and complementary, not ego-centric and isolated.

"How can I apply these architecture principles to the task of Reorganizing in a tough transition?" I ask myself. It takes only a cursory glance of words like *balanced, simple, connected, uniqueness, calm, essentials,* to see a relationship between these "15 Rules for Rebuilding the World" and the steps I must take to rebuild my personal world. One of the sad aspects of having to rebuild our lives is remembering the things we have lost. And one of the happy things is that we can rebuild consciously and according to a new and appropriate blueprint and design.

In Summary: REORGANIZING

WHAT

Reorganizing experiences that are normal in a tough transition include:

Creating a new identity consistent with the changes brought by the tough transition

Thinking in new ways about current situations

Establishing new behaviors to correspond to current conditions

Dealing with new problems related to reorganizing life and with typical problems that are just part of everyday living

Being creative in thinking about and solving problems, using problem space and problem finding

Retrieving threads of purpose and meaning

Jettisoning the outdated

Articulating a considered faith and values

WHEN

Reorganizing is likely to begin along with or following Reviewing experiences such as considering what positive steps I might take or after asserting that I must make changes consistent with the tough transition that has occurred in my life. And Reorganizing continues for whatever period of time it takes for new identities to be established, new values to be articulated, and threads of meaning and purpose to be retrieved and brought forward into the present. If a "working lunch" is the kind of meal break where the business at hand is brought to the table and continued while the sandwich is eaten and the coffee drunk, then Reorganizing is a kind of "working life" where I'm making the required changes and solving new problems related to the transition while I'm doing the rest of life.

WHERE

The further individuals go in navigating the Terrain of Tough Transitions, the more they have to accommodate a whole variety of types of experiences simultaneously. On some days, or during some minutes of a day, experiences from Responding—like haywire emotions—predominate. During that same day—maybe even during those same minutes—serious decisions have to be made ... experiences of Reorganizing. These decisions might trigger Reviewing behaviors—specific ways to deal with stress, or maybe reminiscing. While one group of experiences—Responding, Reviewing, or Reorganizing—tends to predominate at certain points in the sequence of a move through a tough transition, all of the experiences can be a part of daily living most of the time. What's the value, then, of artificially separating out the three distinctions, if they are all going to occur together anyway?

The Chinese have an ancient proverb: To name a thing is to tame it. When we make the distinctions of the Terrain of Tough Transitions, we can learn to identify each type of experience. We can learn what is normal. We can learn what to expect. And, most important of all, we can learn useful ways to think and act that are appropriate for each type of experience. By the time Reorganizing is the predominant action for an individual, with all the changes that requires, it is invaluable to be so familiar with the other distinctions like Responding and Reviewing that you are not undone when you have to deal with two or three of them at once.

HOW

What helps during Reorganizing experiences?

Identifying and using your signature strengths
Talking your way through a hard patch
Constructing a biography of joy
Launching a project
List making
Using music intentionally
Consciously cultivating gratitude

4

Renewing

Corn grows in the night.

HENRY DAVID THOREAU

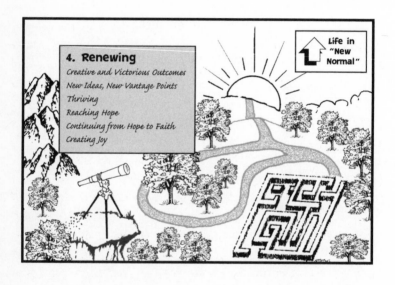

4. Renewing

Creative and Victorious Outcomes
New Ideas, New Vantage Points
Thriving
Reaching Hope
Continuing from Hope to Faith
Creating Joy

Life in "New Normal"

Tough transitions are not periods of our lives that we are supposed to get over—though it may seem that way while we're in them. They are not experiences we are supposed to put behind us. We are not required to pull ourselves up by our bootstraps and go on. Rather, tough transitions are times we have lived that will remain part of who we are forever. The very person we are has been changed by these experiences. To block these events (even if we could) would be to black out some of the most significant times of our lives. And to create an incomplete picture.

Does this mean we are thankful that we had the tough times? Well, maybe sometimes and for some people, but not for all and certainly not always. What is there to say, then, about the way something undesired comes finally to be a source of renewing in our lives? Who can talk about this without being a Pollyanna or sounding like a walking cliché?

Interestingly enough, doctors and scientists talk a lot about the possible positive outcomes of tough transitions if—and it is an if—individuals choose to move actively through the process it takes to find a new normal, a new equilibrium. They use words like "change-creative gain sequence." They talk about a "normal transformational adaptive process with an outcome of gain and freedom once the process is completed." They assert that people do "reestablish balance" and that there is built into the very physicality and mentality of human beings a "universal means of adapting to unwanted change."

What are these learned folks saying?

That we have available to us a way to make meaning out of the experience of a tough transition and to live through this difficult time not just to survive but to find a new coherence and a sense of continuity in our lives.

"Oh, sure," I can hear my own doubting self say, "make lemonade out of lemons . . . every cloud has a silver lining . . . you're better for having lived through this . . ." No one wants to go through all the hard work and pain and confusion and emptiness of a transition time in one's life only to have everything tidily summed up in the words of a commonplace adage. But I don't think this is what researchers are saying. They are talking about the outcomes of thousands of studies of people who have lived through experiences of loss and transition, studies that have documented how these people say they have been changed in most positive ways.

Creative and Victorious Outcomes

What are some of these outcomes? In the work of the late Dr. George Pollock, who had been dean of Northwestern University's Feinberg School of Medicine, people who have successfully integrated a tough transition report what Dr. Pollock calls "creative outcomes":

Ability to feel joy, satisfaction, and a sense of accomplishment
Return to a steady state of balance
Experience of increased capacity to appreciate people and things
Assessment that one is more tolerant and more wise
Desire to express oneself creatively
Ability to invest in new relationships

Experience of new sense of play and freedom
Achievement of a considered faith

Dr. Heinz Kohut uses the term "victorious outcomes" and talks about "an enlarged capacity for empathy, ability to think beyond oneself, new outlook on life, increased ability to hold life's ups and downs in perspective, and heightened capacity for humor." Dr. Susan Nolen-Hoeksema lists: "sense of personal growth, a personality change, realization of personal strengths."

Robert Weiss says that we have every reason to expect that at some point in working through a tough transition we will experience:

Ability to give energy to everyday life
Psychological comfort, as demonstrated by freedom from pain and distress
Ability to feel pleasure when desirable, hoped-for, or enriching events occur
Hopefulness regarding the future, being able to plan and care about plans
Ability to function with reasonable adequacy in social roles

New Ideas and New Vantage Points

Let's true up these doctors' and scientists' assertions against the reality of a tough transition experienced and lived through by a real person. First, a few words about the speaker of the words we are about to read: a professional woman who teaches in a medical school, the mother of an eight-year-old, divorced following the discovery of her husband's affair and absence of any success in reconstituting the marriage. Does her experience include any of the "creative and victorious outcomes" we are told are possible? Let's listen to her story:

I have now been divorced seven years. The first few years, I had to work to empty out a lot of negative effects and physical feelings. I chose to do that by writing in my journal, writing lyrics and music for songs that spoke of my pain, and keeping up my disciplines of exercise and quiet time. I also did not allow myself to be isolated. I kept pushing myself to connect with my friends. I have to admit that I had to fight the tendency to pull back.

I also had to work through some of the shame I felt about being divorced. My biggest challenge was changing my perception about divorce. In the beginning I was so full of thoughts and feelings about being a failure at marriage, being someone a partner no longer found attractive, being a person whose spiritual commitments were known to all but who could not make her marriage work. I imagined that everybody I saw was thinking these things.

Then people wanted explanations for why I was divorced. How come? Why? I had to learn how to answer, to sort through, and it took me a while to figure this out. At first you think, "What will they think?" But recently, at my parents' fiftieth anniversary party, an old friend of the family asked about my husband. I said, "Oh, I'm not married." He clearly wanted an explanation. I didn't feel a need to give one. So I left him speechless; but I felt great. It is no longer necessary to talk about this to others.

Things come in waves as you work through the aftermath of a divorce. It was tough at first to do things like go to a retreat alone or take my daughter on a vacation, just the two of us. One thing I did consciously was force myself to take risks. After I wrote a few songs, I started performing on open-mike night at a pub nearby. I signed up for a songwriting school. During all this there were times I thought, "I'm there"; then more grief would come. I'd find out more information about things my ex-husband did while we were married. Or I'd see someone I was close to when I worked in a nonprofit organization devoted to helping teenagers, and I'd have to deal with the shame issue for myself again. Once more the process of emptying was required.

Why did I keep working at this? I wanted to be free. If knew that if I were bitter or obsessing about being wronged I would not be free. One of the hardest things to let go of was that he had an affair. Of course, I felt that I had the moral upper position; I had been wronged, after all. I felt like telling the universe: I'm an incredible human being who has been so wronged. But I knew that wouldn't give me freedom. It would just keep me stuck and bitter. There was a lot of renewal in coming to the place of being at peace and really forgiving the other person. I tapped into my own spirituality too and realized that I have a big life that can unfold for me with endless possibilities and options.

Renewal. How does this come? As emptying happens, you start to get a new set of eyes that can see new potentials and new possibilities and you start to listen to some of your desires. Oh, this would be something for me to do or something I would like to learn. You see more of these things and can act on them. Like dancing. I had never moved my body much, so I took a sacred dance class. I took a vacation with my daughter to Disney World. Part of me said, "You're not a family and that's a place for families!" But then I said, "Why not?" and grabbed my single-parent sister and her family and said, "Let's do it."

At first I had to do a lot of work reorganizing my life. There was my full-time job, my daughter, child care, house maintenance, finances, and on and on. I realized early that I had to put aside anger feelings and establish good relationship with my ex for the sake of our daughter. Some days it was, "Fake it until you make it," but I did my best to start with good habits of being respectful. Even when I didn't feel like being respectful I found I could do it.

I also found out I could do some things that I had always depended on my husband to do. Like a light socket cover. I learned I could actually use a screwdriver and put that cover back on. And things in the yard that had always been his to do. I learned how to start the weed eater and run the lawn mower. I also found that I had to open myself up more to community and let people around me help me. I had a neighbor who was kind and helpful and watched out for my house. If there was a storm, he made sure the shingles got back on. But I had to be willing to call on him and other friends to help me do things. I also discovered you can always hire a handyman. Sometimes that's more simple than having a husband!

About having a life: There's a root and wing thing. You want to hold on tight to old relations, old familiar things. And that's good, but I always also needed to have something a little new. I risk, open up a bit—like calling a friend who wouldn't be the normal person I would call. In my daily spiritual discipline I listen for new ideas and write them down to make sure I don't lose them. This takes energy; I have to push myself. But it keeps me alive. Related to my music I've had to fight thoughts like: I'm too old; I'm not good enough; Music is not my primary thing. But music is also something I really love, so I'm going to take some chances on it. I'm crazy enough to follow this crazy thing that I love so much. My youth is renewed.

Pouring out at the beginning is in the nature of the process. You are self-focused. My focus now is on lots of interesting things and people and what's going on with others. I like who I am. After you work to integrate a divorce, you become so grounded in your new identity, or maybe it is that you reclaim your identity and "come back home." My response to my divorce is now a part of my story that I am proud of. I am a better person because of it. I like who I am because of having gone through it. I've been made a deeper, richer person because of it. I learned new thinking because of having to deal with the divorce, and I became more deeply connected to others and to my spirituality because of it.

What creative and victorious outcomes has this woman achieved? Let's relate some of her statements with a few of the outcomes professionals tell us are possible when we work through a tough transition:

She says,	Professionals identify creative and victorious outcomes
"I like who I am."	Sense of personal growth Ability to feel satisfaction
"It is no longer necessary to talk about this to others."	Ability to function well in social roles
"There was a lot of renewal in coming to the place of being at peace and really forgiving the other person."	Enlarged capacity for empathy Assessment that one is more tolerant and wise

"I've tapped into my own spirituality too and realized that I have a big life that can unfold for me with endless possibilities and options."

Achievement of a considered faith
Hopefulness regarding the future

"You start to listen to some of your desires."

Desire to express oneself creatively
New outlook on life

"I learned I could actually use a screwdriver."

Ability to feel new sense of accomplishment
Realization of personal strengths

"I learned new thinking and became more deeply connected to others."

Ability to invest in new relationships
Experience of new sense of play and freedom

The suggestion that good things can come out of tough transitions, we can see from this comparison, isn't a Pollyanna gloss and wishful thinking. People do experience creative and victorious outcomes when they reflect on how they have changed and what they have learned.

At the age of ninety-three, the cellist Pablo Casals explained how, for the past eighty years, he had started the day in the same manner. He went to the piano and he played two preludes and fugues of Bach: "It is sort of benediction on the house. But that is not its only meaning. . . . It is rediscovery of the world in which I have a joy of being a part. It fills me with awareness of the wonder of life, with a feeling of the incredible marvel of being human."

Renewing is that place we reach when we can once again—on more days than not—feel what Maestro

Who is your hero? It sounds sentimental, but I feel that the real heroes in the world are not the famous people but the people in our own families, people who never wrote a book, never published an article, never painted a picture, but who have made a household with what is the highest measure of creativity.

Joyce Carol Oates, novelist

Casals calls "a feeling of the incredible marvel of being human."
But what it has taken to get there! I had to laugh one day when I
looked up *renewing* in the dictionary and read the suggestion to
compare *renewing* with *renovating*. Be-

Which apply?
Synonyms for *Renew*
(a) invigorate
(b) heal
(c) furbish
(d) fortify
(e) enliven
(f) continue
(g) all of the
above

cause *renovating* is exactly what we
had to do when we were Reviewing
and Reorganizing our lives. And who
has ever known a renovation process
to go smoothly? Now, at this time of
Renewing, we live with new percep-
tions, with different goals, and with
plans based on who and where we are
now.

*Renewing: being restored to freshness,
feeling vigor and rejuvenation, experiencing a transformation that leaves you feeling regenerated.* That's a lot to ask, isn't
it, as an outcome of something painful, hard, confusing, and often
just downright infuriating? But one day, perhaps after weeks,
months, or even years, there it is. Active interchange with life
again, on new terms, from a new vantage point, with new ideas
about what makes life worthwhile.

Thrivers: Doing Something More Than Just Surviving

Researchers have located a new tribe! People who find themselves
integrating tough transitions not just by surviving but actually
thriving. Who are these folks? Maybe they're like that woman we
sing about in "Delta Dawn," sweet but addled—"Delta Dawn,
what's that flower you've got on?" Or like Forrest Gump with his
"life is a box of chocolates"? Or maybe like one of the Sisters of
Mercy carrying on Mother Teresa's work around the world? No,
this tribe are just normal folk who are sensible, awake, uncompro-
misingly honest. So what makes them different?

Well, let's start with how thrivers approach life: as students and philosophers, not as patients, victims, or even warriors. When thrivers are students, what are they studying? If they are philosophers, what do they philosophize about? Thrivers come up with new ways to view a situation they have found themselves in during a tough transition. They learn to apply a new explanatory system to what happens to them, creatively disputing default ways of thinking and inventing new views of the situation. They think like philosophers, asking questions such as, "How can I make sense of this? What can now, in this circumstance, give my life meaning?" Thrivers reflect on where they find themselves at this present time. They know absolutely that it is in their power, and in their power only, to construe—explain, interpret, translate, define—what happens to them in life.

Thrivers know that they have more than just the typical fight-or-flight responses available to them. They possess a third kind of response: relax, wait, think, listen, focus. Many of them—especially women—even know about and practice a fourth response: connect and relate. Thrivers know they can create a context for their situation by using their innate talents (which researchers assert are available to everyone) for framing, evaluating, and interpreting. They come to know through experience that they can count on their strengths: the ability to wait, think, imagine, tolerate, forgive, learn, and change. In researchers' terms, thrivers have (a) comprehensibility—being able finally to make some sense of what happens even though life is chaotic and unpredictable; (b) manageability—being able to find a way to think that is an appropriate match for the event that is impacting them; and (c) meaningfulness—realizing that investing energy in really engaging with a tough transition is a worthy thing to do because from this work they are able to add new meaning to their lives. Thriving is reconstructing life's meaning in response to life's most destructive occurrences.

How can we spot a member of this thrivers' tribe? I think back into my own experience. When did I know a thriver? When did I know someone afflicted with the "failure to thrive"?

What responses do you make?
Flight
Fight
Relax, think, and wait
Connect and relate

On business in another city, I once had dinner with a widowed woman who clearly was failing to thrive. She cried all through our meal. At the end of the evening, as we were walking out of the restaurant, I said, "I'm sorry about the death of your husband. How long has it been?" When she answered, "Eighteen years," I knew something was wrong. Now, it isn't that we can't feel grief years after a loss ("shadow grief," people call it—like the sun going behind a cloud when you're on a picnic), but instinctively I knew this was different. Here was a woman who had chosen to make a lifestyle of being a griever. Who had chosen not to replan her life consistent with what had happened to her. Who had no current and active interchange with life. Here was a person who had chosen a lifestyle of failure to thrive.

Then I think about my dear friend who at fifty has found herself chronically ill. "Catastrophe living," she calls her situation, alluding to the title of a book she has found invaluable. "How do I live well even while I have to live differently?" she asked herself. Of course she railed against the illness. Of course she spent time feeling down and even depressed. But mixed in with these reactions were new ways of thinking. I was having coffee with her one cold morning when someone called from her church. Could she take the lead this week in organizing Freeze Night, a program that brought homeless people in to eat and spend the night in the church when the temperature fell below thirty-two degrees? She considered and knew that she didn't have the strength and reserves to take on the project. But I heard my friend offer, "Give me something to do that I can do from home, even from my bed." A bit more conversation and she was set to e-mail and call everyone on the Freeze Night team to alert them that tomorrow the standing plan would go into operation and they would be needed. For the long term my friend has made other thriver-type decisions. "Since I can't work in the corporate world"—where she had been a wildly successful senior vice president—"I've asked, 'What kind of work can I do? What can I do in this situation that satisfies and even excites me?'" She decided to return to school and get her certification in adolescent counseling. She has also made some new friends who talk to her about things more meaningful than weight loss and business competition. She recognizes the power she has to say what her life is going to be like, albeit in a different—and unwanted—circumstance. My friend is without question a thriver.

> What a wonderful life I've had! I only wish I had realized it sooner.
>
> Colette, French novelist

Reaching Hope

Not too long before the tennis great Arthur Ashe died of AIDS, which he contracted through a blood transfusion, I watched a television interview with him and his wife. Ashe was asked where he was finding his sustenance in this hard time, what was buoying him up. Without a moment's hesitation, he answered, "The writings of Dr. Howard Thurman." Until then I had not heard of Howard Thurman. I didn't know that he was one of the great spiritual leaders of the twentieth century, a poet, a mystic, a dean at Boston University, a prolific author, a black man who founded the first interracial, interdenominational church in America. Once I bought his books, I could understand Arthur Ashe's answer. Howard Thurman was a man who knew the hardest of the hard in life but a man who also knew about reaching hope.

> The important thing is the fact that beyond the zero point of endurance there are vast possibilities. There is a bottomless resourcefulness in individuals that ultimately enable them to transform "the spear of frustration into a shaft of light."

Thurman gives a specific example of the power of hope to fortify oneself for action. Reminding his readers that the prophet Jeremiah asked a hopeless question—"Is there a balm in Gilead?"—Dr. Thurman points out that the black slaves turned that depressing question into an adamant assertion—there *is* a balm in Gilead—that they sang day after day as they worked.

There is a balm in Gilead
To make the wounded whole;
There is a balm in Gilead
To heal the sin sick soul.

Talk about optimism. Talk about faith. *Is there a balm in Gilead?* To respond so certainly—*There is a balm in Gilead*—is an act of sheer audacity. An act of reaching hope.

> "There is no use trying," said Alice. "One can't believe impossible things."
> "I dare say you haven't had much practice," replied the Queen. "When I was your age, I always did it for half an hour a day. Why, sometimes I've believed as many as six impossible things before breakfast."
>
> Lewis Carroll

What is hope, when we are slogging along through the process of a tough transition? An illusion? An infantile want? Or something else entirely? Can hope be the mark of a person of humility who has to say, if truth be told, "I cannot know what is going to happen or when, so who knows when good might come?" (I often say to myself, and to my friends, "You never know when the Divine might break through!") Hope stands on the truth that there are always "as yet unborn possibilities." A person who hopes feels that somehow it is meaningful to carry on, while a person who does not hope lies "in a stupor of postponed reality."

Hope can sometimes sound like revolt. People who say, "I will not be defined by this event that has happened to me; I will take the risk of thinking things will improve. Now, so how can things get better?" are people showing resistance and revolt. They will not accept any idea that how they experience a situation now will be forever permanent. *To hope is to take a "creative leap out of a dead-end situation into a situation of new promise." Hoping is having an "apt attitude":* Things are apt to change for the better, or at least be the best they can be.

> Sometimes the quality of our lives depends on our ability to make a one hundred percent commitment to something about which we are only fifty-one percent sure.
>
> Albert Camus

Martin Luther said that everything that is done in the world is done by hope. And the metaphors we find in all spiritual traditions—waking up from illusion, being touched by grace, becoming free, release from suffering, being born again of the Spirit—all shout out a promise: that we can experience new possibilities and see the world in new ways. What is that but hope?

In her powerful memoir *The Liars' Club*, Mary Karr describes this kind of hope—hope based on "some ancient sense of possibility." There was little reason for Mary to hope. Growing up poor in Orange, Texas, with the smells and ugly sights of oil refineries always around her, she found herself shuttled from one caretaker to another, sometimes way across the country. In the following passage she describes a moment in her childhood when she and her sister are in an airplane, flying yet again from one parent to another. It is night. Mary describes the sudden emergence of hope in this most unexpected circumstance:

> I woke to clouds. A whole Arctic wasteland of clouds bubbled up in the round airplane window toward which my sister's head was tipped. The clouds seemed to have seized up in violet motion, like some cauldron that got frozen mid-boil. A full moon shone across them. The full moon cut a

wide white path straight to us, the beauty of which flooded
me with some ancient sense of possibility. Maybe there was
hope for me yet, even from the vantage point of being a
kid, hurtling across the black sky with my sister. . . . When
mystics talk about states of grace, surely that's the feeling
they mean—hope rising out of some Dust Bowl farmer's
heart when he's surveying the field of chewed items that lo-
custs left. This hope lacked details. From it came neither
idea nor impetus. I only felt there was something important
I had to do, held by the clear light of that unlikely low-
slung moon.

Metaphors of Hope

Leonardo Boff, even while working for social justice with the
poorest of the poor in Brazil, can say:

> The Spirit appears . . . hoping against all hope. The Spirit is
> that little flicker of fire burning at the bottom of the wood-
> pile. More rubbish is piled on, rain puts out the flame, wind
> blows the smoke away. But underneath everything a brand
> still burns on, unquenchable. . . . The Spirit sustains the
> feeble breath of life in the empire of death.

The poet and writer Raymond Carver, told at age fifty that he
would soon die of cancer, illustrated this kind of hope when he
asked himself in one of his final poems if he had gotten what
he wanted out of life. The answer is, "yes, he has felt beloved on
the earth." After his death, Carver's companion found an "errand
list" in his shirt pocket. I would call this "errand list" a Manifesto
of Hope:

Eggs
Peanut butter
Hot choc

Australia?
Antarctica??

There's a line in the Old Testament that asserts: "But there is hope for someone still linked to the rest of the living." There have been times in tough transitions when that was about all I could say—"Well, I am still living and breathing." But this means everything. For so long as I am living and breathing, there is possibility, something new can come, my spirit can be touched by Spirit. By the time we reach Renewing in our process of working through a tough transition, we have experienced this kind of hope: the sense that I can rise and do a new thing.

The Continuum from Hope to Faith

Can we, to use the philosopher Kierkegaard's phrase, be "crazy-human with hope"?

We can draw a line and put a progression of different kinds of hope on that line. At the far left end would be *hope as fantasy*. I hope I win the lottery. I hope it doesn't rain on their wedding day. Hope shouting both my wishes and my impotence. Hope where I can—and where I must—do nothing. Then further on the line is *hope as expectation*. Expectation can be a bit like "you owe me." Or at best it's based on predictability, fairness, and control. Then there's *hope as vision*. I hope for the future I am envisioning now. I connect my hope with something concrete that I can move toward. I am energized by the hope that I can make a change soon. Further across the line is *hope as work*. I hope these trips to the infertility clinic result in our having a child. I hope these months I've spent studying for the bar will allow me to realize my dream of becoming a lawyer. Recognizing the chance and uncertainty always present, I nevertheless, in hope as in work, am willing to do everything I can to bring about the thing I so desire.

> We die on the day when our lives cease to be illuminated by the steady radiance, renewed daily, of a wonder, the source of which is beyond all reason.
>
> Dag Hammarskjöld

Near the right-hand end of this line of progression we can place *hope as trust*. I plant the tulip bulbs in hopes of a pleasing riot of color in the spring. I volunteer with Habitat for Humanity in the hope that providing a home for a poor family will bring the stability and sense of security this family needs. I risk a new relationship because I know that somewhere in me is the ground for hope. Then at the far end of the line is *hope as absolute*.

Another word for *hope as absolute* is *faith*. This can be faith in the surprises and opportunities in life. Faith in the Mystery that surrounds my life. Faith in the possibility of the resurrection of dead hopes and redemption of a lost past. Faith that we are always carried by life. Faith based on a sense of oneness with other people and with the cosmos. Faith based on a relationship—even a friendship—with God, the Divine, the Holy Other. Faith is trusting in the love of God, in spite of the fact that we often cannot understand the whys and whats of daily existence. Faith rests on an assertion that there is purpose and meaning. Faith is foundation for a life of vitality, fullness, and assurance. Faith joins us with something larger than we are, and the larger that something is, the more meaning our lives have. When that something is the Holy Other, our faith is absolute; it is ultimate. Faith is joyful, energetic, and patient. And, perhaps, most of all, faith is expanding.

I once knew someone who exuded absolute hope, who lived joyful, expanding faith. Her name was Bernadette Muller and she was a member of the cloistered Poor Clare order, whose occupation is prayer. Bernadette was one of the members of the order who had commerce with the outside world since she was responsible for the care and maintenance of the sisters and the monastery. What a character she was—wearing cowboy boots under her habit as she worked the miniature horse ranch that was the source of sustenance for the order; playing a mean blues saxophone in the Friday night sisters' rock-and-roll band; talking to Dan Rather for a segment on his newscast or John Burnett for a spot on NPR; being interviewed by *Le Monde* or the London *Times* for a feature article. I always told Sister Bernadette that she would have been a millionaire if she weren't a nun; she was a brilliant and shrewd businesswoman. Her spiritual philosophy was definitely active, not passive: "If I think of doing something," she would say, "I go ahead and do it. If God doesn't want me to do it, He can stop me." And over the years I knew her, when she thought that had happened—that God had stopped her—she was total obedience. Until then, however, it was . . . Bernadette thinks it; Bernadette does it.

There came the day she found out she had pancreatic cancer. Knowing that time was short, she made appointments to have a good-bye talk with loved ones and friends. I drove onto the ranch one bright September day to sit with her on the ranch office porch where red geraniums were still blooming in the flowerbox and the light out across the yard toward the barn glowed luminous. Sister Bernadette and I talked for several hours of this and that. We laughed about the time my husband inadvertently rubbed up against her hips at a crowded reception and she replied to his embarrassed apology, "Oh, I rather liked it." We recounted the day the reporter who doubted the pregnancy rate figures of the miniature horses was stopped in his tracks by the words of the president of the American Miniature Horse Association: "Yes, the certified records show these numbers." "And how do you explain this high pregnancy rate for these horses?" the reporter asked. The official replied, "They say they pray for them." We grinned again at the telling.

Finally, it was time for me to go. Bernadette and I hugged, and I was crying. She held me at arm's length and said, "Elizabeth, I don't know how it is going to work when I get up there, but if there is any way I can help you, I sure as hell will." And then she said, "I am sad to leave all this, all of you. But I am so happy. Going to be with God is the culmination of my life as a nun; it's what I've wanted most my entire life as a nun. Now it is about to happen."

There was no buoying up here. No putting the best face on things. Bernadette was dying as she had lived. With hope and faith absolute.

Sadako Ogata, former United Nations High Commissioner for Refugees and Japan's special representative on Afghan issues, was once asked to define security and surprised her interviewer by talking about hope:

> My goal is to live the truly religious life and express it in my music.
>
> John Coltrane

Real security is not about weapons. It's about the widest possible range of people having enough faith about living to see tomorrow—that they actually start to think about the next day, the next week, the next year. Feeling secure . . . is about having enough hope to plant in time for the spring season, because you know that spring will come.

This knowing that spring will come lies in our hearts, perhaps dormant or just beginning to bud from the roots. We know hope, then, at the rhizome level of our being, and this hope shows up as faith that spring will come.

Creating Joy

Someone once said, "We should seek joy by reasoned decree, regardless of how foolish and unrealistic the quest may look." But how do we seek joy by reasoned decree?

Joy—gladness, exhilaration of spirit—comes from finding harmony between our inner and outer lives. From redirecting our life stories. From paying attention to what Einstein called "a sort of intoxicated joy and amazement at the beauty and grandeur of this world, of which man can form just a faint notion." He went on to say, "This joy is the feeling from which true scientific research draws its spiritual sustenance, but which also seems to find expression in the song of birds."

Is not the best life we can live then the life where we are committed to something larger than our own interests? A life in which we act as if it is our responsibility to combat suffering in the world? Over and over people tell me that this is where they find themselves when their lives reach a "new normal" after integrating a tough transition: Committed to giving back some of what they have received. Committed to making whatever contribution they can make out of what they have experienced. Committed to wonder, thanksgiving, playfulness, and service.

Wonder, thanksgiving, *playfulness*, and service? How did a concept as frivolous as *play* make it into such an exemplary lineup? Someone has said that silliness softens suffering. The ancient Hindu scripture reminded us a long time ago, "There are three things which are real: God, human folly, and laughter. The first two are beyond our comprehension. So we must do what we can with the third." And it's reported that Socrates' last words were: "Please the gods, may the laughter keep breaking through."

There is, of course, a whole field of study on the value of laughter to our health. "Gelontology," it is called (*gelos* is the Greek word for laughter). I remember once when I was in the middle of a tough transition—a move to a community where I knew no one, had no work, and not enough energy to "make things happen." One morning I decided to start reading the newspapers in a different way, not just to know what the news of the world was, but to look for things that were genuinely funny. With an eye turned toward the humorous, I noticed stories I probably would have passed over otherwise. There was, for instance, the account of the woman taken to court for drunk driving who claimed she was innocent because she had, in ignorance, eaten three pieces of a Christmas cake laced with whiskey! The story gave these details:

Ms. Wynne was stopped by police and given a positive breath test, despite claiming she had drunk only two half-pints of lager that evening. But a scientific analysis of the cake she claimed to have eaten confirmed that the three hefty slices of "Grandma's Original" consumed by Ms. Wynne explained her erratic driving. The court was told that the 12–inch cake, baked to a recipe concocted by the 86-year-old grandmother, contained sultanas, mixed peel and the magic ingredient: half of a large bottle of whiskey.

I also read the words of hockey coach Harry Neale, speaking to the press: "Last season we couldn't win at home and we were losing on the road. My failure as a coach was that I couldn't think of any place else to play." And later I heard a Lily Tomlin joke, "I always wanted to be somebody, but I now realize I should have been more specific." Yes. That morning, during a really tough transition, silliness did soften suffering.

So we actually create joy in our lives through our commitment to making a difference in the world, through being kind, generous, forgiving, helpful to others. And, probably, because we do want to balance the seriousness of that avenue to joy with laughing at ourselves and the wacky, wonderful world around us, we best needs take note of E. B. White's humorous observation: "I arise in the morning torn between a desire to improve (or save) the world and a desire to enjoy (savor) the world. This makes it hard to plan the day."

People who do the work of tough transitions create more joy because they do fewer things they don't want to do, hang out less with people they don't enjoy, commit to activities that they find meaningful rather than expected. And they are much more outrageous.

> There are only two ways to live your life. One is as though nothing is a miracle. The other is as though everything is a miracle.
>
> Albert Einstein

PEOPLE TELL THEIR STORIES OF RENEWING

Isak Dinesen once said that all sorrows can be borne if you put them into a story or tell a story about them. The individuals whose stories follow have navigated truly difficult times. They have certainly borne all kinds of sorrows. Yet they are not undone. They have not checked out of life. They are not bitter or in constant despair. These are honest people, not skirting the truth of the challenges that they have been through, *and* they are thrivers. They have achieved creative and victorious outcomes after navigating their way through very difficult times. Let's listen to some of their stories:

RENEWING: AT THE END OF BEING UNEMPLOYED

It took me fifteen months to find a job. At least nine months longer than I anticipated in my worst-case scenario. After all, I was living in a large city where I had been successfully employed in various high-profile positions for seventeen years. At the time the international company I worked for downsized, I was a senior vice president there and was blessed with a huge network of friends and associates. So I thought that it might take six months to replace my income, since I knew I was willing to work as hard to find another job as I had worked all the years previously. How wrong I was! Instead of six months, it was almost a year and a half before I was on a payroll once again. And what a tough—and life-altering—fifteen months it was!

But today I have the clarity to know and see where things are in my life, and I feel so peaceful. I was speaking with my friend Olivia tonight and told her I was going to put things down on paper to remind myself of the process and what I've learned. All the wonderful people who have supported and prayed for me. All the kindnesses of strangers. The chance to have a clean slate, live a simpler life. Remembering that when I kick back, the mind is free and able to process information. Remind-

ing myself that I can embrace change and love what happens with change. Oh, so many thoughts . . .

I've talked about simplicity for years, wanting to slow down and make time for things that were more meaningful. I got that in spades! The past fifteen months gave me the time to do just that . . . stop and see what meaningful really means . . . that the simple things are so wonderful. Being able to be with my sweet aging dog Cotton; joining a new book club that forced me to read more, something I've also enjoyed and hadn't slowed down to do before; and spending more one-on-one time with good friends.

Part of this new simplicity is buying a new house. The house I have had is luxurious and beautiful. But it's isolating, being located in a gated community. My home has always been one of openness and the gate here is a barrier to me and to my friends. I've found another home that I think I'll love more than any house I've ever owned. Simpler, more welcoming, and not isolated by gates and entrance phones.

One of the biggest changes this transition brought was my learning to ask for help, something that's been hard for me to do for a long time. Accustomed to living independently, I've always taken care of myself.

But because I did learn how to ask for help, I was rewarded. One person I had never even met before took me under her wing and opened doors, offered thoughts and good humor, and checked in just to say hi and see what was up. Many friends called or sent e-mails on a daily basis sharing how they prayed for me every morning. So many prayers from so many people bolstered me. So many people offered their contacts. Even people I didn't really know offered to help—friends of friends who would pass an opportunity along. I want to remember their generosity and extend the same to others that may come into my life.

I will remember the kindness of strangers. I remember being completely flustered over what I'd done wrong that resulted in my not getting my unemployment check. I simply fell apart on the phone. This stranger, in of all places, the Employment Commission, was calm and warm, ensuring me we were going to fix the problem and not to worry. Somehow I'd expected people in this government outfit to be completely jaded, and such was not the case. What generosity of spirit.

I learned a lot of things about myself. For every interview, I felt compelled to prepare, read, and be completely conversant about the company. I wanted to be sure to ask the right questions and to be "smart" about the operation. When I finally got a job, I had gone in feeling completely unprepared. I had answered the questions out of my experience, not from a strategy I'd planned in advance. What I learned from this is that I think I had been trying to be too smart in the previous interviews, trying to sell myself, and hadn't listened in the moment and responded with no plan in mind. What I do know is that I landed this new job—which I absolutely love—in a week's time. When I'd been a finalist for other jobs, it had taken at least six weeks to move through the process, only to find that I hadn't been chosen. This was a lesson that having an easier, lighter thought process works.

Through this experience I have realized that in a work environment not everything needs to be so deadly serious. I notice that I sometimes make things hard when they don't have to be. Or I complicate a situation with extraneous details, feeling as though I have to have all the answers and work harder. I want to remember, now, to be realistic but also to take things more at face value and add some lightheartedness to the process.

When I got my job, the word got out and the calls poured in. I knew people were supporting me, but I just had no idea how many cared. I realize now that my community is far larger than I ever knew. I want to remember how being grateful feels. That I felt grateful when someone returned my phone call. Grateful when a lead came in. I want to repay those acts of kindness.

In retrospect, I know that the journey is supposed to be part of the fun. But I will have to say it wasn't fun for me. I think I was so methodical and obsessive that I became mentally burdened with myself. I want to remember a saying someone told me: that only when there's a crack does the light come through. I know I've had guidance, that I've been led and shown a path. God has given me strength when I thought there was none. And now it's so clear and the blessings are so big.

RENEWING: LIFE AFTER SEPTEMBER 11

You know, it's poetry that sustains me when I think back today on the trauma and tragedy of 9/11. Two poems in particular. One, written by Billy Collins, the poet laureate of the United States in 2001, honors the dead. It's a poem called "The Names," and contains a name of someone lost in the World Trade Towers for every letter of the alphabet. The first stanza goes:

> *Yesterday, I lay awake in the palm of the night.*
> *A soft rain stole in, unhelped by any breeze.*
> *And when I saw the silver glaze on the windows,*
> *I started with A, with Ackerman, as it happened,*
> *Then Baxter and Calabro,*
> *Davis and Eberling, names falling into place*
> *As droplets fell through the dark.*

I treasure this poem because it is a way for me to remember, at any time, the ongoing sadness and loss that exist in the world as a result of that day. And to pay homage. To mark and remark the absence—and the presence—of those names.

But there's another poem about 9/11 that gives me courage to connect with life fully and make meaning of this event in my own mythology. The poem is called "Try to Praise the Mutilated World," and it's by Adam Zagajewski. The first and last lines read:

> *Try to praise the mutilated world.*
> *Remember June's long days,*
> *and wild strawberries, drops of wine, the dew.*
>
> . . .
>
> *and the grey feather a thrush lost,*
> *and the gentle light that strays and vanishes*
> *and returns.*

The line that means the most to me, I think, as I have "joined life" again after this life-changing event is "Try to praise the mutilated world," which the poet changes near the end of the poem to "Praise the mutilated world." Yes, I'm different after 9/11. Life is different. And I can remember a spring shower, a cloud shaped like a rabbit, a night lit by the full moon. I do praise "the mutilated world."

One of the things I notice the most when I listen to people talk about the outcomes of their tough transitions is this: Not even the worst thing imaginable—death, incurable disease, disaster, loss of homeland—has destroyed the human spirit. "Blessed be laughter," speaks the mother who lost two children. "There are more roads out there," asserts the man without a job. "What has sustained me over the years has been true friendships," says the immigrant who can't go home again. These individuals live in a place of Renewing, although their lives have been full of the toughest of transitions. "It is such a miracle that we are alive," one speaker tells us. "It's a Mystery. Life is so precious. So I do the best I can to appreciate life while I have it."

RENEWING: FROM STAY-AT-HOME-MOM TO CAREER WOMAN

When my children were in middle school, I decided to go back to school myself. I got a bachelor's and then a master's degree. My husband was supportive until I told him I was going to work. For the last two months of graduate school, my husband didn't speak to me. It was a tough transition.

I had always been active as a volunteer—a school trustee, PTO president, many activities at church. But that I would commit to a job with certain hours and a wage was a slap to my husband's ego. I knew I would never leave my husband and family; I just wanted to fulfill my own dreams. I felt I had to grow wings and fly.

I had a structure in place for care for the children and my husband; I kept my love for them up front. But I didn't give up my dream. I got a well-paying job that brought enormous personal growth. It was tough for months after I started to work. When I would walk into the room, my husband would give me a dirty look and walk out. But gradually he came to see and understand that I wasn't doing this to be independent and get away from my family. I was doing this out of a strong personal *conviction that if a person wants something and it doesn't harm anyone else, it's right for that person to go for that dream.*

Now ten years later it's clear that my family knows that there's never a point in life when we should choose not to grow intellectually and in any other way we desire. Even though I disrupted the structure of the family as it was before I went to work, they saw that I continued to give unconditional love and stayed completely engaged. My family saw this and they internalized it for themselves. In fact, our twenty-seven-year-old son is now back in school for hotel management. It's inspirational to instill confidence so that people know they can make changes in life when desired or necessary. Also, my husband and family have seen that personal growth allows you to give more of yourself. There ultimately was more of me for them because there was more of the true me being expressed by my work.

I am retired now and have a thriving little business on the side in silver plate. I won't ever stop exploring, following my convictions, and becoming more of who I am. It's an amazement to me what that commitment has given to me . . . and to my husband and family, though it continues to require many changes.

RENEWING: HONORING A FATHER ON THE ANNIVERSARY OF HIS DEATH

My sister sent the family this e-mail today, on this seventh anniversary of our father's death.

> *What nice memories I have of Daddy and our life together. It is hard to believe that seven years ago this morning was when he died. I will always remember how sad I was to arrive, after driving very fast to get there, and he had already died. But I will always remember the peacefulness that was on his face. He was always a trouper and that is what I plan to be as well. I got new tires on Monday (Bridgestone) and realized that Daddy would have heartily approved of my choice!*
> > *Love*
> > *Barbara*

And I sent this message to my sister and the rest of the family:

> *I'm eating a baked sweet potato with butter for Daddy today. I love that the last letter he was writing when he died—still on his table at his chair—was to a farmer in Georgia whose picture had been in the Market Bulletin. The man had grown a crop of sweet potatoes in a big washtub, and Daddy was writing to him to find out just exactly what the farmer did to accomplish this. Daddy, at age eighty-eight, wanted to grow some, too. Always the farmer with a love for growing things, including that huge garden he made at Mrs. Cranmore's after he retired from the ministry. Big as a small farm, it always looked to me.*
>
> *I woke up last night near the time he died and stayed awake for a while thinking about Daddy and talking to him. (Fortunately, they've done research at Harvard that shows that talking to a dead person is a healthy thing to do! ☺ That's true; they have done that research! I'm not just covering myself!— ☺)*
>
> *I don't think there could be a more authentic-to-himself man in the world than Daddy was.*
>
> *Love to all today*

RENEWING: AFTER A CAREER CHANGE THAT DIDN'T WORK OUT

I researched and consulted experts to a fare-thee-well, but nothing prepared me for the reality. Leaving the corporate world where I was in senior management to go into business for myself ended up fitting none of my pictures. I was warned that, without that corporate badge, I wouldn't have authority and influence behind me when I made a call to ask for business. But I naïvely thought that the relationships I had built over the years with corporate clients would hold, no matter that my desk was in a home office rather than the executive suite of an international company. After all, the team I had led for the corporation had won all kinds of international recognition in branding, advertising, and public relations. Surely I could parlay this experience and success into a small, thriving business.

It was a stark water-in-the-face wake-up to experience that a lot of *people won't even take your call once you're out on your own, people you have worked with for years. You're just not part of their "family," their work world. You've disappeared. The experts can tell you that you're starting over when you go into business for yourself, but they don't tell you how far down the elevator of starting over that you are dropping!*

There are so many problems you don't anticipate: Feeling a sense of loss and grief, even if you voluntarily left your corporate job. Missing people you shared so much with. They're going out after work, gossiping, being together. You're over here, lonely. And how to maintain momentum? You understand intellectually that you need to stay the course. But it's very difficult to keep motivated. You thought you knew what you were doing, but now you realize that there was a lot you didn't know. So you have to find some kind of motivation, whether it's stubbornness, fear, or concern for people depending on you. "How am I going to keep going in a hopeless situation?" You live this question day after day. It's almost physical—coming up with the energy to make yourself move forward. Digging down to some place to find some force of energy. You never realized how much the infrastructure of corporate life kept pulling you forward, whether you wanted it to or not. There was a constant flow of tasks given to you that served as your momentum.

What's so surprising, too, is how long it takes to do anything when you're on your own. Getting a letter out can take all day. In the corporate world you could ask someone to help and get your part done in five minutes. But by yourself you have to compose the letter, type it, go find an envelope. You have this wonderful brilliant idea, which could change the world, and you're trying to get your printer to work. You can't call tech support or your secretary.

I've learned that I didn't know much! The knowledge you have working in a corporation can be next to useless on your own. You don't get asked to do long-range consultative strategic-type things—what you were good at in the corporation. People now want you to do what they don't have time for, implement something rather than think strategically. And they want you to do it fast.

What I have learned—the hard way, I might add—is that I need to think of everything I do as an independent businessperson as being done in cooperation with someone else. You find a job—say a Web site—and you write it and hire someone else to do the database or the design. Or you come across someone who wants video streaming for a meeting and you say, "Oh, my company does that," and then you find someone who does it and hire them to work with you. I know people who have different business cards—some four, some eight—and they use the one in the moment that they think will get them the opening they need. I've learned that you really have to think outside the box, form ad hoc groups.

I'm asking myself now about what's next. I don't know many people who are happy in what they're doing right now. Were people ever happy in their work? In the past you got a job, worked, retired. We're more conscious now of work's possibilities as a source of fulfillment. My neighbor, who was a geologist with a major oil and gas company for twenty-five years, is now out of work. When we were standing out in our yards this week, one of us said to the other, "Well, could we sell pottery? Start an herb garden?" We were only halfway joking. What can we do and not get caught up in a meat-grinder economy? To do this, you have really to turn your back on consumer society, set your own agenda, and live very differently from any way you lived in the past.

What I see now is that sometimes a change just doesn't work out. But you can't just whine for life. I'm going to start over, with new plans and a new direction. Even though I'm at the end of this particular road, there are a lot more roads out there.

RENEWING: BEING A BREAST CANCER SURVIVOR

I know it's a cliché. But being a breast cancer survivor makes you so appreciate life. You actually get it—you get that we are all going to die. That you might die. I no longer take life for granted. It's been fourteen and a half years now since I had breast cancer—removal of breast, chemo, loss of my hair . . . the whole thing. I see every day of life now as a gift. I do my best to pay attention to what really matters.

Of course, I take care of myself with annual blood work. I down loads of vitamins (which I never took before) and take cholesterol-reducing medicine since I can't take estrogen because of the previous cancer. Recently my husband and I separated, and one of my first thoughts was, "You have to handle your stress; you cannot get cancer again over this." So it's never far from my mind that I will take as good care of myself as I possibly can.

I see now that having breast cancer was a quantum leap in learning for me. Not that you'd ever want to have something like this in order to learn! But it is an outcome. I read widely now in spiritual books; I've discovered a real passion for art, taking classes in looking at art, going to galleries. I go on silent retreats and to conferences in places like Cape Cod where I not only learn uplifting things but enjoy the beautiful surroundings. I have taken up hiking and spent the week after Christmas this past year hiking in Big Bend National Park. I have a little shack on the bay where I spend a lot of weekends just being quiet and looking at the water. I have been changed by this event in the best of ways. I have such a deeper engagement with living.

I'm moved by the love and care of my friends. I'm moved by beauty. I'm moved by life. I am a breast cancer survivor who is filled with gratitude for everything.

RENEWING: LIFE AFTER THE DEATHS OF TWO ADULT CHILDREN

My daughter died at forty-eight of lung cancer; my son at fifty of multiple sclerosis and results of an earlier accident of being hit by a car. Charles was an actor who had performed at the Ashland Shakespeare Festival among other places. Peggy was beautiful and talented. Peggy died one August and Charles died the next August. It was a horrible shock. I was just barely coming out after the first year when the second death occurred.

Some people ask why I'm not bitter and angry. What would be the point of that? It wouldn't make any difference but would just make a horrible picture of a shriveled-up person. That would be such a waste of one's life the way I see it.

My daughter and son are always there in the daily mix of my life. Memory is such an enriching thing. I have a kitschy little angel that my daughter gave me. She carried this little angel with her into the hospital. Now it sits on the windowsill in my study. I think almost every day of stories about my children—seeing my son onstage, getting so many cards from my daughter all the time—and I am happy to remember them. I have written Morning Pages every day since 1993 and good memories of times with my children show up in there.

Since they both died in August, one year apart, I find that month very hard. So I have a project now for every August. I write a poem each morning every day of the month.

I have wonderful friends to laugh with and cry with. Gradually, I've realized just how important laughter is. You know, even in a memorial service, stories will be told about the deceased person and the audience will laugh, even then. Laughter is one of the ways we remember what happened. I'm in a story circle—we call ourselves "Writers of the Purple Page"—and once a month we get together to read what we've written that month. We laugh a lot in that group.

Of course, dark thoughts come. I sit every morning, and through that meditation activity I've come to recognize my thoughts and see their patterns. If the sadness is a kind of thought related to missing my children, I know that's just part of the situation, not bad, just normal. I don't push these thoughts away, and I also don't dwell on them. But if the thoughts are debilitating kinds of thoughts—like "Could I have done anything that would have made things different for either my son or my daughter?"—then I know I can make conscious choices. I can refuse to stick with that thought.

I wrote one poem called "No and Yes" about choosing to be joyful.

No and Yes

I want to say NO
No to regret
No to guilt
No to depression
No to over-commitment

And YES
Yes to knowing when enough is enough
Yes to what is most important
　　and knowing what that is
Yes to taking care
　　to knowing what that is
Yes to living joyfully
　　and making that choice every day.

Yes to the song of myself
　　and to connection
　　to community
　　and living its richness

Yes to this moment
　　Just as it is.

I so appreciate this thing called someone's life, so appreciate having had the chance to be part of someone else's life and having them in my life. So I just don't get bogged down in regret. I remember the good parts of that.

You know, finally, you have just to get the absurdity of life. Life is so different from what I experienced as a child or even in young adulthood. How little we know about why we are here. Life is so precious. And life is so brief. And it is such a miracle that we are alive. It's a Mystery. So I do the best I can to appreciate life while I have it.

RENEWING: EVEN WHILE AGING

I know that, in my late seventies, I'm much closer to the end than the beginning. Aging is bound to come. I get depressed when I look in the mirror. Last year I stopped taking hormones because my doctor thought I might be at risk for a stroke, and I think I've aged ten years in that one year. I see changes in my body, in muscle tone for instance. I got new glasses the other day, and I was astonished at being able to see so many more wrinkles. Aging is just pretty much going to happen. On the other hand, I feel good. I exercise. I eat healthfully. All that is positive.

I have to say there is some sense of urgency. I'm very aware that I haven't got that much time left. So the big question is what to do in that period of time. I decided this week I was going to focus on coming up with a Law of How I Use My Time. I'm going to reorder my priorities. Top priority is going to be getting rid of stuff. I've bought a lot of books on decluttering but so far all they have done is make more clutter, being stacked here and there. But I have a new book called Keeping Life Simple and I am going to put some of that into practice. A second priority is to balance outside and inside activities. I've noticed lately that when I have a block of time in my calendar for something where I have to show up at a certain time, my energy level drops. I'm paying attention to that.

But I know the things—outside and inside—that give me pleasure. There is my writing group. And I go to line dancing at the senior citizen center every Monday and have for three years. I'm in the Listening Ministry at my church so on a regular basis I go to visit a person who is in grief or trouble of some sort. I have friends who are still working, and I go out to lunch with them. I play duets with a friend on the piano, something we have done for sixteen years. There is a huge literature from composers for one piano, four hands. Last year we hired a coach and since then we have played in several recitals. It is pure joy. Such fun to play.

RENEWING: LIFE AS A CHILDLESS COUPLE

My husband and I now know that we will never have children. We never anticipated that this would be the shape of our lives. Surgery precluded my ever getting pregnant. We accepted that. But I still hoped for adoption, although my husband wavered on that subject. We came very close once to getting a three-day-old child but legal and personal complications arose. That experience was the lowest point for me. For weeks afterward, I would stand at the kitchen sink, crying. Scenes would flash in front of my eyes: making molasses cookies with our little girl, teaching her to embroider, walking the nature trail behind the house with her and my husband. It was like a black, empty hole that I was *looking into, knowing every one of those images was a fantasy. I grieved for months . . . well, probably even years.*

I am at peace about our lives today, however. We have now been married almost thirty years, and we consider ourselves a two-person family. We know that we are different from our friends who have children, and we are clear that we've missed both the good and the bad of it. We were talking about some family heirlooms the other day, and my husband said, "Well, who are we going to give them to?" And when I'm making photograph albums sometimes I think, "Why am I still doing this? Who is going to care? Who is even going to want them?" So we do acknowledge the absence of children; we speak sometimes with regret about the end of the genetic line that each of us is. We talk about what we have probably missed. But then when we see friends whose children don't care anything about visiting them or whose children have become addicts or angry dropouts, we realize anew that having a family does not always mean having a close connection with children.

I can still feel times of deep sadness that I was never a mother. I wish I had been. But I read something several years ago that I still rely on today. It was a discussion of gaps in our lives, losses, things we were never able to have that we wanted desperately. The writer, Ann Ulanov, put it this way:

> We must see a way to receive into awareness our gaps, a way that neither represses them altogether nor falls into a state of identity with them. Leaning on God means holding in continuous awareness the gaps that occur in our being. This way goodness comes out of evil, for our awareness extends our continuity of being onto the other side of the gaps, around the gaps, holding them, receiving them in a persistent line like a necklace alternating knots and pearls. We grow around our wounds and come to be able to sustain them in the larger central sequences of our lives.

Then Ulanov goes on to warn of what happens when we do not extend our being to the other side of the gap but instead stay only in the knot of the thread. If we do not go on despite "all the gaps and violations of our being,"

> Where there should be a whole fabric of being, holes appear like lost stitches. Where there should be a firm foundation of being to stand upon, cracks and fissures appear and we fall through. We disregard the larger fabric that holds the holes . . . we extend the dead air spaces instead of building up the solidity within us.

From these words I glean a life-giving truth: that though I will never mother a child, I can over time extend the continuity of my being onto the other side of the gap of that missing. I can say today that not just the knots in the thread but both the knots and the pearls make up the necklace of my life. I have "grown around my wound" and do contain the absence of a child in the "larger central sequences" of my life. For both my husband and me Ann Ulanov's solidity has built up within us.

RENEWING: THREE DECADES AFTER LOSING ONE'S HOMELAND

My family and I first fled Pakistan when civil war was about to break out, thirty years ago. My uncle had already disappeared, and we knew that he was dead. So we felt we had to take our leave as quickly as we could. One day I was a young high school student from a privileged family about to take her A Levels in Karachi, and the next day I was a refugee and immigrant standing in the snow of Grand Forks, North Dakota, where my older brother was studying on a student visa.

The loss of not getting to take my A Levels, tests for which I had been preparing for two years, was profound. For the first time in my school life I had risen to the top of my class. I finally felt I would prove to myself and to others that I was worthwhile and I would achieve something in my life. Putting forth a stellar performance for these exams that I had studied so hard for meant everything to me. But I never got the chance to prove to myself what I could have achieved. I lost this chance all because we wanted to avoid a war that ended up lasting only two months.

It was only when I got a letter in the mail saying I had made the honor roll in the American college I was attending and then when I went on to make a 4.0 average in the next semester that my self-confidence started to rise again.

When I first arrived in America, I had no idea what was in store for me. My first impressions were exactly the opposite of what I had always imagined. Arriving in the small town of Grand Forks, in the farm belt of America, I may as well have landed on the moon. I assumed that, since I thought I knew everything about the U.S., the Americans would also be just as knowledgeable about my country. You can imagine the shock I felt the first time someone asked me where I was from and I replied, "Pakistan." "Oh," the person replied, "Buxton." Buxton was a little farming town, outside Grand Forks. "Maybe this person thinks I am a Native American," I said to myself. "No," I insisted, "PAK-IS-TAN." "Where is that?" was the reply. I answered, "It is a country close to India. You ever heard of India?"

Very soon after we settled into our new life in Grand Forks, we came to realize the enormity of our mistake in leaving Pakistan in such a hurry. The plan was that my father would be able to find a job, and my older sister and I would also work to supplement the household income. My father's government work experience left him with few job options in Grand Forks, North Dakota, but my sister and I landed jobs as waitresses at the Mexican Village, the only local Mexican restaurant.

I still laugh at my naïveté. When I first knew we would have to get jobs, I really panicked. I had never worked a day in my life. I was supposed to be going to school, enjoying life. I had never before given any thought to earning a living. Abbu, my father, was supposed to handle where the money came from. But it did not take long for the seriousness of the situation to hit me like a hard punch in my stomach.

So started my stint at the Mexican Village. The first few days were absolutely disastrous for me. My feet hurt like I didn't know they could. My shoulders and arms ached from carrying the heavy food trays. Once when trying to set down an order, I spilled boiling hot cheese down my right hand. It took extreme control not to throw the plate down. Having never been exposed to Mexican food, I could not tell the difference between a taco and a burrito. When I brought out an order, I had no *idea who got what. I would hold out the order and ask my customers to pick out their plates. For me this experience was humiliating and embarrassing. My customers had a much better sense of humor. They took my total ignorance and incompetence in stride and helped me learn how to recognize the different items on the menu and actually tipped me generously. Maybe they felt sorry for me. All this was far away from my life in Pakistan. How could everything change so quickly?*

But here I am today, thirty years here. My husband from India, whom I met in college, and I are longtime American citizens. Our son was born here. And as much as I am an American, I still feel that Pakistan is "home." I find myself now and then thinking, "What if"—even about those A Levels, if you can believe it—but I know now this is not a good way to live. My life is so full now, and there is always some loss there, too. But I'm able to ask myself now, "If I had not experienced all those hard times as an immigrant, would I have made of my life what I have made?" I still don't like having to spell my name out every time I have to give it to someone on the phone. I still don't like my mail coming addressed to Mr. instead of Mrs. because my first name is not American and people don't know if the name is male or female. I didn't like my son getting detained at airports after 9/11 when he was born here and is as much an American citizen as anyone.

But what have sustained me over the years have been true friendships. And now having the luxury to do things like take a writing class or travel to Europe with a friend for my fiftieth birthday. I'm writing a book about my life as an immigrant, and that helps me understand myself and my past better. There's a sense of accomplishment, too. It doesn't matter if it gets published; I'm doing this purely for myself. And the writing has been selected for a Writer's Gallery by the university where I took the class and people ask to have copies of what they hear me read, so I do know the story speaks to people.

I'm clear that I have something to offer the world. I'm committed to being a good wife, a good mother, a good citizen. And I'm an excellent and successful businesswoman, co-owner with my husband of a home-building firm that has had more than twenty years of thriving activity.

I will always keep Pakistan in my life. I listen every Saturday to radio programs of Pakistani music here in my city. I buy filmi, soundtracks from Pakistani and Indian movies (which are all musicals no matter what else they are). This filmi music has new hits every week. I enjoy the beat of the music. It's lighthearted, romantic stuff. Almost all the songs are love songs with lofty titles like "Joishq ka matlab," which means "The Meaning of Love," or "Main terihoon," "I Am Yours." I also listen to Ravi Shankar's recordings and play CDs of religious chants in praise of Allah. Nusrat Fateh Ali Khan, now deceased, is perhaps one of the most famous singers of Pakistani classical music. He puts famous Urdu poetry to music, and many of his songs are praising God. This master takes me back to a place in time that I almost forgot for many years existed. He sings in a style known as gawli, *where the singers improvise as they go along and the pieces can be as long as twenty-five minutes.*

I make a real effort to explain Islam to people who are interested; for while I'm not a religious person, I am very concerned about the misrepresentation of Islam that extremists have displayed to the world. I tell them that Islam has been hijacked by a few extremists, who interpret the religion in a warped way which justifies their actions. The 1.6 billion Muslims of the world do not agree with the extremists. I try to make people understand that they should try to look beyond the stereotypes. I recommend that people read Dr. Karen Armstrong's book on Islam.

And Pakistani food is phenomenal. If I ever feel lost and want to feel that I am back home I eat chawal *(rice),* dahl *(lentils),* subzi *(vegetables), and* chapati *(flatbread).* Rus malia *is the most heavenly dessert in the world—little balls of white flour and ricotta cheese, a bit like doughnut holes, soaked in milk and sugar and served chilled. For me, the smells of these particular foods are a definite trip down memory lane. They take me home!*

RENEWING: A LOST PERSON ALWAYS PRESENT

He was the first person close to me who ever died. He was my mentor, the teacher I wanted to be. And he just passed right out of my life. He went out so quickly, so irretrievable, so irrevocably. I couldn't go to the funeral, so I didn't get a chance to say good-bye. I did say good-bye one

night out in the backyard of my house, but things still always seemed
unfinished. But something happened recently that allowed me to see the
place Mac has and will always have in my life. It happened as I was
completing a writing seminar prior to taking my doctoral orals.

I started to make peace after an experience in a graduate writing
class. Dr. Graves, a professor in a writing seminar, had instructed us
students: "Read Scott Momaday's tribute to his grandmother—'Now
that I can have her only in memory, I see my grandmother . . . stand-
ing at the wood stove on a winter morning and turning meat in a great
iron skillet; sitting at the south window, bent over her beadwork.' Then
write a model of Momaday's paragraph, using someone as the subject
whom you can have now only in memory."

I chose Mac, my teacher and mentor, as the subject for my para-
graph. This is what I wrote:

Now that I can only have Mac in memory, I recall the sense
of continuity that was shattered when he fell off a road in
East Tennessee and out of all our lives forever. I think of
Mac and I see Kris Kristofferson, grizzled beard, deep voice,
sparkling, deep-set eyes. He was my teacher, my colleague,
my friend, who showed me how to step across a boundary
and leave all the tangled messes behind. It was the crossing
that mattered.

Once we were going into a Japanese restaurant. You had
to cross a little bridge to get to it. Mac was bothered by
something that had happened at the university . . . I didn't
know what it was, but something had disturbed him. As we
started to go into the restaurant, Mac said, "When I go
across this bridge, I'm leaving the problem here and I'm
going over there. It's not going to be with me anymore, and
we're going to go ahead and have our time together."

We did have a wonderful time, and it was one of my
greatest lessons in life, watching Mac do that. What he
taught me was to let go of things and move on. I think that's
why I had such a hard time letting go of him—because he
taught me how to let go and I couldn't imagine letting go of
that. Continuity. The smooth movement from here to

there, from then to now, and on into tomorrow without getting caught in any one place too long. That's what he taught me, and it's always with me.

I'm convinced the reason we are here is to remember, if we understand memory to be that uniquely human ability to create from the past a sense of meaning in the present and an anticipation of possibility in the future.

RENEWING: ILL AND INFIRM PARENTS

Both of my parents are in their late eighties and are not well at all. I stare death in the face with them intimately and often. Yet there is something amazing. Speechless. I experience joy in the very midst of suffering. Now, on one level I would like to live a superficial circus life. I don't want to go deep. Yet with my parents' closing lives I have immense light in my life, as well as sadness. Because of my engagement with their circumstances, I have had profound observations.

So many times I have said, "My heart is breaking." And the truth is my heart has been broken open. This means my heart is now open. I saw a new book the other day titled Breaking Open, *and I thought, "That's it exactly. I've been broken open."*

I know now there are two realities: the reality I live in daily that requires me to take responsibility, to be accountable, and the reality that is Other . . . which I see only in the tiniest glimpses. Last week I visited a homeless shelter and at one point in the afternoon I realized . . . I truly am these people. We are all one. I knew this intellectually but that afternoon I experienced it with a deep understanding. I look at my parents at times and say, on the one hand, "Now, you are not your parents. Don't over-identify with them." Then I will experience that other reality where we are and the same. All connected. Or I will see expressions of immense loving compassion, of sheer unadulterated love. And I know that we all are one.

I've been a seeker all my life. I'm so grateful that I'm not alone in this. I have absolute certainty that if I thought I were alone in taking care of my parents at the ends of their lives, it would be too much, even with family and friends. But I know the angels are there. The community of saints is there. I study the spiritual practices of the Celts and the Native Americans, who knew so much about the Spirit World. So I pay attention to what I can't see as much as what I can. I honor synchronicity. This Other reality sustains me even while I go about the daily acts of living and caring for my parents.

RENEWING: MANAGING AIDS

I have had AIDS for four and a half years, and that means that it's a kind of a little miracle for me. I remember when I was first told I had AIDS, eighteen months was about all I thought I had. And here I am. And I don't know why. I don't know why. I know that I am really grateful. I think my life now is in a place of equilibrium, a place of balance most of the time. And also in a place of continued dealing with new problems. There is so much constant loss in my community. Last week three people died that I cared about. How does one fully integrate that? I don't know. But I do know that I am able now to live my life fully. To dream and to plan for the future. I guess the thing I would want to say to people who have the virus in their bodies . . . I would say to not hold back. To live your life powerfully and fully. To be willing to take whatever risks are necessary for you to feel happy with life and fulfilled. To go for it. To step beyond what you think your limits are. And to those people that are experiencing AIDS in the lives of others, I'd say, "Thank you." I would say that you are our angels. You are the people who are helping us get through this because we can't do it alone. We have to teach you how to take care of us and we need you there to help us through this dark night.

RENEWING: AFTER A FINANCIAL LOSS

Ten years ago, when my family and I first experienced the financial loss that cost us everything we had accumulated for almost twenty years, I felt, first of all, nothing but dumb. How could I have made the business decisions that I made? How could I have thought investing where I did was the right thing to do? In one fell swoop, with one company going under, we had gone from a home with a swimming pool and private schools for the boys to living with relatives. I mean, it was total devastation, total loss. On many days I could feel nothing except despair. And I spent so much time wondering about my own worth and worried about what others think when they see where I am now.

But I had props that never let me down: My wife's sticking with me even though my decisions had cost us everything. My siblings' constant actions and words that said, "You are a good man and we believe in you." The response of a gentleman to whom a friend introduced me who, even though he and I had just met, spent several months helping me work out a business plan for a new future. That plan ultimately didn't work out, but this man's commitment to me, a stranger to him, changed how I thought about myself. Another businessman, a friend of one of my siblings, gave his time to me, both in person and on the telephone, helping me think through what my career options were and what first steps I might take.

I had to start from the bottom; I mean, the bottom. Instead of a six-figure income, I now made $6.50 an hour doing temp work in an area that wasn't even my field. Then it was three years on the road in a job that left me almost no time with my family and with little energy to do anything but meet the demands of my work. But, you know, something funny happened along that road. One day, as I was working, an absolutely new thought hit me: Perhaps as I did this traveling job, going into many different types of businesses, I might find just the kind of work I'd like to do in the future. This new idea put a whole different spin on the daily drudgery of my work. Now whenever I went into a place I not only was trying to sell the product I was there to sell but I was looking around and thinking, "What about this industry? What about this kind of company?" These questions gave me a lift and made the job I was doing only temporary in my mind, though in reality I worked at it for three long years. But I was now imagining something else, thinking about something new.

And sure enough that's what happened. On one of my trips, I did business with a firm that was tops in its field, a field I didn't even know existed before. That field is where I ended up getting a really good job. Sometimes I think of it as penance—that long journey from $6.50-an-hour temp work to a five-days-a-week-on-the-road sales job that often felt like garbage compared to the work I do now—but I think of the life my family and I have now as the reward.

I make much less now than I did in those fly-high days before the financial fall. One thing that I have learned, though, is that my worth is not tied to my paycheck. It's been a process to gain that belief. And I still have to manage my thoughts sometimes when I think about where we could be now if I hadn't made that stupid financial mistake. But I don't stay there long. I turn as quickly as I can to what are the good actions to take now. And I also turn to thoughts of gratitude that my family and I are where we are now. Sure, I have to be a financial realist, and we do have concerns and worries, and we've given up things so I can have a job that is fulfilling but not as lucrative as my earlier career. But I'm internally satisfied much more than I'm worried, and as long as that's so I'll feel good about continuing to do what I do.

Someone asked me the other day how a person can feel any personal power when you're down, feeling the lowest you've ever felt. I answered, "The personal power comes from knowing that I made the choices that led to good things in the past and I made the choices later that led to bad things happening. And I can make new and different choices today." There is something strong in knowing that your choices matter and that you can make new ones. I said to myself early on in this process, "You screwed up. Now you have to do what's necessary to get to where you want to be from here. Start right here. Move yourself forward from this point." So every day it's a matter of getting up, determined to keep going. You've got to keep getting up and keep on doing whatever there is to do today, the best way you can do it.

I'm a different person today, and I think a better person. I know I'm much less afraid. My attitude is now that the light at the end of the tunnel isn't a freight train; it's the light of a beautiful, wonderful day.

WHAT ARE THE POSSIBILITIES IN RENEWING?

CELEBRATING

Well, the first order of business is to celebrate, wouldn't you say? When we can say that the tough transition is no longer something we have to deal with every day, it's time to acknowledge the work that has been done. It isn't that there is no aftermath. It isn't that everything is now behind us. It's not that we aren't still sad or mad or worried on occasion. But we do experience now a "new normal." We feel more balanced. Clearly our equilibrium is more steady.

Ten of my women friends and I got together one night recently to discuss the tough transitions we had moved through in the last while, and the evening did turn into a celebration. It was like that children's song . . . "Count your many blessings, count them one by one."

What was there to be happy about?

We now had more confidence in our ability to deal with change.
We were much clearer about what really mattered to us.
We honored how important certain people had been to the success of our process.
We relied on the power of our ability to make choices.
We connected more with God, Spirit, Holy Creator—whatever name by which each of us called the Mystery that was bigger than all of us.

Celebration for your tough transition may be as simple as telling a coworker that you feel more yourself than in a long time. It may be as enjoyable as having a backyard barbecue and inviting friends and neighbors. It may be going on a weekend retreat. Or setting out a big bowl of berries and whipped cream for everyone to enjoy. Going on a trip. Having a next-step graduation party. The important thing is to take notice. To name. To draw a line of demarcation. That was then; now is now. And I'm well . . . capable . . . whole . . . settled . . . full of hope . . . energetic . . . anxious to serve others . . . whatever is the forward place you now find yourself.

So, in whatever way suits, the thing to do when we know Renewing has occurred in a tough transition is to celebrate.

CONTRIBUTING TO OTHERS

Among the creative and victorious outcomes scientists tell us we can expect when we work to integrate a tough transition are:

Assessment that one is more tolerant and more wise
Experience of increased capacity to appreciate people and things
Achievement of a considered faith
Capacity for empathy
Ability to think beyond oneself
Increased sense of humor

What better to do than to contribute to others from these outcomes? There is no better volunteer for a local grief support group than someone who has not just *gotten through* a tough transition but who can talk about a genuine renewed commitment for living. Programs that help welfare recipients make the transition back into the workplace; centers that serve women working to create a new, safe life for themselves; tutoring programs for

If the success or failure of this planet and of human beings depended on how I am and what I do, how would I be and what would I do?

Buckminster Fuller

young adults who need a hand up to get a job and learn basic life skills—to volunteer in such environments would be to take one's own experience and multiply that exponentially in helping others.

People who renew their active interchange with life after a tough transition do all kinds of wonderful things. They start support groups; they write books and songs and paint pictures; they volunteer in hospitals and hospices; they teach tap dancing at the senior center. There's a bigness about these people, a generosity, that—like the fabled honey found in the lion's carcass—came after meeting and facing danger and coming out a victor.

IDENTIFYING WHAT SUSTAINED

It's very satisfying to make a list of those things that sustained us when we were in the thick of our tough transition. My friends and I, on our celebration night, made this list of what we called "containers that held us" during the hard work of the change:

Remembering specific ancestors as a touchstone for courage

Returning often to a powerful image: for example, a yellow forsythia bush in a dream; cupped hand holding us

Recalling a sacred word: for example, On the day I did call, you did answer me: strength of soul you gave me.

Thinking about words spoken to us by others who had been in a similar situation: Find three things to be thankful for every day; imagine that if she has done that, I can do that, too.

Praying: feeling enfolded like a bear hug

Reading: Tolstoy, James, Dostoyevsky, Jane Austen

The Aztecs have three spiritual laws:
Thou shalt not lie.
Thou shalt not be a coward.
Thou shalt acknowledge the wonder.

Listening to "information" around me: yoga, wise person, art, good
     smells
Doing things that gave a sense of vacation from your hard life at the
     moment
Playing music: Opera Goes to the Movies, Moonstruck, Mahalia
     Jackson, The Pearl Fishers

When you make your own list, it can serve as a touchstone
for the future, when you are once again going to find yourself in
another tough transition. These things, you can remember,
helped in the past and they can help later.

ACKNOWLEDGING ALL WHO HELPED

"These are the beings through whom God loved me," Saint-
Martin, the eighteenth-century philosopher, once said, speaking
of those who had cared for him. It is a wonderful thing when we
find our balance after a tough transition to think of everyone who
helped us, knowingly or not, as we worked through the challenging time. Recently I received in the mail a small, beautiful book
of Celtic morning and evening prayers. In the flyleaf the gift giver
had written: "A year ago my mother died. A book you wrote about
grief and loss has been like a bible for me, always on my night-
stand. I wanted to send you this small token of my deep appreciation for the help you have given me." I was touched. The act of
this distant reader inspired me to think of people I could acknowledge who had been particularly helpful in the tough transitions of my own life this past year.

COLLECTING MEANINGFUL WORDS

Ralph Waldo Emerson once said we should "select and collect all
those words and sentences that in all your reading have been to
you like the blast of trumpet." This is a most consolidating thing

to do when we reach the Renewing experiences of a tough transition. And really an ancient one, too. The Greeks believed that you could actually form your character by quotations, bits of conversation, sections of a play or a book that you chose to copy. But form your character or not, words and sentences that hit us "like the blast of trumpet" when we traverse a tough transition exist like a treasure chest of jewels always available to us.

I keep such a book for myself—I call it my commonplace book. In addition to my journal entries, I copy lines that I like, quotations I come across, things that teach me or entertain me or lift my spirits. I can follow the trajectory of a tough transition I've experienced by following the pages of my commonplace book. Here are examples:

An editorial in the *New York Times*:

> Good Boll Weevil News: Over a century ago, the mighty boll weevil left its home in Mexico and began devouring cotton fields across the South and West. Now, after 25 years of spraying and more sophisticated antiweevil weaponry, the federal Department of Agriculture has finally forced this wily little beetle into submission.

First of all, how does this announcement merit a place in my commonplace book? And how in the world could it speak to me in a positive way as I faced a transition in my urban life?

The boll weevil was central in our family mythology: how the Harpers lost everything and yet how they persevered. My father remembered the first day anyone ever saw a boll weevil in the cotton field. Daddy was only seven years old when he spotted the strange little winged creature; but when he was near ninety he could still describe the scene as if it had been yesterday. Such a tiny insect . . . such a devastating victor. Cotton production on the family acreage in Georgia went from three hundred bales per acre to ninety-eight bales per acre within the year. The next year it was even worse. Grandma finally had to make bread out of pig shoats (rough grain bought for the hogs) and pick wild poke salad for greens. It got so bad that one day the man from the bank in Brooks came and repossessed the mules. So there was not even a way to pull the plows except for the men and boys to harness themselves and strain back and forth across the fields.

In my own childhood, though those devastating years were far in the past, Grandma and Grandpa would tell me the stories of the boll weevil while we sat in the farm kitchen eating a piece of Grandma's apple stack cake. The climax of the stories my grandparents told was always the way they found to go on even during those toughest of times. So no wonder that when I saw the announcement in the newspaper about the conquering of the boll weevil I would cut it out and put it in my commonplace book. What better story could I mull over as I summoned up the courage to take steps forward in tough transitions?

I had to laugh at the cartoon I had put in my commonplace book at about the same time. Four dogs are pictured, each in a separate frame. The title of the cartoon is "Insomniac Dogs: Why They Can't Sleep." Each dog gives his reason for lying awake at night. "I'm not where I expected to be in life right now," says the dog who looks like a German shepherd. "Why aren't there more pugs on television?" laments the bulldog. "Other dogs always seem to be having all the fun," complains the spaniel. And then there's the dachshund: "I think I might be color-blind."

Yes, I was laughing at the cartoon but I was also laughing at myself. Which has to be good for you when you're struggling with all that heaviness of a tough transition.

I come upon a page of newsprint taped into my commonplace book. "Fruits of the Desert Sun," is the headline. The article is all about making tasty dishes out of spiny, bristly leaves of a prickly pear cactus. Boiling the pulp of the red fruits of the cactus, blending with lemon juice, straining out the seeds, and then drizzling the warm red syrup over a piece of cheesecake. I see the lesson here, at this point in the tough transition of moving. I must take the things that feel like cactus spines at the moment—not enough room for everything in our new place; missing old friends who haven't called; crystal glasses broken in transit that we can't re-place—and make something useful out of them.

The lines of an ancient poem given to me by a friend seem like a lovely end punctuation, marking the integration of our tough transition. "I am back," the poem reads. "I am back, anchor in the sand, face washed with dew. I hear you." It was a new life, a new day.

SEEING LIFE AS ONGOING NEW TRANSITIONS

One of the creative and victorious outcomes researchers tell us we can expect when we have navigated our way through a tough transition is increased wisdom. One piece of that new wisdom has to be a recognition that we will never be finished with tough transitions. Yes, we will work our way through this particular difficult time and that particular change. But we'll never get to a place in life where there are no more transitions. We aren't going to get so good at the skill of navigating through hard places that the changes don't show up for us as a challenge. Even though I've studied, thought, and written about tough transitions for almost twenty years, I still have to be reminded from time to time by people who love me that I will get through a particular difficult transition. My husband will sometimes jokingly say to me, "You need to sit down and read your own books." There's no life insurance policy one can take out and certainly no author one can catch on to that will bring freedom from the hard work of dealing with tough transitions.

What can we come to understand through our gained wisdom? That there is a process that can conclude with victorious outcomes and a sense of Renewing. That I can make the decisions and the choices that allow me to navigate as smoothly or as roughly through a hard time as is possible in that moment. That a transition is about so much more than what appears. Yes, circumstances and situations around me change, and that launches me into the necessity to navigate myself through a difficult time. But something much more profound is taking place. I am being changed myself. And those changes in me stand to make me more capable, compassionate, and increased in my capacity to put life's ups and downs in perspective. When I begin another tough transition, I have all these learnings and all these valuable experiences at my disposal.

LISTENING TO A FESTIVAL OF MUSIC

What a plethora of choices we have for music when we reach Renewing. Music that celebrates. Music that sounds out gratitude. Music that dances. Music that enlarges. Friends and professionals have suggested selections like these:

Alison Krauss's bluegrass recordings
Ragtime music
Irish jigs
Anything by June or Johnny Cash
Daniel Kobialka's "Path of Joy"
Beethoven's Ninth Symphony (*Ode to Joy*)
Mozart's Coronation Mass
Mascagni's Intermezzo from *Cavalleria Rusticana*
Rimsky-Korsakov's symphonic suite *Scheherazade*, op. 35, third movement
Rachmaninoff's Piano Concerto no. 2
Khachaturian's Adagio of Spartacus and Phrygia from *Spartacus*
Anything by Willie Nelson, but particularly "On the Road Again"

These suggestions are only that. The real fun in Renewing is picking your own music!

DOING NEW THINGS

To consolidate our gains after finding equilibrium we might take note of the research of Gregory Berns, MD, at Emory University in Atlanta. Dr. Berns suggests that novelty is the key to a satisfying life. If we want to cultivate happiness, we can seek new things to do that stimulate and engage us. This doesn't mean crazy things that require one to risk life and limb, just things that are new. Things that you've never done before. Not only does doing new things keep the pleasure areas of the brain stimulated but the action also helps build emotional resilience since some novelties turn out to be great and some turn out to be something you wouldn't be interested in repeating. These new things can fall into categories such as: trying a sport or physical activity you've never done before; doing something intellectual, like attending a lecture on a subject you've never thought about before or reading a book or watching a movie that you would not have thought of reading or viewing in the past; making a connection with someone new; and doing something that takes you into the transcendent, such as spiritual experiences, art, or music. Doing new things is not a quick fix that promises eternal happiness, but it is an avenue to satisfaction, which is a very fine foundation on which to build ongoing happiness.

> Start at least one new hobby every two years. Start early and by the time you retire you'll have at least 15 options of things to do.
>
> Anne Durrum Robinson

LIVING OUT OUR VALUES

I don't think I have ever met anyone who has done the hard work of moving through a tough transition and has reflected on her or his experience who doesn't want to make some kind of contribution out of what he or she has just gone through. There's just something about weathering a difficult time and reaching a place where one finds a new equilibrium that makes us want to be of use to others who find themselves in a similar situation. I think this is one of the true hallmarks of reaching Renewing.

I saw this in action recently. Parents whose twenty-one-year-old son had died in a freak accident at a concert spoke to me about their pain and confusion and I remembered a lovely woman who had told me over lunch a few months earlier how she and her husband had dealt with the death of their eighteen-year-old son in an automobile accident many years before. I said to the couple in front of me, "Let me call Mary Grayson. I feel sure she and her husband would talk with you, and I know you will enjoy meeting them." I made the phone call. The two couples—total strangers to each other—met for an early Sunday morning breakfast. They talked for three hours and made plans to meet again. The newly bereaved parents called and thanked me for making the connection. But what was remarkable—but not at all surprising, for I've seen it so many times—was how much gratitude Mary and her husband expressed to me for the opportunity they had to share their experiences and what they had learned from them.

People's priorities clearly have changed by the time they find a place of "new normal" in their lives. And so often these new priorities flow out of a deepened commitment to the inner life. Perhaps it's a return to church after a long absence. Perhaps it's a commitment to a period of quiet and reflection before going to work. Or a new interest in theology or world religions or journal writing or dream work. Whatever the expression, the life of the Spirit, the pull of the heart begins to take precedence. It is intangibles that matter more now—a sense of freedom, of having space and time just to be, of going deep to experience what's there and what it's good for. Joseph Campbell told us a long time ago that our inner world was as fascinating and vast a domain as outer space. Part of our time in Renewing is spent exploring that inscape, recognizing for each of us that it is completely unique.

Finally, Yes

On the first Christmas after 9/11, my husband and I just couldn't find it in us to send our usual holiday letter, full of thises and thats about our lives. But we wanted to be in touch with our friends. So we wrote this communication:

> That Love is all there is,
> Is all we know of Love . . .
> Emily Dickinson

When it was time for us to sit down and write our 2001 Christmas letters to you, we found that we could not write the kind of letter we usually send. But we also were unwilling to forgo a Christmas message completely, since the events of 9/11 and after made us profoundly aware that our families, friends, acquaintances, and colleagues are at the center of what really matters in our lives. So from our hearts to yours, we would like to send these passages . . .

1. At the memorial service in New York City for British citizens who were lost in the World Trade Center attack, Prime Minister Tony Blair read from a novel, *The Bridge of San Luis Rey*, written in 1928 by the American novelist Thornton Wilder. The book takes as its starting point the true story of the collapse in 1714 of a rope bridge in the Andes—"the finest bridge in all Peru"—sending to their deaths in the gulf below the five travelers crossing at the moment the rope snapped. Mr. Blair read:

" 'Soon we shall die,' reflects a kindly survivor of the tragedy at the end of the novel, 'and all memory of these five will have left the Earth, and we ourselves shall be loved for a while and forgotten. But the love will have been enough; all the impulses of Love return to the Love that made them. Even memory is not necessary for love. There is a land of the living and a land of the dead and the bridge is love, the only survival, the only meaning.' "

2. I know this. Death, life, angels, rules, things happening now, things that will happen, high things, low things, nothing else in all the world can come between us and God's love. (Romans 8:38–39, World English translation)

May you be surrounded by Love this holiday season.

Then we signed our names.

Once Leonard Bernstein spent several weeks giving the Charles Eliot Norton Lectures at Harvard. His subject was "Whither Music," and in these lectures he explored the origins of music and the relationship between music and human physiology. I was fascinated by the entire series, which was published as a book, *The Unanswered Question*, following the lectures, but what I remember most was how Bernstein ended his last talk. "I no longer know what the question is," he said, "but I do know the answer is Yes."

"If I can keep in touch with possibility in my life," John S. Dunne reminds us, "if I can keep a sense of the road going 'past the view,' going 'ever on,' I can say 'Yes!' I can come to peace without losing hope."

The theologian Howard Thurman tells us that within each of us is a world where the great issues of our lives are determined. "It is here," he says, that "at long last the yea and nay of our living is defined."

The tough transitions we experience all throughout what we hope will be a long and fruitful life do call forth from us, ultimately, *a nay or a yea*.

For all the tearing up and tearing down that these transitions result in,

> Be joyful, though you have considered all the facts.
> Wendell Berry, poet, author

they do, in the end, become our growth points. It's like the wise person said: "For a long time it had seemed to be that life was about to begin—real life. But there was always some obstacle in the way, something to be got through first, some unfinished business, time still to be served, a debt to be paid. Then life would begin. At last it dawned on me that these obstacles were my life."

Transitions are the stuff of living.

And *Yes* is the way to live them.

In Summary: RENEWING

WHAT

Renewing experiences that are normal when we reach a steady state of balance after a tough transition include:

Recognizing that we have achieved some creative and victorious outcomes: ability to think beyond oneself, experience of new sense of play and freedom, achievement of a considered faith, increased ability to hold life's ups and downs in perspective, heightened sense of humor, among many others

Having new ideas and new vantage points

Acknowledging that we can be thrivers, doing something more than just surviving

Gaining insight into the many facets of hope and faith

Creating joy

WHEN

How do we know when Renewing arrives? There's not a magic equation . . . well, when I've done this much Responding and that much Reorganizing, it must be time for Renewing. The process is unpredictable . . . and different for every person. When does the experience of having a steady state of balance again occur? For some, it's a moment in time. Sitting at a picnic table under a lime tree, bright sun overhead, eating an Easter lunch, friends surrounding . . . suddenly there is an actual physically felt shift and you know that you are now in a different place. You sense a new equilibrium. You know that some integration of what had felt previously like pieces of yourself, fragments, has occurred; you now feel whole. For others it is a gradual, almost imperceptible movement toward Renewing. Perhaps it's on one day the desire to redo a room after months of lethargy, and at another time it's the awareness that you can now laugh about a situation that months before would have made you only angry. Maybe the new place or the new job or the new budget now seems like a "new normal." However Renewing shows up, it is our heightened awareness of life that makes possible the recognition.

WHERE

Reaching Renewing does not mean that we no longer have experiences of Responding, Reviewing, and Reorganizing. We can feel integrated and still break into unexplainable tears. We can be in a steady state of balance and be carried back by some event or thought to a past where there is yet something we can learn or see through reminiscing. We can be swept by gratitude and have a renewed interest in being with others at the same time that we are solving another sticky problem or retrieving another thread of purpose. Navigating your way through a difficult time is a dynamic, not a static, experience. And in Renewing, our experiences of all the places on the map continue to be present in a kind of spiral, some days less, some days more. The difference is that by the time we assess that we are in Renewing that spiral is upward-moving.

HOW

What are the possibilities in Renewing?

Celebrating
Contributing to others
Identifying what sustains
Acknowledging all who helped
Recollecting meaningful words
Living out our values
Listening to a festival of music
Doing new things

NOTES

PART ONE: PRELIMINARIES

Surveying the Terrain

Page 27

Although observers: See Institute of Medicine, *Bereavement: Reactions, Consequences, and Care*, p. 48.

PART TWO: NAVIGATING THE MAP

1. Responding

Page 34

Emotions Haywire: To read about these facts and more, see *Looking for Spinoza: Joy, Sorrow, and the Feeling Brain* by Antonio Damasio, pp. 27–80; *Shattered Assumptions: Toward a New Psychology of Trauma* by Ronnie Janoff-Bulman, pp. 64–69; and "The Heavy Cost of Chronic Stress," *New York Times*, December 17, 2002, p. D1.

In a positively regulated life; a deep and defining part; maintain the coherence: See Antonio Damasio's *Looking for Spinoza: Joy, Sorrow, and the Feeling Brain*, p. 36.

Page 35

120 milliseconds: See Antonio Damasio's *Looking for Spinoza: Joy, Sorrow, and the Feeling Brain*, p. 61.

"Emergency-mobilizing" chemicals: See Jonoff-Bulman's *Shattered Assumptions: Toward a New Psychology of Trauma*, p. 66.

Page 40

Some people's brains secrete special neurohormones: See Institute of Medicine, *Bereavement: Reactions, Consequences, and Care*, p. 162, and *The Anatomy of Bereavement* by Dr. Beverley Raphael, pp. 34, 40–42.

Page 42

Social emotions: See *Looking for Spinoza: Joy, Sorrow, and the Feeling Brain* by Antonio Damasio, pp. 43–46.

Page 43

Transition and commotion; terrible advisors: Ibid., pp. 63, 40.

Page 44

What kinds of assumptions: For a discussion of fundamental assumptions, chapters 8–10 in *Prospect and Retrospect*, edited by Gordon Pradl; and Ronnie Janoff-Bulman, *Shattered Assumptions*, pp. 3–25.

Page 53

W. H. Auden: To read this poem in full, check the Web site, http://poetry-pages.lemon8.nl/life/musee/museebeauxarts.htm

Page 73

Illnesses and accidents: See Raphael's *The Anatomy of Bereavement*, pp. 59–62 and 219–21; Parkes's *Bereavement*, p. 16; the Institute of Medicine's *Bereavement*, pp. 21–22, 26, 35, 40, and chapters 2–3; Davidson's *Understanding Mourning*, pp. 21–22, 70–72.

Page 76

William Sunderman: See *The Economist* magazine, March 20, 2003.

Page 78

The Story of the Weeping Camel: See *National Geographic* magazine, "Behind the Scenes," June 2004.

Page 80

Research shows: See John Bowlby's *Loss*, pp. 193, 243.

Page 81

Web sites dedicated to collecting true stories: See the *New York Times*, July 17, 2003, p. E3.

Page 84

Parma violet: See Caroline Desnoettes's *Colors*, pp. 4–5.

Page 85

A soprano: See Victoria Finlay's *Color: A Natural History of the Palette*, pp. 5–6.

Page 86
Aspirin, meditation, ceremonial rites, shared assembly: Selections made by Elizabeth Neeld from Antonio Damasio's *Looking for Spinoza: Joy, Sorrow, and the Feeling Brain*, pp. 124, 284, 286. All interpretations and applications of Dr. Damasio's work are mine and should not be attributed to his authorial intent.

The spiritual is an index: Ibid., p. 284.

Page 87
Make our way to a happy ending: Ibid., p. 283.

Page 89
Hildegard of Bingen: See Elizabeth Johnson's *She Who Is*, pp. 124, 127, 128.

Peter Kreeft: See www.peterkreeft.com.

Page 91
"Slow is the step of the going": Celtic Spiritual Verse: Poems of the Western Highlanders from the Gaelic, G. R. D. McLean, p. 331.

2. Reviewing

Page 100
Correlation between certain diseases and emotional experiences of change and loss; physical and mental cost of chronic stress: See Elizabeth Neeld's *Seven Choices: Finding Daylight After Loss Shatters Your World*, pp. 86–104; Antonio Damasio's *Looking for Spinoza: Joy, Sorrow, and the Feeling Brain*, pp. 63–65; Ronnie Janoff-Bulman's *Shattered Assumptions: Toward a New Psychology of Trauma*, pp. 64–69; and "The Heavy Cost of Chronic Stress," *New York Times*, December 17, 2002, p. D1.

Page 102
When you reminisce: For an in-depth look at reminiscing, see Pietro Castelnuovo-Tedesco's "The Mind as a Stage: Some Comments on Reminiscence and Internal Objects," *International Journal of Psychoanalysis*, vol. 59, part 1, p. 22.

Page 107
Kant's three questions: I am indebted to *Love's Mind: An Essay on Contemplative Life* by John S. Dunne for making me aware of Kant's three questions.

Page 114
Barbara Brown Taylor: See Rev. Taylor's book, *God in Pain*, pp. 115–19.

Page 115

Elie Wiesel: See the New York Times, October 2, 1997, p. A15.

Page 116

Rabbi Marc Gellman and Father Tom Hartman: See Self, September 1997, p. 68.

Page 118

Why solitude: See Anthony Storr's Solitude, pp. 20–21.

Page 119

Even babies need solitude: See D. W. Winnicott's "The Capacity to Be Alone," in The Maturational Processes and the Facilitating Environment, pp. 34–35.

Page 120

The Jewish mystical writings: For fuller discussion of silence and solitude, see Elizabeth Neeld's A Sacred Primer: The Essential Guide to Quiet Time and Prayer, chapters 7 and 8.

Page 121

Anthony Bloom: See Anthony Bloom's book Beginning to Pray, pp. 92–94.

Page 126

The tendency to go over the events: Colin Murray Parkes, Bereavement, p. 85.

Page 127

Pupil of possibility: The Kierkegaard quote is adapted by Elizabeth Harper Neeld from the original version.

Page 130

Clarissa Pikola Estes: For this quotations and several others I am indebted to the website www.dailycelebrations.com.

Page 148

HeartMath: See The HeartMath Solution by Doc Childre and Howard Martin, pp. 64–86, and also www.heartmath.com.

Page 149

Art: See Andrew Weil, "Healing with the Creative Arts," Dr. Andrew Weil's Self Healing newsletter, May 2000, pp. 1, 6–7.

Writing: See James Pennebaker's Writing to Heal: A Guided Journal for Recovering from Trauma and Emotional Upheaval. Also check his Web site: http://homepage.psy.utexas.edu/HomePage/Faculty/Pennebaker/Home2000/

JWPhome.htm. For those people who would like to write essays, poems, stories, books, memoirs, or even anecdotes, see Elizabeth Harper Neeld's audiobook *Yes! You Can Write*.

Page 152

Music: These suggestions (and some of the headings) come from a variety of places, including the work of Ann Racklin; Louise Montello's book *Essential Musical Intelligence*, pp. 231–43; colleagues; and my own choices.

Page 154

Making lists: See *List Your Self: Listmaking as the Way to Self-Discovery* by Ilene Segalove and Paul Bob Velick.

Page 155

Mindfulness: See *Full Catastrophe Living: Using the Wisdom of Your Body and Mind to Face Stress, Pain, and Illness* by Jon Kabat-Zinn, pp. 33–40. These seven attitudes are summarized here by Elizabeth Neeld.

Page 156

Thomas Merton's story: See *Raids on the Unspeakable* by Thomas Merton, pp. 9, 10.

3. Reorganizing

Page 173

Problem space and problem finding: For more information about these distinctions, see David Perkins's book *The Mind's Best Work*, pp. 185–87; 216; 249; 270; 272; 285.

Page 178

Specific problem-solving approaches: For more information, see Martin Seligman's *Authentic Happiness: Using the New Positive Psychology to Realize Your Potential for Lasting Fulfillment*, pp. 88–101.

Page 185

Many human beings require: Ibid., pp. 268–69.

Page 205

Signature strengths: See Martin Seligman's *Authentic Happiness*, pp. 134–61.

Page 208

Biography of joy: See Dr. Verena Kast's book *Joy, Inspiration, and Hope*, pp. 54–63.

Page 212

Using music intentionally: These suggestions (and some of the headings) come from a variety of places including the work of Ann Rachlin; Louise Montello's book *Essential Musical Intelligence*, pp. 235–43; colleagues; and my own selections.

Page 216

The work of Christopher Alexander: See *Wired* magazine, March 2004, pp. 64–65.

4. Renewing

Page 223

Change-creative gain sequence; normal transformational: See George Pollock's "Process and Affect: Mourning and Grief," *International Journal of Psychoanalysis*, vol. 59, pp. 267–73; "Mourning and Adaptation," *International Journal of Psychoanalysis*, vol. 42, pp. 345, 354–55; "The Mourning Process and Creative Organizational Change," *Journal of the American Psychoanalytic Association*, vol. 25, pp. 13–28.

Page 274

Creative outcomes: See George Pollock's "Mourning and Adaptation," *International Journal of Psychoanalysis*, vol. 42, pp. 354–55; "The Mourning Process and Creative Organizational Change," *Journal of the American Psychoanalytic Association*, vol. 25, pp. 13–28; "Process and Affect: Mourning and Grief," *International Journal of Psychoanalysis*, vol. 59, pp. 267–73.

Page 225

Victorious outcomes: See Heinz Kohut's "Forms and Transformations of Narcissism," *Journal of the American Psychoanalytic Association*, vol. 14, pp. 243–72.

Susan Nolen-Hoeksema: See "Growth and Resilience Among Bereaved People," *The Science of Optimism and Hope*, edited by Jane E. Gillham.

Robert Weiss: See his "Loss and Recovery," *Journal of Social Issues*, vol. 44, no. 3, pp. 37–52.

Page 230

Thrivers: See *The Beethoven Factor: The New Positive Psychology of Hardiness, Happiness, Healing and Hope* by Paul Pearsall, PhD, especially pp. 128–42, 158, 195.

Page 231

Comprehensibility: Ibid., p. 190.

Page 236
  Raymond Carver: See *Spirituality and Health*, April 2003, p. 51.

Page 240
  Sadako Ogata: Quoted in *Fast Company* magazine, June 2002, p. 72.

Page 246
  The "Names": To read this poem, go to http://www.loc.gov/poetry/names.html

  "Try to Praise the Mutilated World": To read this poem, go to www.poemhunter.com and search the name Adam Zagajewski. For a discussion of the poem, see Esther De Waal, *Lost in Wonder: Rediscovering the Spiritual Act of Attentiveness* (Norwich, UK: Canterbury Press, 2003).

Page 274
  Novelty is the key: See Gregory Berns's book on novelty and happiness, to be published by Henry Holt in 2005.

Bibliography

Bowlby, John. *Loss: Sadness and Depression*. New York: Basic Books, 1980.

Childre, Doc, and Howard Martin. *The HeartMath Solution*. San Francisco: HarperSanFrancisco, 1999.

Cleary, William. *Prayers to She Who Is*. New York: Crossroad Publishing Company, 1995.

Damasio, Antonio. *Looking for Spinoza: Joy, Sorrow, and the Feeling Brain*. New York: Harcourt, 2003.

Desnoettes, Caroline. *Colors*. Houston: Museum of Fine Arts, 2003.

De Waal, Esther. *Lost in Wonder: Rediscovering the Spiritual Art of Attentiveness*. Norwich, UK: Canterbury Press, 2003.

Dunne, John S. *Love's Mind: An Essay on Contemplative Life*. Notre Dame, IN: University of Notre Dame Press, 1993.

———. *The House of Wisdom*. New York: Harper and Row, 1985.

———. *The Reasons of the Heart: A Journey into Solitude and Back Again into the Human Circle*. Notre Dame, IN: Notre Dame University Press, 1978.

Finlay, Victoria. *Color: A Natural History of the Palette*. New York: Ballantine, 2002.

Gillham, Jane E. *The Science of Optimism and Hope: Research Essays in Honor of Martin E. P. Seligman*. Philadelphia and London: Templeton Foundation Press, 2000.

Janoff-Bulman, Ronnie. *Shattered Assumptions: Towards a New Psychology of Trauma*. New York: Free Press, 1992.

Johnson, Elizabeth. *See Who Is*. New York: Crossroad Publishing Company, 1992.

Jung, Carl. *Letters*, Vol. II, Princeton, NJ: Princeton University Press, 1975.

Kabat-Zinn, Jon. *Full Catastrophe Living: Using the Wisdom of Your Body and Mind to Face Stress, Pain, and Illness*. New York: Bantam Doubleday Dell, 1990.

Kast, Verena. *Joy, Inspiration, and Hope*. College Station: Texas A&M University Press, 2004.

McLean, G. R. D. *Celtic Spiritual Verse: Poems of the Western Highlanders from the Gaelic*. Cleveland: Pilgrim Press, 2003.

Merton, Thomas. *Raids on the Unspeakable*. New York: New Directions, 1976.

Montello, Louise. *Essential Musical Intelligence: Using Music as Your Path to Healing, Creativity, and Radiant Wholeness*. Wheaton, IL: Quest Books, 2002.

Neeld, Elizabeth Harper. *A Sacred Primer: The Essential Guide to Quiet Time and Prayer*. Nashville: Abingdon Press, 2005.

―――. *Seven Choices: Finding Daylight After Loss Shatters Your World*. New York: Warner Books, 2003.

Osterweis, Marian, Fredric Solomon, and Morris Green, eds. *Bereavement: Reactions, Consequences, and Care*. Washington, D.C.: National Academy Press, 1984.

Parkes, Colin Murray. *Bereavement: Studies of Grief in Adult Life*. New York: Tavistock Publications, 1972.

Pearsall, Paul. *The Beethoven Factor: The New Positive Psychology of Hardiness, Happiness, Healing, and Hope*. Charlottesville, VA: Hampton Roads Publishing Company, 2003.

Pennebaker, J. W. *Writing to Heal: A Guided Journal for Recovering from Trauma and Emotional Upheaval*. Oakland, CA: New Harbinger Press, 2004.

Perkins, David. *The Mind's Best Work*. Boston: Harvard University Press, 1981.

Pradl, Gordon, ed. *Prospect and Retrospect: Selected Essays by James Britton*. London: Heinemann Educational Books, 1982.

Raphael, Beverley. *The Anatomy of Bereavement*. New York: Basic Books, 1983.

Segalove, Ilene, and Paul Bob Velick. *List Your Self: Listmaking as the Way to Self-Discovery*. Kansas City: Andrews and McMeel, 1996.

Seligman, Martin E. P. *Authentic Happiness: Using the New Positive Psychology to Realize Your Potential for Lasting Fulfillment*. New York: Free Press, 2002.

————. *Learned Optimism: How to Change Your Mind and Your Life*. New York: Pocket Books, 1998.

Stafford, William. *You Must Revise Your Life*. Ann Arbor: University of Michigan Press, 1986.

Taylor, Barbara Brown. *God in Pain*. Nashville: Abingdon Press, 1998.

Thurman, Howard. *The Creative Encounter*. Richmond, IN: Friends United Press, 1978.

————. *The Inward Journey*. Richmond, IN: Friends United Press, 1990.

Winnicott, D. W. *The Maturational Processes and the Facilitating Environment*. New York: International Universities Press, 1960.

INDEX